RECONCILIATION WITH WAR:
A Family Journey

RECONCILIATION WITH WAR:
A FAMILY JOURNEY

From WWII Heroism to PTSD and Transformation

Janelle Kaye, MA
Charles Sidney Willsher

Copyright © 2013 by Janelle Kaye.

Library of Congress Control Number: 2013914116
ISBN: Hardcover 978-1-4836-8113-9
Softcover 978-1-4836-8112-2
Ebook 978-1-4836-8114-6

All rights reserved. No part of this book may be reproduced or transmitted in any form or by any means, electronic or mechanical, including photocopying, recording, or by any information storage and retrieval system, without permission in writing from the copyright owner.

This book was printed in the United States of America.

Rev. date: 10/28/2013

To order additional copies of this book, contact:
Xlibris LLC
1-888-795-4274
www.Xlibris.com
Orders@Xlibris.com
135641

My father never set out to be a war hero. He didn't like being in the spotlight or the center of attention. He just always did what was expected of him. He was one of the reluctant "humble heroes" of WWII who saw unspeakable horrors and who desperately wanted to forget about them, and couldn't. Dad stated at the end of the war that all that he and his war buddies wanted to do was "Just get on with our lives." It is because of these humble heroes that we are able to get on with ours! "Thank you, Dad!" And "Thank you to all who served in World War II and later wars! My gratitude is deepened by knowing more about your experiences." And a special "Thank you!" to the families of all veterans. Your sacrifices have gone unnoticed and unappreciated for too long.

Dedication

To my parents, Charles and Norma Jean Willsher
My greatest teachers!

Jean and Charley

War has been the background of my life. Both my parents were deeply affected by my dad's war experience. For decades, I ran away from war because I couldn't handle it. "Too much war isn't good for you," someone once said. Telling the story of my dad's war experience and how it affected our family is my way of reconciling with my family's experience with war, paying tribute to my family, and offering hope and possibilities for healing and reconciliation to other families who might be experiencing similar circumstances.

"When we go to war, our imaginations are shaped by government, media, and popular beliefs for months and years beforehand in order to prepare us, or any people, for the terrible act of going to war. When troops come home, veterans most commonly do not speak—they do not tell us the truth about their horrible experiences in war. We see them come home changed, disordered, disturbed, perhaps unable to function . . . Many have an identity disorder . . . and still live in war consciousness."

—Edward Tick, PhD

"The first casualty of war is truth."

—Edward Tick, PhD

"Veterans carry the truth about war. We, as civilians, do not know the truth. Violence, suffering, and destruction will continue and veterans and other victims of war will continue to suffer until others know the truth about war. We are responsible to help (veterans) come home and restore life . . . Veterans do not have to live in a psychic war zone for the rest of their life."

—Edward Tick, PhD

"One person's suffering should be enough to make us doubt and stop!"

—Faust

"The truth shall set you free."

—John 8:32

"Only you can change the world that you create, and by changing your world, the world will change . . . and that is the Truth that will set you free."

—Don Miguel Ruiz

CONTENTS

Acknowledgments 11
Introduction 15

Part I
The Depression Years: 1929-1941

Chapter 1 Growing Up 29

Part II
World War II: 1941-1945

Chapter 2 Training Camp at Fort Bragg, North Carolina 50
Chapter 3 Our Support for our Mission 56
Chapter 4 Our First Battle in French Morocco 58
Chapter 5 Moving on to Algeria and Tunisia 62
Chapter 6 Sicily 72
Chapter 7 England 80
Chapter 8 France and Normandy 83
Chapter 9 Ardennes 93

Part III
The Boom Years: 1946-1964

Chapter 10 Coming Home 107
Chapter 11 Jeannie 111
Chapter 12 Family Life 128
Chapter 13 Post-Traumatic Stress Disorder 139
Chapter 14 Secondary Post-Traumatic Stress Disorder 192

Part IV
Escape: 1964-1984
Chapter 15   Escaping my Roots 205
Chapter 16   Marriage 217

Part V
Healing: 1984-2003
Chapter 17   Healing Mind, Body, and Spirit................................233
Chapter 18   Charley's Healing Process...250
Chapter 19   Jean's Healing Process 266
Chapter 20   Janelle's Healing Process...273

Part VI
Reconciliation: 2003-Present Day
Chapter 21   Reconciliation with the WWII
              Experience of my Father 373

APPENDICES
A: WWII Timeline and Wartime Statistics 377
B: Distinguished Service Cross Award 383
C: Facts and Figures about the 9th Infantry Division........................385

Nonmilitary Notes and References 389
Glossary of Military Terminology
       and Other References from WWII 395
Bibliography..415

ACKNOWLEDGMENTS

The following people have been helpful in the writing of this book. Some offered their comments and helpful criticism, some offered their support and encouragement, some listened with empathy and prodded me to keep on writing, some offered legal advice, and some suggested various resources. I am deeply grateful to each of these people and want to acknowledge them for showing up in my life at an opportune time to help me complete this project: Michael Martin, Ken Speake, Karen Gilden, Jeff Johnston, Cathy Peterson, and Lorri Cole.

I also am grateful for the many words of encouragement and interest from family members and friends, and for the numerous hints to keep on writing, and ways to explore and learn about PTSD that appeared on the media and in my e-mail at various times when I needed them the most.

In addition, I would like to acknowledge Edward Tick, PhD, who has helped me understand myself, my family, and our mutual and extensive war experience. After Dad returned home from WWII, an unnamed war of a different kind, post-traumatic stress disorder, (PTSD) and secondary or trans-generational PTSD, waged in our household for decades. Thanks to Tick, I have greater understanding and compassion for my entire family and for families of other veterans. I also have greater concern about our nation's and any nation's war strategies and commitments.

Edward Tick, PhD, is a clinical psychotherapist, author, and director of Sanctuary: A Center for Mentoring the Soul in Albany, New York. In his book *War and the Soul*, he offers many insights that have helped me to understand my father and my family. His belief that

PTSD, which many veterans experience, is an identity disorder reflects the experience of Dad.

My dad came home from the war a fundamentally changed man who didn't know if he was a bad person because he had killed or if he was a good person because the army had given him a medal for extraordinary heroism.

Dr. Tick further states that war's violence can cause the soul to flee and be lost for life. I believe this insight completely explains my father's experience. After reading Tick's book, I highly recommend it to anyone searching for insight and practical help in healing severe combat trauma. Tick believes that many of the best models for healing are holistic, psycho-spiritual, and outside of mainstream therapeutic models. He offers many suggestions about the healing process.

There are five people I would especially like to thank:

Jan Deardorff, whose friendship, words of wisdom, and belief in my project have impacted and encouraged me more than I can express. More than once, her impeccable timing provided me with the resources or support I needed to continue on with writing. More importantly, her understanding and empathy, not only of my experience as a victim of PTSD, but also of my transcendence, has convinced me that there are others who may be touched by my experience.

Lynne and Bill Jeffrey, lifelong friends and companions on the road to healing, whose careful first reading of this book encouraged me to persevere in the second part of my literary journey, getting published. They have never failed to offer not only friendship, but hospitality, truth-telling, healing and spiritual inspiration, wisdom, and laughter. They are the sister and brother I never experienced biologically.

Leila Levinson, who authored *Gated Grief: The Daughter of a GI Concentration Camp Liberator Discovers a Legacy of Trauma*, which is the first book I read that has similar subject matter to mine. After talking with her, we were both amazed and profoundly moved by the realization that not only did we, as daughters in a PTSD family, have similar kinds of experiences, but our fathers did as well. The result of both of our journeys is to help others transcend their war-related wounds. I am so grateful to Levinson for sharing her story, her encouragement to me to tell mine, and for all the resources and guidance she has offered. When we summon the courage to tell our story, we find we are not alone.

My mother, Jean Willsher, who always had faith in me and in the crafting of this book. Her memory, her stories, her patience in listening, and her willingness to have her story told were so valuable to me throughout my entire writing process. Without her love and support I would not only not be here, I also wouldn't have been motivated to heal.

Thanks to all of you who have contributed in any way to the writing of this book. It is my hope that all that I have learned through our collective effort and written down here will be an inspiration and source of information for other individuals and families who are experiencing PTSD and the many effects of war.

Slave camp at Nordhausen, Germany

INTRODUCTION

"Dad, what are these pictures?"

At four years old, I was exploring the back corners of a bedroom closet on a wintry day in 1950 and had drawn out a large scrapbook that I had never seen before. I remember opening it as my dad rushed toward me to grab the scrapbook out of my hands. The first pictures I saw puzzled me. They depicted bare-boned bodies piled high in a mound. I could not imagine what they were.

My dad mumbled, "They were people who were killed in the war."

At four, I barely knew the word *war*, but I did know that my dad had been in one.

"Why are they in a pile, Dad?"

"Because some Nazis put them there."

I may have questioned "Why?" or "What is a Nazi?" but I don't remember all the details after that. Dad took the book from my hands and put it on a high shelf in his closet.

Decades passed before I saw it again. I understood that I was not supposed to see those pictures. Rather than fading from my memory, however, those pictures became the background of my life's existence and purpose. As the years rolled by, the horror of those pictures remained with me. I could not imagine a group of people killing other people and piling them in a heap to be disposed of like a ton of garbage. Could that happen to me or anyone I knew? What would it take to stop that kind of possibility?

Years later, when I was taking a German class in high school, I asked Dad if he had ever been in Germany. By this time I knew that he had been in WWII, and I had heard about concentration camps in my history classes. "Did you ever see a concentration camp, Dad?"

Dad told me that he had taken the pictures I had seen at four at Nordhausen Concentration Camp and smuggled them out of Germany when the war was over. He didn't say anything more about his experience though. I was reminded of the horror of those pictures in the scrapbook during this conversation, and the desire to make a positive difference in people's lives began to develop within me.

As I grew older and witnessed the effects of being in "the war" on my parents, that desire started to solidify. My major life's work had at its core the healing of psychological and physical wounds and the teaching of skills to help people deal in positive ways with conflict within diverse relationships. These skills included interpersonal communication skills as well as a variety of holistic self-help and spiritual skills such as meditation and mindfulness, and physical skills such as massage and energy work.

By the time I reached forty years of age, I also knew that the healing and teaching work that I was doing was not only on behalf of others, but for me as well. I had my own wounds to heal even though at the time I started my healing process, I did not recognize my wounds as war wounds. It took twenty more years and the decision to write this book to open my eyes to the truth behind my wounds. They were war wounds gained as a result of living with a combat veteran who was deeply troubled by his experience in the war. Later I realized that not only did my dad have war wounds, but that our entire family was affected.

I believe that other families of combat veterans also have their war wounds, recognized or not.

This book is the account of our family's journey to healing and reconciliation with the war experience of my father. It is not about reconciliation with war. Indeed, reconciliation with war may be impossible to attain.

To my knowledge, Dad was never able to fully reconcile his role in WWII. He served as battalion sergeant major for two years for the Third Battalion Headquarters Company Sixtieth Infantry, Ninth Division. He saw combat in Algeria, French Morocco, Tunisia, Sicily, Normandy, Rhineland, and Ardennes. He received several medals for his service including the Distinguished Service Cross, which is awarded for "extraordinary heroism in military operations against an armed enemy of the United States." This is the second highest medal that can be earned after the Medal of Honor. Eighty-six men from the Ninth Infantry in WWII earned the DSC. Four earned the Medal of Honor. He also received the Purple Heart with two Oak Leaf Clusters for being wounded in the war twice, once in 1943, Africa, and once in 1944, Normandy, and the EAMET Service Medal (European-African-Middle Eastern Campaign Medal), which was awarded for service in this theater for at least thirty days or for receipt of any combat decoration, a Good Conduct Medal, a Bronze Star Medal which is awarded for an act of heroism in a combat zone, a Bronze Arrowhead which is a replica of an Indian arrowhead which denotes participation in an amphibious assault landing, a Combat Infantry Badge for the performance of duty in action against the enemy in a major operation, and five Overseas Service Bars.

He was honorably discharged from the army on September 14, 1945. Today he is recognized as one of many highly decorated WWII veterans from Minnesota.

The above words tell where he was and what medals he earned while in WWII. They do not tell the story of the man, the hero who was afflicted all of his postwar life with untreated post-traumatic stress disorder (PTSD). Like most WWII veterans, my dad was silent about his experiences for decades after the war. But his inner rage, depression, sleepless nights, pain, debilitating headaches, nightmares, thoughts and threats of suicide, and other symptoms of the trauma he experienced shouted out his torment to us. While my family knew that something was wrong with Dad, he wasn't diagnosed until the 1980s as having PTSD.

Unfortunately, before the medical community recognized PTSD as an emotional disorder in 1980, most doctors and laypeople thought that the anxiety described by many veterans was simply nothing more than cowardice or personal weakness. If their anxiety was taken seriously, the solution was thought to be rest and relaxation. "Just get some R & R and you'll get over it," most veterans were told.

My dad was a victim of this kind of thinking. He thought he should just be able to tough out the rough spots, and he didn't talk with us, nor did we talk with him about his experiences. We thought that to seek help would expose him as being personally weak, which would contradict his image as a war hero and label him as "crazy," a stigma that none of us wanted to apply to him. We also didn't have the skills to talk with him in a meaningful or therapeutic way, although we didn't fully realize that at the time. We tried to cope the best we could with no understanding of the problem or how to make it better. We didn't know how or where to seek help.

On one occasion before the 1980s, my mother, in an act of desperation, asked the family doctor if he could do something about Dad's depression and threats of suicide. The doctor said in a demeaning voice, "Don't you worry about this, Jean. We (meaning the doctor and Dad) will take care of it." Nothing was done.

I also tried to reach out to my Aunt Amy, Dad's only sister, when I was a teenager, and begged her to "talk with Dad." Nothing happened.

I didn't realize that she probably had her own issues with Dad and didn't know what to do for him either.

Instead, we all endured large segments of time lasting from a few days to three months of consecutive silence on his part. During this time, Dad's jaw would lock down in an effort to suppress his emotions, and my mother and I avoided him as much as possible. We didn't know what was wrong, or why Dad wouldn't talk. We noticed, however, that the longer the silence continued, the more likely it was that it would end in an episode of rage.

My mother and I also had our own emotional health problems as a result of living with my dad. Our best coping mechanisms at the time were passivity and repression. We were afraid to speak up to my dad and to admit to others that we had problems. "Don't tell anyone!" were words I heard frequently. Fear dominated our lives. We grew very close as we tried to handle the effects of living with Dad. Unfortunately, for us and for Dad, our solidarity largely negated and omitted him. I am certain that he felt ostracized and unimportant in our family relationships, which compounded his emotional problems.

Finally, in 1980, the medical community identified PTSD as a legitimate disorder in the *Diagnostic and Statistical Manual* (DSM). The Vietnam War was over, and war trauma symptoms were noted in returning combat veterans. It was imperative to name and legitimize the problem experienced by thousands. One of the effects of the diagnosis was that some of the stigma connected with PTSD began to disappear, and some veterans began to seek help for their psychological wounds.

Early help for this disorder included "talking about the war," which Dad began to do through writing about it. Unfortunately, ideas about how to help the families of veterans who had PTSD was not typically a part of a therapeutic process. Nor was dealing with issues that included any form of spiritual, emotional, and mental wounding for the veteran or the family. It never occurred to my mother and me that we should seek family counseling or that we had a problem too. We saw Dad as having a major problem, and we saw ourselves as the victims of "his problem." We thought that help for him would make our problems go away. Therapy for veterans was in its infancy and did not address any of our needs.

In our family, it took two generations and forty-plus years to bring healing and reconciliation to what Dad experienced as a combat soldier in WWII. His experience profoundly affected his health, outlook on life, and relationships. How he related to my mother and me affected how we thought about ourselves, each other, and how we treated my dad. How we treated Dad further provided some family wounds that compounded his war wounds.

We lived in a secretive nightmare that had no explanation and no relief until the 1980s. Not only did my dad begin to seek therapy at this time, but I did as well. Unfortunately, my mother did not, and it wasn't until much later in her life, after Dad's death, that she consciously began to heal some of her trauma. She recently stated that she wished that there had been some support groups for family members of war veterans dealing with PTSD. This kind of support is finally beginning to be available.

During the writing of this book, she helped me recall the past, which has resulted in her understanding that she wasn't at fault for Dad's behaviors. Unfortunately, too many people believe that they are the ones to blame if a family member abuses them. As this understanding grew within her, she found it easier to let go of past memories and put my dad's behavior into the framework of a mental disorder rather than something personal he directed at her.

Understanding has led to compassion for Dad and relief for her. Understanding has also led to our desire to tell our story in hopes that others may also find healing and reconciliation with their loved ones who have experienced the trauma of combat war.

Although some veterans today may be treated for PTSD, many of their family members go untreated. It is not enough to show families how to cope with a loved one who has PTSD, or to teach them communication and relational skills, even though both of these efforts are very important. Family members also may need to become emotionally healthy after living in an abusive PTSD household. In my personal experience, as a result of living with a parent who was physically ill much of the time, and emotionally and spiritually ill all of the time, and another parent who didn't know how to cope with it in a healthy way, I was emotionally damaged and needed therapy in later years in order to heal my wounds.

I am grateful that my mother tried to protect me as much as she was able, and that she provided a powerful antidote for the abuse in our family by ensuring I knew she loved me. She spent countless hours teaching me fundamental survival skills like cleaning, cooking, laundry, and sewing. She wanted to make sure I could take care of myself when I left home. We also spent some time almost every day where she entered my world and helped me to create doll clothes or play age-appropriate card games. Through playing and talking, we bonded as she instilled in me values of honesty, courage, independence, and perseverance. Her love and attention helped me to be constructive and successful in school and to leave home with survival skills and hope for the future. Unfortunately, she couldn't help herself.

PTSD is a family problem. As more and more veterans suffer PTSD today, I hope we begin to understand and approach it as a family disorder and that treatment will be available for the entire family.

Ideally, when a family unit seeks therapy, they receive the opportunity for spiritual, mental, emotional, and physical transformation that benefits all the members of the family. Fortunately, a gift can emerge from the pain: by working through the wounds of war, a family can realize greater love, forgiveness, tolerance, patience, and spiritual development through healing and reconciliation than they might have otherwise discovered.

Reconciliation means settlement, resolution, compromise, reunion, or bringing together. All of these meanings of the word *reconciliation* were part of my family's experience. I offer my journey and my family's journey in hopes that other people may be able to recognize the similarity between their journey and ours. Our family's journey may even provide inspiration for another family's healing and reconciliation with their war experience. When one family tells the truth about their experience, other families may also find their truth and speak it. That is my hope and my inspiration!

None of our lives are untouched when we send a family member to war. Perhaps when enough people tell their common story, humanity will see that war has profoundly negative spiritual, psychological, and physical effects on generations of families. We may even come to the decision to stop going to war! Only we as individuals can do that.

Since this is a family story, I wish to start with my dad's family and his family circumstances while growing up. All of our beliefs and values start within the home, and my dad's upbringing had a profound influence on his role in the war and on our life as a family after the war. Since 64% of "America's Greatest Generation" grew up in small towns and rural areas, the story of my father's upbringing was similar to the story of many people of his generation.

The years of the Great Depression, World War II, and the boom as experienced by my family are probably a familiar experience to many. The last part of our journey, healing and reconciliation, may not be so familiar.

Part I on the Great Depression depicts my dad's growing up years and how poverty and religion influenced his values. His values influenced his experience in WWII and in postwar America.

Part II tells the story of Dad's WWII experience in his own words. Whenever I read his words, I am touched by the sparseness of emotion in his story. Reading what is not expressed as well as what is expressed is part of his story. In this section of the book, I have also included some letters that Dad wrote to family members and a few friends that illustrate some of the differences between what he was writing about to others and what he was experiencing firsthand. In addition, there are a few newspaper articles from the time that give even a different perspective.

Part III tells the story of the boom years and my growing-up years. Although there is much to admire about my dad, I didn't realize this until I reached forty years of age. The boom years tell the story of the hidden family trauma we experienced.

Part IV tells the story of my escape from a troubled household and how I established roots elsewhere that led to my healing and reconciliation with Dad.

Part V on healing and Part VI on reconciliation tell the story of how we were able to heal and reconcile as a family. The processes discussed here were not always easy to accomplish, but they were filled with grace. Whatever was needed showed up at the perfect time.

I hope that this account of our family's experiences will be a source of inspiration to anyone who is struggling with their own family trauma, for we truly can be healed. To this end, I have included some suggestions for healing that are based on the processes that our family experienced but are written about generically so that anyone can use whatever is suggested according to their needs, values, and beliefs. I don't know what would be useful for anyone else and have no intention to suggest that the practices I mention are the only possibilities that will facilitate healing or that they should be followed universally or in any particular order.

Throughout this book, I make several references to God. By God, I mean a Higher Power, Higher Self, or a Supreme Creative Force. Until I understand it differently, I believe that there is an Intelligent Creative Force of our universe, a Supreme Being who is called many different names in different parts of the world among different peoples. As you read this book, know that I have chosen to use the word God because it is short and reflects my heritage. It is not because I am referring to a certain fatherly depiction of God as illustrated in the Christian religion. As you read, please substitute another word for God that depicts your understanding of a Higher Power, Higher Self, or Creative Force, if needed, so that what I say will have relevancy for you.

At the end of the book, there are three appendices and additional notes and references that may be helpful in understanding the history and details of the years discussed.

It is my hope that by reading my dad's story, others may know of one silent hero who sacrificed much for his country. For those who have not experienced combat war, it is hard to imagine what veterans and their families sacrifice for the rest of the population. Perhaps there will be a better understanding of the truth about war and its effects after reading our story.

Once we recognize the truth, perhaps we as a nation will work harder at solving our problems with each other and with other nations in ways that do not include violence and killing each other. Finally, by reading our family story, other war veterans' families may come to recognize some of their own story and be able to find their own way to healing and reconciliation with each other and with their family's war experience.

PART I

The Depression Years 1929-1941

In 1929, the stock market fell and the Great Depression began. The Willsher family, like other families in southwestern Minnesota was particularly vulnerable because they lived in a rural and agricultural area. Commodity prices dropped, and jobs and social services were scarce. Wages began to fall in 1931, and the bottom was reached in March of 1933. Families and neighbors helped each other, and everyone did the best they could to survive. Multi-generations frequently lived together and helped address the needs of the entire family. The economic depression was often accompanied by a psychological depression among the adults who were trying to make a living in difficult times. Children, for the most part, did not know they were "depressed". They thought their lives were "normal". When the United States entered WWII, the Great Depression ended.

ONE

Growing Up

When I was a young girl, my dad took me to see the cemetery in the town where his family had once lived. After seeing the gravestones of his grandparents, I noticed a small gravestone off to the side of the larger stone. It had my dad's name on it. "Dad, why is your name on this gravestone?"

"That's the place where my brother was buried."

"I didn't know you had a brother."

"He died in infancy. It always bothered me that I was named after a dead person. I wanted to be my own person, not a replacement for a dead person."

Dad didn't care, or maybe didn't even know, that this had been a common practice throughout history. He didn't feel valued for himself because he thought of himself as a replacement for an older son. "Having my own personal name would have made me seem more valuable to the family," he told me. "I would have been my own person, not a replacement."

Many years later and well into the writing of this book, it occurred to me that seeing his name on a gravestone was similar to having a premonition about his adult life. After his war experience, he was numbed and dissociated from his prewar self, and large segments of his personality seemed missing. What happened that led to his becoming one of the walking dead for many years of his life?

Robert and Minnie Willsher with daughter, Amy, and son, Charley

Dad's story began with his parents, Minnie Myrtle Rand and Arthur Robert Willsher.

Minnie was born in November of 1886 in Mason City, Iowa, the tenth child in a family of eleven children. The Rand family was poor and hardworking, as many families of that era were. They lived in Mason City until 1902 when her parents, Charles and Amelia, and their youngest children moved to southwestern Minnesota to farm in an area that was being touted by the newly developed railroad system as great farmland. Charles loved to grow produce and flowers, and having their own land to cultivate and harvest seemed promising. Charles and Amelia lived there until 1915 when Charles died.

Minnie was sixteen when the family moved to Minnesota. She already had received her education in the Mason City public school system, so her time on the farm was spent in helping the family and taking care of a younger sister. As soon as she was able, she returned to Mason City where she met her future husband.

Robert was born in September of 1882 in Tollesbury, Essex, England, the youngest of four children. In February

Young Charley

of 1901, he immigrated to the United States on a cattle boat and found his way to Mason City where some of his family had settled before him. For thirteen years he lived and worked in Mason City until he married Minnie in August of 1914. Shortly after their wedding, they moved to the home of Charles and Amelia in Minnesota to help them farm.

One month after Charles Rand died, Minnie and Robert's first son, named Charles after his grandfather, was born and died in infancy. A year later, Minnie gave birth to a daughter, Amy Ruth.

Shortly thereafter, the family sold the farm and moved back to Mason City where in November of 1918, a second son, who they also named Charles, my dad, was born. Minnie and Robert deeply mourned the loss of their first child and thought that my dad was his replacement.

In 1922, Robert and Minnie moved their small family, Amy and Charley, back to Minnesota to another sparsely populated, agricultural town in the same county where they had previously lived. This time, the move was motivated by getting a fresh start in a town where there were no previous sad memories. They also realized that they didn't have all the money and family labor help that was needed to successfully farm, and Robert thought that he could make a better income by being self-employed.

The town itself seemed like a desirable place to live. A railroad provided a connection to Minneapolis and St. Paul and other states and made marketing products more convenient for area farmers and businesspeople. Items like food and other necessities were more readily available than in locations where there was no railroad.

A regal courthouse stood in the center of a block, which was surrounded by small businesses on all four sides which locally was called "the square." Some of the businesses of that era included a hardware, furniture, clothing, grocery, and drugstore, a bakery, and a bank. A hotel, meat market, creamery, ice house, photo studio, piano and music store, a cafe, wallpaper and paint shop, confectionary shop, jeweler, laundry, tailor shop, barbershop, harness shop, grain elevator, a saloon, and a lumberyard were available, as were a doctor, lawyer, and a real estate developer. The town's businesses promised a bright future for those who lived and worked there.

Since there were no franchises at that time, and traveling to larger communities was an all-day event, the town's business owners were prepared to take care of all of the needs of the community. During the weekdays, when the businesses were open, shoppers filled the area around the square—people looking for the excitement of making a connection with a friend and spending a nickel or two for a treat at the cafe or the bakery after having purchased their necessities. On Saturday night, the area farmers and their families came to town to buy goods and swap stories with other farmers, while their children roamed the streets or hung out at the confectionary shop.

The courthouse and the businesses around it formed the heart of the community. One block away, a brick school stood ready for the education of the youth of the town. All the children in the area attended the same school. Most of the town's activities took place in the downtown area or in the school.

The east hill in the town was primarily inhabited by Lutherans, and a Lutheran church proudly stood on the center of the hill. In Minnesota towns, Lutheran churches were often built on hills in order to be closer to God and a beacon of light to the townspeople. The small homes built around the church were the first homes of many Norwegian immigrant families.

There was a sprinkling of other protestant churches in the town, primarily around the downtown area. A Catholic church stood alone on the north side of town surrounded by many small houses filled with Catholic families. These Catholic families in the early 1920s were victims of prejudice and discrimination. For a brief time around WWI, local Ku Klux Klan members rode the streets terrorizing the families who were thought to be different from the protestant families. It wasn't until after John F. Kennedy became president of the United States in the 1960s that local prejudice against Catholics began to fade.

The close proximity of businesses, school, and churches was not an accident. The builders of the town wanted to make it easy for the townspeople to get to all three. Cars were rare, and everything needed for living, socialization, inspiration, and education had to be within walking distance. During Minnesota winters, one did not want to walk far!

Even though there was a tendency for segregation by faith in the community and some discrimination, the townspeople generally were peaceable and cooperative in helping their neighbors and building their community. Everyone knew and trusted their neighbors, and there was so little crime that doors went unlocked, and children roamed all the streets and alleys without fear or threats to their safety.

Robert and Minnie were satisfied that they had discovered a perfect town in which to raise their children and earn a living. They purchased a modest house—complete with a chicken house, a cow and hay barn, a woodshed, and a large plot for a big garden—close to the downtown area and settled in with the intent to make it their home for years to come. (Many homes in the villages and small towns at this time had chicken houses and a building to store hay and house a cow. Hay was used in the chicken nests. Chickens were a source of eggs, meat, and possible income. Cows were necessary for their supply of milk.)

Robert and Minnie found work as custodians for the First United Methodist Church, a local bank, and a lawyer's office, and Robert also did various odd jobs around the community such as working with the dray service (a horse and cart used to transport goods like groceries from the railroad depot to various stores and small towns in the area) and digging graves. He did not have a steady job doing one thing but managed to make a humble living for the family by serving the needs of others, a lesson he taught to his children. He had a reputation for doing every job he undertook well, so he was often given more work than he could do while others were looking for work.

Like many of their era who lived in rural America and belonged to various Protestant denominations, they thought of their church as the centerpiece of their community. Not only was the church a source of inspiration, spirituality, and community support, but also a gathering place for social activities.

Robert and Minnie were devoted to their church and its teachings, and lived stalwart and upright lives. Some of the religious principles that formed the foundation of their faith included the Ten Commandments, the seven deadly sins, the Golden Rule, and the idea that every person should be their brother's keeper. Service to others was an admired virtue, as was humility, honesty, and hard work. "Thou Shalt Not Kill!" one of the Ten Commandments, was impressed firmly in the children's minds. They saw this ethic as being "Truth," and any kind of killing of another person was considered a sin that would result in dire consequences (eternal life spent in hell) for the soul of the killer. This belief enormously impacted Charley's life after the war.

Minnie and Robert also provided for Minnie's mother, Amelia, who had lived with them since 1920. Amelia was blind, obese, diabetic, and later developed cancer and was a constant care to Minnie. In June of 1931, Amelia died. The only memory of Amelia that Dad shared with me in later years was his recollection of her sitting on a porch smoking a pipe and chewing snuff. Charley, as a young boy, liked to spend his time away from home as much as possible, partly because he was embarrassed by his grandmother.

Later that year in December of 1931, two years into the Great Depression, Robert died from a cancerous growth on the brain. Charley never fully recovered from the loss of his dad. I remember him telling me that he always missed having his dad available to do things with him. (I find it sad to realize that I thought the same thing about my dad!)

Charley never talked about how the multiple deaths in her family affected his mother. My guess is that some part of her died too. I only knew her for the first nine years of my life and have no memory of her other than sitting quietly in her wooden rocking chair off to the side of the rest of her family. No words, no touch, no laughter accompany that memory. My maternal grandparents, on the other hand, were very loving, and I have many fond memories of spending time with them during that same time period.

At thirteen, Charley became the man of the house and had to find ways to help support the family. Nearly every one of his generation worked hard in order to survive. Kids were no exception. Charley chopped and delivered ice in the summertime and did assorted jobs such as yard work, weeding gardens, and shoveling snow in the winter. When he was in high school, he worked for the school system where he sanded floors, painted, washed windows, and did daily maintenance chores. He also worked for his uncle by mowing grass at the local cemetery and digging graves and filling them in again.

After Robert's death, Minnie continued working as a custodian, and moved her small family in with her brother, Alvah Rand, "Uncle Al," who helped to make a living for the family for a few years before he moved to Tennessee and started his own family.

When Charley enlisted in WWII, Minnie continued to live with her daughter, Amy, until Minnie's death from cancer in 1955.

The home of my father's youth was humble, caring of family, and filled with hardships of various kinds: the Great Depression, harsh Minnesota winters, lack of formal education, illness, deaths of family members, and a struggle to stay alive. With all of the conveniences that people have today, it is difficult to imagine the living situation of my father's family: a small poorly insulated two-story dwelling where heat from the coal stove rose to the second floor through a ventilation grate in the floor, where there was an icebox in the summer to cool produce and milk, where food was cooled in the winter outdoors, where a cellar was the refuge for a family when there was a threat of a tornado and where all the root vegetables and other foods were kept cool in the summer, where rising in the winter mornings was accompanied with brushing off ice from the bedcovers, and where there was little money to make any improvements. The other families in my dad's neighborhood lived the same way, so life was "normal" to them. The children of this era did not feel deprived or unfortunate or poor.

Instead, they experienced multiple generations living together and helping each other, with the emphasis on working together to make a life for the whole family, rather than on the individual. Each member of the family did their share of the work that was needed for the family to survive. Hard work, cooperation in the family and community, honesty, always doing the best you can and giving the most you can, and perseverance were values practiced by my dad's family and in most rural communities around the area. Deals were sealed with a handshake, and trust formed the background of most relationships.

There were few joys and happy times. I asked my Aunt Amy once about her happy memories as a child, and she had none to share other than spending time with relatives in Mason City. She did, however, have some accounts of mischief that she and Charley instigated.

In an essay written for her high school English class, she wrote about how during one summer she and Charley (he was called Chas then) and two other neighborhood boys formed "Our Gang," inspired by the popular movies by the same name which later became known as "The Little Rascals," with Amy as the leader. They dug trenches in the front yard to make it more realistic when they played "war" until they were stopped by Minnie. They converted the hayloft into a "real pirates ship." And they planned revenge for the next-door neighbor who foiled their attempts at mischief "by keeping the telephone wires sizzling until we were punished." Amy wrote, "With no regard for her hours of labor to create a perfect lawn and garden, we seized her garbage can and distributed the contents up and down the walk, which extended from the house to the chicken coop. With this completed to our satisfaction, we let all the chickens out where they proceeded to have as much fun as we did with their newfound freedom. Finally, we gathered stones and threw them at the back door where they sounded like hail." The neighbor came outdoors to find the gang disappearing from view. She called their mother, and Minnie made Amy and Charley and the two other boys chase the chickens and bring them back to the coop, clean up the garbage, and put it back in the cans. Then they were paraded to the woodshed where they were punished. Amy wrote, "Everyone of 'our gang' can still describe the woodshed perfectly."

Not only did children create their own entertainment, most adults took responsibility for their children and meted out punishment that they thought appropriate when the entertainment turned to mischief. They did not side with the children if another adult complained about a child's behavior. Children were taught to respect their elders and to take responsibility for their own behavior. If they made a mess, they cleaned it up. If they hurt another person or property, they made amends. Neighbors, and the entire community, acted together to raise the children so that they had morals and were respectful of others.

My dad had a few tales of how he and his buddies (a group of nine boys who were called the River Rats) banded together and roamed the town and got into mischief; in the winter snow, they slid or skied down Plum Creek Hill, a small hill outside of town near the Des Moines River, and in summer they learned how to swim by being dunked into the river and telling each other to "Sink or swim!" The River Rats, named for the amount of time spent by the river hunting and fishing with their boats and rafts, dared each other to try new things and spent every free moment exploring the area in which they lived. With the help of their imagination, like most children of their generation, they made their own fun by playing tag, kick-the can, anti-over, searching for arrowheads while following Indian trails along the Des Moines River, playing baseball, making up games, and getting into mischief. They did not expect others to arrange their games for them. Instead, they roamed free in a safe environment and benefited from creating their own adventures. The River Rats became lifelong friends.

One of Dad's earliest memories of the times the River Rats had together was when he was in second or third grade. In later years he wrote about that time. "We built ourselves a tree house out of some old lumber. We went down to the river, which was close by, and gathered some weeds that were white in the middle. We thought they would make good smoking, so we cut them into the proper length and climbed up into our tree house. We lit up, and with our first breath, we inhaled pure fire down our throats. We were hacking and coughing when Mrs. Larson came out of the house and yelled, 'Are you boys smoking up there? Come down, and Charles, you head for home!' We were in the doghouse for a week or two."

When they were a little older, they often hung around the fairgrounds where "there was a good racetrack, both for cars and horses and for us to run around." Charley wrote, "There was a big racing stable in the northwest part of the grounds where the horses were kept, and manure and straw were piled high not too far away. We liked to watch the horses and often hung around the stable. One day one of the guys brought some Bull Durham with him, so we went behind the stable to roll our own and light up. I guess someone was a little careless because a fire started and soon was out of our control. One of the men from the stables must have turned in the alarm, for we could hear the fire trucks coming. We took off for the safety of Perkin's Creek, which was nearby, and hid there until dark. When we got home, we were really in the doghouse, both for starting the fire and for being late. We didn't talk about that episode for many years."

During the winter, Charley escaped the hardships of the times by reading. His Aunt Jennie, his father's sister who lived in England, sent him volume after volume of children's stories, which he devoured and treasured. (Years later, they were handed down to me along with a love of reading, and cherished deeply.) When reading of different times in England, he could escape the difficulties of his own life and dream of a future where he could be an adventurer or hero. When he grew older, Charley visited the local library weekly, a practice that he later encouraged in me.

Charley always had a thirst for adventure and a desire to better himself. He enjoyed learning and graduated in 1937 from high school where he distinguished himself by lettering in football, track, and wrestling, although he only weighed 135 pounds and was five feet and six inches tall.

The River Rats
Charley is the middle boy in the first row

Charley's High School Graduation in 1937

He enrolled in Mankato State University in Minnesota after graduation but quit after one semester because the need to earn money for the family was so great. At that time, it was more important to eat than to study and aspire to something better. For the next three years, he worked as a soda jerk in the local drugstore and later for a few months at a local plumbing and heating business, which was owned by the family of some of his friends. These two jobs provided him and his family with necessary income before he enlisted in January of 1942 for WWII, one month after Pearl Harbor.

Drugstores in most communities of his generation were the town's gathering place and a source of news and socializing, as well as a place to purchase necessary items. Townspeople gathered there to play the jukebox and listen to the radio. While working, Charley socialized with the town's young people because the drugstore was a favorite hangout. Some of the people who frequented the soda counter included his future wife and her cousins. He really liked this job and grew close to the owners, Clifford and Vern Lewis, and thought of them as father figures.

While Charley was in WWII, he sent a letter to Cliff and Vern in February of 1944 that depicted his fondness for them and his appreciation of their role in his life.

> I want to say a few things to you fellows, just in case I never get to say them firsthand. As you know, my father died when I was fairly young, and until I started working in the drugstore, I never had anyone to go to with my troubles and for advice, except of course Mother, and you know how young guys are with their mothers. After I started working for you, I always felt that no matter what I did, you two fellows would back me to the limit, and you always treated me like I was one of the family. I know several times when I could have done better work, but never once did I receive a 'calling down' from either of you. You always treated me and my family with the utmost generosity, and it is really appreciated by both myself and them. I don't think you realize just what you have done for me, but I really want to thank you both.

At a very young age, Charley learned about the value of the dollar, and a hard work ethic, about the value of teamwork, and how to adapt to difficult circumstances, and to do your best in whatever circumstances you find yourself. Most importantly, he learned to put his own hopes and dreams aside for the good of his family and, later, his country. Hope and optimism for the future underlined his motivation to succeed as it had done in previous generations of his family. He understood that he was responsible not only for himself, but also for the welfare of others.

These values helped him in the next aspect of his life, serving in the U.S. Army with honor in a time of war.

I don't remember his telling me about how he heard about the U.S. declaration of war. Since the war began in 1939, he had been hearing and reading about it for about two years before the attack on Pearl Harbor on December 7, 1941. My guess is, like many Americans, he heard about it on the radio while he was at work.

This announcement was a life-changing moment for thousands of young men and women and their families and communities. For Charley, it brought up feelings of fear, patriotism, and a willingness to participate in a cause greater than himself. The posters depicting the picture of Uncle Sam pointing his finger to the young men of America, declaring "Uncle Sam wants you!" was a powerful image. It offered an opportunity for young men to become a cultural hero whose service was blessed by the Divine and who made the world safe for its people. It was hard to resist. The thinking of the time was that men were not men if they resisted this call to arms.

I remember his telling me once about the day he left home for war. Up until this time, he had never been further from home than Mason City, Iowa. "Naturally," he said, "I had some fear. My mother told me,

'Be a good boy, now!' when she sent me off to war. I wanted to hear, 'I love you!' or 'I'll miss you!' or even, 'Be safe!'"

His family had never been affectionate, nor did they show emotion. Life was hard, and to show emotion was considered a sign of weakness.

At twenty-three, he left for training with fear, excitement, sadness, and a commitment to "fight for America!" Charley didn't completely comprehend that fighting for America meant learning to kill people. That was and is the basic reason for going to war.

PART II

World War II
1941-1945

This part of the book is not intended to be an historical account of WWII. Rather, it is the story of one man's experience in WWII told in his own words. Even though he wrote most of what follows in the 1980s, he used the vernacular, slang, and cultural references of the war years. In fact, his way of expressing himself never really changed after the 1940s and 1950s.

To help the reader understand the context of the battles and campaigns that Charley took part in, a partial timeline of WWII is provided in appendix A. This timeline does not include information about battles fought before Pearl Harbor, nor does it include every battle after Pearl Harbor. In appendix B, there is a copy of Charley's Distinguished Service Cross paper, and appendix C offers a few facts and figures about the Ninth Infantry Division. Before the bibliography, there is a glossary of military terminology and other references from WWII that will help the reader better understand the times discussed. Numbers after possible unfamiliar terminology refer the reader to the glossary at the back of the book.

Early in January of 1942, Charley left home for Fort Snelling in St. Paul, Minnesota. For the next three years, he experienced horror and hardship that are incomprehensible to me. He also experienced extreme physical trauma as a result of the demands on his body that his service required. "I am amazed at what the human body can endure," he stated in his diary written during the war. After reading his story, I am amazed too.

I would like to tell his story in his own words that came from this diary written during the war and his memoir that was written in the late 1980s. His diary contained sparse words about some of his major experiences during the first two years of his service. After that, he stopped writing for some reason. My guess is that his experiences were so horrific and so indelibly imprinted on his mind that he couldn't bring himself to write about them at the time, or perhaps, he thought that he would never forget them and so didn't need to write them down. After reading some information that was obtained by some WWII researchers of the Ninth Infantry, I also realized that perhaps Charley didn't keep a personal diary after his first two years of service because he kept a journal of events for his unit. Maybe he didn't have the time or the inclination to write a personal journal too.

His account of his experiences written in the 1980s was far more detailed. In fact, they were written as though he was living through the experience again, which he probably was. He doesn't speak much about his emotions, however. Through what is not said, the reader can imagine the horror and trauma of the situations described.

After the war, Charley didn't speak of his experiences for many years. After three decades of unnamed and untreated PTSD, he finally spent three months in the 1980s in a veteran's hospital in hopes that he could be cured. One of his physicians told him to write his story and to talk with people about his experiences. Thus began what became a somewhat cathartic experience for him. He typed out his story and gave it to anyone who wanted a copy. He also told his story to many local groups and, as a result, seemed to find some relief. When he told his story to schoolchildren or at Memorial Day celebrations, he was honored for his service. I believe that this honoring helped him to feel better about his role in the war.

In 2006, after my father's death, I found the memoir of his war experiences in a box in a closet along with the pictures he had taken of the Nordhausen concentration camp and smuggled out of Germany, and other war-related pictures and memorabilia. After reading his story again, I finally understood more about him and how his experiences affected our family life. I also realized that it was important for me to tell his story from his perspective along with our family story. How he writes is not only characteristic of him but also is characteristic of the times of which he wrote.

Putting together our family story is part of the reconciliation process between us. For years I kept myself separate from my family. The bringing together of our story has reunited and reconciled us in ways that I wouldn't have thought possible earlier in my life.

Training camp

Private Willsher

TWO

Training Camp at Fort Bragg, North Carolina

January 1942

A total of more than three hundred thousand Minnesota men and women served in the military in WWII. Out of the country's male population, seven in ten eligible men served. After enlisting, they typically spent five days in a reception center before moving on to training camp.

In Minnesota, they had mental and physical exams at Fort Snelling where they were inspected, tested, weighed, measured, questioned, and inducted in wartime service. They were issued clothing from the skin out, some of which didn't fit very well, and told to "learn to do things the army way, and you will get along!" After five days, they were sent to a training camp without knowing where that camp was located. They did know that some of them would not be returning to their homes in Minnesota. They did not know how many. Nor did they did know that those who returned from combat would be changed men.

In 1988 Charley wrote of his war experiences and said of those beginning days . . .

In 1941, the Germans were trying to conquer as much territory as they could from the northern tip of Norway to the southern part of

Greece. Italy had joined the Germans after France was occupied and was helping them fight the British in North Africa. The British had sent part of their African force to Greece to help fight the Germans, and they had suffered large losses at Dunkirk. The United States had not entered the war yet but was trying to supply the British. We were also trying to prepare the fortress of Corregidor to fight off the Japanese. After Pearl Harbor, the Germans declared war on the United States, and the Americans lost the Philippine Islands. The Japanese were spread all over Asia and were moving toward Australia. It seemed awfully bleak for Britain and the United States which were at last forced into war.

I was sworn into the United States Army at Fort Snelling (1), Minnesota, early on January 15, 1942. After receiving numerous shots and being issued clothing, I boarded a train, along with hundreds of others, bound for Camp Wolters (2) in Texas. We traveled for two and a half days with sore arms from all the shots we received at Fort Snelling, and some of the guys were running a fever. It was twenty degrees below zero when we left Fort Snelling, and we were loaded down with heavy underwear, wool uniforms, and a big barracks bag with all our extra stuff packed in it. When we arrived at Camp Wolters, it was sixty degrees, and we had to march about three blocks loaded down with everything. That first night we were badly in need of a good night's sleep!

The next morning we were awakened at five o'clock, told to wash up, make our beds, and fall out at six to march to our breakfast. When we fell out as ordered, we were told to go on a one-mile run before breakfast. After our run, we marched into the mess hall to be greeted by over a hundred other poor, sad sacks who had been there for a week or more. We were also greeted by a large platter of scrambled eggs, which was a curious green color and didn't smell good. Needless to say, none of us ate much. After six o'clock that evening, nearly all of us visited the post exchange to stock up on good things to eat to tide us over when we didn't have good meals.

The first part of our training was devoted to getting our bodies in shape. Every day we ran before breakfast. It wasn't long before we ran three miles. After breakfast, we had close order drill for a couple of hours. Early in the training, we were given rifles and other weapons and learned how to use them. We had to able to take them apart in the dark and put them together again. We learned the use of hand grenades, mortars, machine guns, gas masks, bayonets, and how to disarm the enemy in hand-to-hand combat. We learned how to dig foxholes, put up tents, run the obstacle course, peel potatoes, and how to keep ourselves and our equipment clean.

The highlight of the day was mail call, usually after supper. Some of the guys received "Dear John" letters, which left them sad for a few days. There were a few fellows who were not cut out for the infantry, and they were weeded out and sent to other parts of the army. One fellow in our company was very quiet and didn't make friends. One day he turned up missing. A few days later when we were hiking through the woods, we found him hanging in a tree. He was homesick, I guess.

After a few weeks, we were allowed to get a pass to go to the nearest town, Mineral Wells.

Another time we traveled by convoy to Fort Worth to attend the Stockman's exposition, my first rodeo.

It was during these times away from camp that I saw a colored person for the first time. They walked in the gutter whenever we met them on the sidewalk and had their own drinking fountains, latrines, and would ride in the back of the bus.

We received our infantry training in thirteen weeks. During the eleventh week, we began to think we were real soldiers. Our sergeant, who had been treating us kind of mean, became a little friendlier and turned out to be a regular guy. We started to think that our outfit was just a little better than the other ones, and we thought we were pretty sharp. Little did we know of what was yet to come.

At the end of the training, we boarded another train, and after about three days, we arrived at Fort Bragg (3), North Carolina, where we stayed for six months of intensive training. We found out that our training at Camp Wolters had just been a starter. Within the first week at Fort Bragg, we went on twenty-mile hikes and ten-mile speed hikes.

Early in this training, we were assigned to the Ninth Division and into three regiments, the Thirty-ninth, the Forty-seventh, and the Sixtieth. I was assigned to Company K, Sixtieth Infantry, which was a rifle company and was given all the various little jobs that a new guy in the outfit gets from the old-timers.

The Ninth Division was a regular army division and at that time was attached to the Amphibious Force of the Atlantic Fleet. Our main training consisted of making amphibious landings at various places up and down the East Coast and Chesapeake Bay. We made daylight and under-cover-of-darkness landings, the night landings under strict blackout discipline. Those could get scary and did most of the time.

We made all types of landings from rubber boats and Higgins boats (4), to Landing Craft Infantry (5), and destroyers and troop transports. For instance, we would go over the side of a troop transport on huge landing nets and drop into the various boats we were using. We were carrying everything a soldier carries into combat such as extra ammunition, hand grenades, rations, a full field pack, a gas mask, our weapons, and various other items.

Then we would proceed up the coast to the landing site, hike eighteen to twenty miles inland, and set up a road block or capture a small town. Then we would wait until dark the next night to withdraw and return to the transports waiting for us. We had to find and signal our recovery boats to once more approach the shores where we could wade out to them. Of course there were many accidents. Time and tide worked against us, and sometimes the waves were eight to ten feet high. If one of us lost our grip on the nets, there was almost no chance of rescue, for all the gear we carried would drag us down at once.

One night we were working off a destroyer using rubber boats when a larger-than-usual wave washed a couple of guys off into the water. We always had a rope dragging in the water from each rubber boat, and one GI (6) was lucky enough to grab it by hand. We were able to get him back into the craft. The other GI was lost. That was not an uncommon experience. Sometimes some of the men would freeze on the nets, and someone would have to go down the nets after him and pull him up on the deck.

After a couple of months of training of this sort, I was transferred to the Third Battalion Headquarters Company. This company was responsible for keeping the rest of the battalion supplied with food, ammunition, and reinforcements.

Once, when we had pulled landings for a few weeks, we had to break off and were sent to the Virginia National Forest to fight a large forest fire. The regular firefighters were not able to control the fire and had asked for help. The division commander sent in about a thousand men, and for two days we fought the fire. We finally got control of it and gave it back to the forest service to mop up. We then returned to Fort Bragg for a few days of rest and to clean up.

When we returned to Fort Bragg, we found that the Eighty-second Airborne had moved into our barracks. All our gear had been transferred to a bivouac (7) area called Chicken Road. For a short while we were told to sleep in pup tents. Naturally, there were some hard feelings because we considered the airborne to be "glory boys" (8).

That Saturday evening the town of Fayetteville was visited by guys looking for trouble, and it erupted in a place called the Town Pump, a very large beer palace. There were a few cross words spoken, and soon our first battle of the war took place. Lots of exits were made where there were none before, right through plate glass windows. Fists, bottles, and steins of beer were thrown. Even women had hair-pulling contests. The local police were not able to handle the situation and called for help from the military police. Several rounds of tear gas were fired, and lots of GIs were carried off to jail.

The next morning, a Sunday, we got called out about 07:30 for a battalion formation. The first thing that the battalion commanding officer did was to dispatch all the company commanding officers to town to get all our men out of jail. Then he told the rest of us who sported black eyes and bruised knuckles, and who were expecting a tongue lashing, that he was real proud of us and the way we had handled the situation. We liked our leader.

Following our tour at Fort Bragg, we were loaded on troop transports at Norfolk, Virginia, and left the United States on October 23, 1942. After two days at sea, we were told that we were going to North Africa. The officers and men were given the battle plan, and our objectives were spelled out, so that the NCOs (non-commissioned officer or sergeant) could begin to prepare their men for battle. The Thirty-ninth Regiment was directed to go through the Strait of Gibraltar along with troops from the First Division and land at Algiers to secure the airport and gain other prizes. The Forty-seventh Regiment was directed to capture the airports and subdue the shore batteries located at Safi and Casablanca. The Sixtieth Regiment's directions were to subdue the shore batteries at Mehdia and Port Lyautey in French Morocco and capture and hold the airports there.

THREE

Our Support for our Mission

All three regiments of the Ninth Division had been made into combat teams. Each team was an artillery, a combat unit which used big guns, and had light tanks for scouting, and supply units and other companies so we could fight on our own without division control. Each team had naval units to support them as well.

The artillery was one of the most important parts of an infantry division. Each company had handheld grenade launchers, BARs (Browning Automatic Rifles), 60 mm mortars (1), 30 caliber air-cooled machine guns, and other small weapons. One company in each battalion had 81 mm mortars and 30 caliber water-cooled machine guns.

Platoons, typically made up of around forty-two men, were assigned to the three infantry rifle companies. The battalion headquarters company had an anti-tank platoon, with 37 mm shells.

There was also a pioneer platoon, which was responsible for supplies and ammunition, a communications platoon with radios and telephones, an intelligence platoon, and the motor pool gang.

Each regiment in the artillery had an anti-tank company and a cannon company with larger weapons than the battalions had. Each regiment also had a battalion of field artillery assigned to it.

When our mission was to take a high point, usually the field artillery would lay down a barrage on the crest of the hill. This would last from a few minutes to a few hours. Sometimes all three of the division's field artillery battalions would concentrate on one sector. When they spoke, everybody listened.

Several different kinds of shells were used. Sometimes smoke was used to conceal a ridge. Tracers were used to designate a target. High explosive firing was used for effect while armor piercing was used for tanks and other objects. Phosphorous shells and air-burst shells, which would explode a certain distance above the ground, were used.

When the artillery had a mission, they would fire all night if needed; consequently there wasn't much sleeping in the vicinity. Our nights were never very restful, and those "big boys" made it worse. We began to recognize which was incoming or outgoing "mail", as we called it. Sometimes a firing ring would come loose on a large shell, and it would sound like a train going by. Our hair would stand on end. One of the more frightening weird sounds would come at dusk when six barrel rockets were fired at us. When these were fired, we would curl up in our foxholes. The artillery would receive a lot of return fire and would have to change position many times.

FOUR

Our First Battle in French Morocco

November 1942

The French, whom we opposed, had been forewarned that we were coming in hopes that they would not give us any resistance. They decided to fight as a matter of honor.

Early on the morning of November 8, 1942, we made an amphibious landing near Port Lyautey in French Morocco. Our commander was Lt. Col. John J. Toffey, Jr., and our first mission was to capture and hold the airport there. Our ship was the *USS Susan B. Anthony*, and we landed at three in the morning and started for shore in a heavy groundswell and full tide.

Around five thirty, two French fighter planes dived on the destroyer that was escorting us, strafing and bombing, and causing the loss of two landing craft, but without casualties among their occupants. We opened up with everything we had, driving them back up in the clouds. As we neared shore, they dove on the Higgins boats, and one plane headed our way. A bullet knocked the canteen out of one of our boat team's hands.

At six in the morning, we landed on the beach. As I jumped off the boat, a big wave caught me. I had a box of MG (machine gun) ammo besides three rounds of AT grenades (1) and a regular combat load. I nearly drowned.

We hurried up the sandy slopes seeking cover from attack by more strafing planes, which were taking off from the airport. Everyone was shooting at the planes, and we did shoot one down with small arms fire. It landed in the ocean seventy-five yards from shore. When some of our men later swam out to the wreck, they found it had over two hundred holes in it from rifles and Tommy gun fire. The pilot had twenty-seven holes in him.

Our headquarters company with their medical detachments didn't stop to reorganize but continued as a boat team until we had struggled up the steep escarpment east of the sand dunes to high ground, about 165 feet above the sea. Two hours after the first landings, we completed the climb, about seven miles, carrying our equipment, which was much more than our regular load, and were ready to advance to the bluffs north of the airdrome. We then discovered that we had not been brought to Red Beach, but instead to a point five miles farther north. What lay ahead was an arduous cross-country march of approximately five miles with the necessity of hand-carrying everything over ridges and through scrub growth. We met no resistance and were in position (but without supporting artillery) on Hill 38 by noon.

After our journey, we were relieved to see the airport and Port Lyautey. We stayed on a hill overlooking the airport for the rest of the day. That night, as we were trying to take the airport, we were brought under fire from mortars, and the shore batteries were firing at the various landing boats and ships that were bringing in our men and supplies. We slept about two hours.

On November 9 in the morning, we went to Hill 38 where we had a lot of casualties from machine gun fire. It rained most of the next day and night. We were cold and miserable.

I had a raincoat that I shared with a buddy. It didn't help much, for by morning we were soaked and cold. This continued to be the typical pattern for the rest of the time we spent at Port Lyautey: wet, cold, and miserable. It was the rainy season, and sleeping on the cold ground where we only averaged a few hours of sleep at night was the norm.

We had naval support from one of the biggest ships of the time, the battleship *USS Texas*, which fired her big guns at the shore batteries and soon silenced them. On November 10, we finally got near the airport, and our planes started coming in, and we engaged with machine gun and mortar fire. The first five planes cracked up. Artillery fire from the Kasba (fortress) landed to our left less than one hundred yards away. The airport was next to the Sebou River, which opened to the ocean. The navy put fifty men on a destroyer-transport, *Dallas*, which came up the river, and fired point-blank at our opposition until the firing ceased during the morning on November 11, 1942.

We had taken the airport, and our planes were landing, and our other units were still encountering gunfire from light tanks when the French called for a truce. The first fight for Africa was over in three days. It was learned that we had three hundred men who were lost or wounded. The French lost over one thousand men.

These first deaths, seen on such a large scale, I carried with me for the rest of my life; they taught me the meaning of "war is hell!" The cold and rainy circumstances under which we fought underlined that idea.

The Sixtieth and Forty-seventh rested for a few days and then turned to the East. We still had a few thousand miles to go before meeting up with Rommel (German Field Marshal Erwin Rommel (a.k.a. "The Desert Fox") and the African Corporation.

Before heading out to Algiers and Tunisia, we had an opportunity to see Martha Raye (2), a comic actress and vocalist who came to entertain the troops with the USO (3). We were camped in a cork forest, and it was primitive. The latrines were just slit trenches, but when we heard Martha was coming, we constructed a wooden seat to put over the trench. She entertained us for an hour and a half from the back of a truck, and she had us in stitches! She was wearing a fur coat because it was so chilly. When she had to heed the call of nature, our battalion commander escorted her over to the wooden seat, and she sat there in her fur coat and carried on a conversation with the commanding officer while waving to the troops. A great gal she was!

Christmas of 1942 was low-key. Since it was the first Christmas away from home for the boys, many spent it by getting drunk.

On January 14, 1943, President Roosevelt came to Morocco to attend the Casablanca conference where various leaders of the Allies met to plan their strategy for the war. He also reviewed the American troops.

There was no more action except for a few casualties from mines in the Kasserine Pass and a few strafing attacks by Messerschmitts (4), German fighter aircrafts, as we moved up to Maknassy.

FIVE

Moving on to Algeria and Tunisia

February 1943

On February 1, 1943, we started moving toward the front. Rommel (German Field Marshal Erwin Rommell (a.k.a. "The Desert Fox") was trying to break through the Kasserine Pass to capture a big supply depot at Tebessa, Algeria. We were moving closer but still were hundreds of miles away. Our division artillery, which was behind us, was almost eight hundred miles from the pass when they were alerted to stop the Germans at all costs. All of our transportation was taken away so that the artillery could move faster. They had to take an incredible journey over the mountains, under blackout conditions, through rain and sleet. They lost a few trucks and guns by slipping off the roads. They reached the pass where a few British troops were sacrificing themselves to slow up the German tanks. Our artillery went into action immediately and fired point-blank at the tanks, which had 88 mm guns. One battery was overrun, but the rest punished the tanks so severely with their 105 mm guns that the Germans had to withdraw, leaving many burning tanks behind them.

We, in the infantry, moved by truck, train, and foot across French Morocco to Algeria then Tunisia. Most of the time, we were on foot. Once again we were made into combat teams, this time with the First Armored Division. We also had some help from Moroccan Goums (1), or native soldiers. They used to go out at night and slit throats or collect ears. The Italians and Germans were really scared of those fellows.

When we reached the pass, we dug in along the sides and spent a few days taking potshots at the German planes that came through the pass to take shots at our artillery. At this time of the war, the only allied planes we saw were Boston Liberators (2), flying really high, so as to cross the Mediterranean to make their bombing runs.

The mission of the Sixtieth was to capture the mountaintop east of the town of Maknassy, Tunisia, that was held by the Germans. There were two ranges of hills, one higher than the other, with numerous ravines running up the slopes. The Germans had fortified the highest of the hills to protect the flank of Rommel's army while he was fighting General Montgomery much farther to the south.

The British army had captured the Port of Tripoli and were trying to build up their supply lines when they were halted for about eight weeks. While Montgomery was building up his troops, Rommel with two hundred thousand desert veterans decided to break out of the ring of mountains and go through the Faid Pass and Kasserine Pass to chop up the American army and capture supplies. For the first six days, he almost succeeded in outflanking American forces. The Germans cut off a combat team of the Thirty-fourth Infantry Division of the 168th Infantry. The regiment was overrun, along with one of the Thirty-ninth Infantry Cannon companies that had been helping out.

The First Armored Division was greatly outnumbered and lost quite a few tanks and had to fall back. We lost a couple of airplane fighter strips or bases. At Kasserine Pass, the Third Battalion, the Thirty-ninth Infantry, and the anti-tank company were hit by two panzer (3) divisions. The Thirty-ninth Division was overrun completely and the cannon company lost all of its guns. Rommel was loose and about to capture Thala and Tebessa, which were two of our bigger supply stations. Just beyond the Kasserine Pass on the road to Thala there was a ridge where a small unit of British light tanks was located. They sacrificed themselves and delayed the Germans for one day.

A portion of the British Twenty-sixth Armored Regiment moved into Thala, along with a few infantry men to form a line of defense. That was the situation on February 20, 1943, and it really looked bad for the Allied soldiers.

Our division artillery was eight hundred miles away at Tlemcen in Algeria. Word was received on February 17 to send all the available artillery and cannons to Tebessa by forced march. The roads were narrow and slippery from frost and rain, but the men kept moving, stopping only for food and fuel until the morning of February 21. In less than one hundred hours, they had moved almost eight hundred miles and had lost some of their guns and supplies over the sides of the road and down the mountain. They finally approached the battle zone and got into position, spreading out the artillery units as well as they could so they could take advantage of the reverse slope of several low hills. The only things between them and the enemy were three platoons of British troops, which were not as big as ours, and a few light tanks.

On the morning of February 22, 1943, the Germans opened up with an artillery attack and started to move forward with their tanks and the support of their dive-bombers. When they started, they were only twenty-five hundred yards away. For three hours, the Stukas (4) tried to silence our guns, but could not. A battery of the Eighty-fourth Field Artillery (FA) lowered its guns and fired point-blank with its 105 mm guns to help stop the oncoming tanks. Two of the guns of the Eighty-fourth were hit and put out of action, but the rest of the battery kept fighting. Rommel tried to break through all day, but our 105 mm and our 155 mm kept on putting tanks out of action. Finally, our infantry started to help out, and some B17 bombers polished off a few. Rommel started to retreat through the Kasserine Pass.

During two days, the First Armored Division lost one hundred tanks, and at least two thousand Americans were taken prisoner, along with our destroyed guns and dead and wounded. But Rommel suffered even more and lost a lot of his armor and retreated toward the east.

It was also during this time period, on February 27, 1943, that I was made staff sergeant (5). (Recorded in Charley's diary with no further information about this event.)

In the meantime, the infantry of the Ninth Division was hurrying to catch up, but we had nearly eight hundred miles to go and not much transport to speed up the process. Finally, a few trucks were dispatched to help us out. They would shuttle a company at a time about twenty miles forward and go back for another company while we kept hiking.

Picture two files of dead tired soldiers walking, walking, walking, until we did not know if we could take another step. We were heavily laden with all the things needed to fight a war.

Picture German soldiers, prisoners, walking from the other way, and they looked as tired as we were. One of our men who was carrying an 81 MM mortar barrel in addition to his other load suddenly smashed the barrel of the mortar against the head of a prisoner. We could see his brains run out. The GI said, "You SOB! You're the cause of all this misery!" The rest of us passing the body lying there didn't give a damn.

After arriving, we were given the task of holding what had been gained. The Sixtieth was given the job of holding two airports. At this time, the American forces in Africa consisted of the Thirty-fourth Infantry Division, the First Infantry Division, the First Armored Division, and the Ninth Division with some special units. At this time, General Patton took command of the II Corps. The Third Battalion, Sixtieth Regiment, attempted to take the high ground at Maknassey.

We jumped off in the attack as dusk fell late in the month of March. Our boys successfully reached the high slopes of the high range around midnight, with a moderate amount of resistance from the Germans. Then all hell broke loose. Our own artillery started to shell the crest lines of the hills where some of our men were. That was before the forward artillery outfits reached the infantry. The fire caused many casualties in our rifle companies, and it was decided to withdraw from the hill so the wounded could be cared for. We tried to take that hill for twelve days, but the Germans had reinforced it and were determined to hold it.

On March 22, twelve medium tanks were brought up to bring superior fire power on the enemy while our boys were attacking. Two tanks were knocked out. Our artillery again fell on our own troops. Our battalion commander, Colonel Toffey, had both legs broken when his jeep was blown up by a land mine. There were many casualties.

On March 23, our artillery concentrated very heavily on the hill. No attacks were made on either side. Snipers got a few, however.

On March 24, I went up with Captain O'Rouke. Our own artillery fell among us, bouncing me off the ground several times. I was lucky and didn't get wounded. We were shot at by machine guns and rifles. I got a few targets myself. When we came back to camp, we got shelled by mortars dropping in the wadi (6). A dud landed six feet away.

On March 25, we were relieved by the Sixtieth Infantry and withdrew to reorganize. About thirty men had been killed and one hundred wounded and evacuated. We continued to rest and reorganize on the Twenty-seventh and moved back to our position on the Twenty-eighth.

On March 29, we received small arms and mortar fire. There were many casualties, and eleven Germans were captured. Company L caught heavy artillery fire for about an hour.

They had heavy casualties including officers. Only forty men were left in that company. Our rifle companies were down to about half strength, and the acting battalion commander asked if I would take a group of the headquarters company personnel up to help them out at the scene of the heaviest fighting.

I agreed and took fourteen volunteers from the Ammo and Pioneer Platoon up the hill just as the enemy attacked again. Lying on the back slope of a high hill, we strained our eyes into the night looking at the skyline. We could hear the Germans walking a short distance away. We were scared and felt alone while we threw hand grenades over the top of the hill and received some from the enemy. We heard the rush of the enemy coming at us. I stood up, fired, and used a bayonet (7) as I had been taught so long ago. I killed or severely wounded three Germans.

Helping my friends who were wounded was my next priority. I could feel blood running down the right side of my face where my ear had been wounded, and I realized I was partially deaf in that ear. Blood was also running down the inside of my leg from a bayonet wound. I was shaking so bad from the aftermath of the nervous tension that I could hardly hold on to my gun.

For the rest of the long, cold night, we laid on the hill, shaking and waiting for the same thing to start all over again. We were scared, and afraid to show it. I prayed a lot. We got relieved from our defense of the hill around two in the morning. We lost fifty men that day.

The next day we carried our dead and the seriously wounded to the bottom of the hill. Of the fourteen men I took up, two were killed, and five of us were wounded. I was lucky that my wounds were only superficial.

For the next several days, we were engaged in battle, and casualties were quite heavy. On March 30, we changed our attacking position to a defensive one. On the Thirty-first, there was much artillery and mortar fire. We made a fake attack and were counterattacked by the enemy. On April 1, we received light mortar and artillery fire. Patrols were sent out, but they received heavy machine gun fire. We did locate a mine field. On April 2, the enemy and our boys were quite active. There were a few casualties. On April 3, the enemy threw heavy mortar fire on our troops. Casualties were quite heavy. During the night we put up barb wire and caught a few bullets in doing so. On April 4, we spotted some enemy trucks and artillery and opened on same. We laid land mines that night. We got some replacements and sent out a strong patrol. On April 5, there wasn't much change. Casualties light. On the Sixth and Seventh, our patrols caught it. Several were killed.

On April 8, we got some replacements. I guided them into the wadi and bedded them down. At about seven in the morning, smoke landed in our wadi, and I yelled at the men to take cover. New men didn't jump fast enough, and three were killed as several Eighty-eights landed in the wadi. We were shelled heavily all day long. It was really getting on my nerves since I had averaged only two hours' sleep a night for over two weeks.

A few days passed, and we were relieved by troops of the Sixth Infantry. Patrols were sent out and encountered no enemy. It was over for a while. Eighty-five men had been killed, and 215 were evacuated.

For several days, we were busy picking up our dead, and burying them in shallow graves, so they could be transferred by the grave registration people. That was the hardest job of all, rolling bodies of our friends into blankets so we could carry them down the hill. Their bodies had laid decomposing in the sun for days, and were filled with maggots and smelled so terrible that we had to wear gas masks. The only way we could identify most of them was by dog tag (8). A bulldozer dug a shallow trench, and the bodies were placed in a common grave. Our battalion chaplain gave a short burial service with all the men gathered around. The bodies would later be transferred to a regular GI cemetery. As the battalion sergeant major (9), I had known a lot of them personally. It was hard. I still dream about that day.

We rested for a week or so and then moved north to the head of the Sedjeanne Valley.

In an article that was printed on September 15, 1943, in the *Cottonwood County Citizen*, Charley's hometown newspaper, his valor was celebrated.

> ### Willsher Wins Coveted Army D.S.C.
> ### Soldier Cited for Bravery During Campaign in Tunisia
> ### Extraordinary Heroism Displayed by Sgt. Willsher
>
> News that the Distinguished Service Cross has been awarded to Charles Willsher, makes (his community) very proud, indeed, and yet very humble. His mother, Mrs. Robert Willsher, and his sister, Amy, just recently had a short letter from Charles telling of his award and the action in which he had taken part.
>
> Of all the boys who have gone from (our community), perhaps none have seen more of the war than Charles. Leaving (our community) in January of 1941, he has been overseas since November of 1942, when he was one of the group landing near Casablanca. He has taken part in the campaign of North Africa and has seen action in Sicily.
>
> It is hard to believe that our boys are being called upon to face such danger and that they find themselves where they must risk their lives in such hazardous undertakings. We print below the account of Charles' part in the action, taken from his camp newspaper:
>
> Charles S. Willsher, Staff Sergeant, Headquarters Company, XXXX Battalion, XXXX Team, United States Army, for extraordinary heroism in action during the campaign at XXXX Tunisia. On

> the afternoon of XXXX March 1943 Staff Sergeant Willsher, upon learning that the enemy had launched an attack on the position held by Company XXXX requested that the Battalion Commander allow him to take forward a group of volunteers from Headquarters Company to assist in driving the enemy to the rear. Permission was granted and Staff Sergeant Willsher helped lead a group of 14 men. They arrived at the scene of heaviest fighting at about 1530 hours where they were led by Staff Sergeant Willsher to the crest of the hill over which the enemy was attempting to storm. Using hand grenades and rifles, the volunteer group succeeded in driving the enemy from this hill, inflicting severe causalities on them. Staff Sergeant Willsher was seen to follow the withdrawing troops and either kill or severely wound three. During this brief engagement five members of the group were wounded. Staff Sergeant Willsher received a piece of shrapnel in the right ear but refused to be evacuated. He remained on the scene of the battle personally supervising and assisting in the evacuation of the wounded and dead. Having satisfied himself that all of his men were accounted for and his assistance no longer needed, he returned to the Battalion Command Post to resume his duties as Sergeant Major.
>
> *Cottonwood County Citizen*, September 15, 1943

Charley, in his own words, characteristically played down the importance of his role in the event just described. According to the *Cottonwood County Citizen*, in the November 7, 1984, issue, Joann Eaton wrote that "In August of 1943, Staff Sgt. Willsher earned his Distinguished Service Cross at Maknassey, Tunisia. In a pitched battle with the Germans, the Americans took the mountain at night. The strategic battle point belonged to the Allies until US heavy artillery blew the Americans off the top of the mountain by mistake. The Germans reinforced the mountain after the American retreat, and it was twenty-one days before the GIs regained their position." In an interview with Charley about his war experience, she wrote that he said, "We found dead Americans who had been lying out in the sun for twenty-one hot days. I still have dreams about it."

Eaton continued to write,

> During the Battle at Maknassey, a group of GIs were pinned down and in danger of being overrun by Germans. Willsher rounded up a group of volunteers and led them into the area, turning the threatened defeat into a victory. When the Germans retreated, Willsher followed and killed two German soldiers. That act of bravery earned Willsher the second highest military award, the Distinguished Service Cross. He was decorated by General Patton. He also received his first Purple Heart after taking shrapnel in the ear.
>
> Even though he was wounded, he refused to be evacuated. Wanting to help his buddies took precedence over his own safety. Willsher doesn't consider his actions such a big thing.
>
> "They needed help. I couldn't just leave them there. Someone had to go," he said simply. Then he added, "It doesn't feel very good to know you have killed somebody. I don't know how you reconcile that with anything."

SIX

Sicily

April 1943

From April 21, 1943, through May 9, we hiked northward toward the Mediterranean through the mountains and toward the city of Bizerte in Tunisia. It was really tough going. We traveled through underbrush four to six feet high, and the stiff branches soon had our clothing in tatters. By May 4, some of the men had no shoes, trousers, or shirts.

There were no roads, and we were supplied by mules that had to go forward with the supplies and come back to get more supplies in order to go forward again. Soon the mules were even more worn-out than we were.

There were many days when we did not average a meal a day. I remember one day sharing a can of C rations (1) with a buddy, the first food we had eaten in four days. At one point, I took some men back, and we handcarried some forty pound boxes of rations back to the troops. We had enough food for one meal. Water was also scarce. Mules bringing rations were shelled, and ammunition was running low. We went back to get rations and found just enough so that every five men would get one ration between them. One day we passed a field where some cows were grazing. One of the men slit some steaks out of a cow, and we had a meal, promptly followed by the runs.

The men were becoming very tired and fell asleep while hiking. They would fall into the ditches, wake up, and fall back into line. I lost about fifteen pounds at this time. By April 30, the mules had finally caught up with the men, and everyone got two meals that day.

On May 1, we dug in and set up mortars and machine guns and gave them the works.

The first battalion on our right got caught up even with us. On the second and third, we were able to move forward, rest, and get more supplies. We were able to eat some food for a change. We then received orders to attack. On the fifth we moved into position to attack at about 1900 hours. On May 7, we captured fifteen prisoners, were fired on by tanks and artillery, and moved on to a hill overlooking Ferryville. On the eighth, we moved out at about 1900 hours toward Bizerte. We cut the Coastal Highway and started down the mountains toward the Mediterranean. Trucks were finally able to bring us some supplies including our duffel bags with our extra clothing. We came to a small river flowing toward the Mediterranean where we jumped in, shaved each other's heads, got rid of our lice, got into spare clothing, and almost felt like we were humans again.

That night, May 8, we attacked and captured the airport at Bizerte at 2200 hours, and then laid down in the grass around the airport to sleep. When we awoke, everyone was covered with sand flea bites. I imagine they wouldn't have bothered us if we hadn't had that bath. We stunk too bad after eighteen days of hard travel. We had the bright idea of going to the buildings of the airport and getting gas in our helmets to dip our clothing in to get rid of the fleas. It worked great, but when we didn't have water to rinse them, there was a great deal of cussing when the gasoline hit those raw flea bites. And of course, the smokers didn't dare light up for a couple of days.

On May 9, we guarded the airport at Bizerte while the artillery and planes took over. In the meantime, the Germans had surrendered at Tunis. The fighting was over in Africa.

Throughout this period of being under attack, we had twenty-five casualties, and 110 were wounded and evacuated. We captured seven prisoners. It was especially hard to fight when we were so tired and hungry. There was no more action until we reached Sicily in August.

By July 10, 1943, we were trucked back to a place called Magenta, Algeria, 125 miles south of Oran on the edge of the Saharan Desert. We went into training for the invasion of Sicily. Many of us, including myself, were suffering from dysentery caused by the flies. They would fly up into our noses, into our mouths when we were eating, or crawl into our mess kit. When a cramp hit, it was impossible to reach the latrine in time. More cussing.

The windup of our training for Sicily was a hike of 125 miles to Oran during the hottest time of the year. We were to hike it in five days. The first day we hiked in the daytime and made twenty-one miles. The plans were changed, and from then on, we hiked at night and camped in hot wheat fields by day. The fourth day was the toughest for me. I fell asleep hiking as did most of the boys. Can you imagine nearly half a battalion of men walking down the road, two and one half miles an hour, asleep? We would wake up in the ditch, and our buddies would help us fall back in line. Fortunately, we rode the last fifteen miles to camp. It took us six days, and then we rested before moving on to Sicily.

I think that the only thing that saved us was that the Arabs would come down the road with two-wheeled carts piled high with melons to eat.

About the fourth night out, the regimental commander came rolling down the road in his jeep between two columns of men. I am sure, if he is alive, that his ears are still burning from the tongue lashing he got. It gave us incentive to make that hike, no matter what.

We rested on the beaches near Oran for a couple of days; then we moved to the Tofouroui Airport at Oran. We slept in a Spanish house on straw-filled mattress covers. I think this was the best sleeping I had overseas even though it was on a cold, cement floor.

We boarded a ship for Sicily on July 26, 1943. The fighting had been going on for a few days before we pulled into Palermo Harbor on August 1, 1943. One of the transports with our vehicles was pulled up at the dock where an ammunition train was being loaded. We anchored near there for the night.

At about one o'clock in the morning, the German planes flew over and started to bomb. Every ship in the harbor started to fire everything they had at them.

I had been sleeping on deck like most of the other GIs because it was cooler there. We woke up to the most beautiful fireworks display as the navy and transports all fired at the bombers. The navy got seven of them, and they got one of our tankers.

Soon our ship was out of ready ammunition, and the soldiers started bringing up shells from below the deck. We kept those guns hot until the bombing was over, about one and a half hours later. Then it took the rest of the night to clean up. The navy shot down seven bombers that night, and they exploded as they hit the sides of the mountains as they came down. It was quite a night and hard for the men to quiet down afterward.

The next day we unloaded and were soon heading for the hills where the Germans were waiting. In a day or so, we were in the mountains of Sicily being supplied by mules again. This time there were enough roads, so there was no difficulty in being supplied. It was cold up in the mountains, especially when the clouds came down at night. Many a mule had his feet tied, was flopped to the ground, and a couple of GIs hunkered down beside the mules to keep warm. The after-smell on the GIs wasn't too great!

From August fourth to the fifteenth, we marched through the hills over rough terrain. On some days, there would be heavy artillery fire, blown bridges, and roads that were heavily mined. On other days there was no action. By May 7, we reached Mount Paleto where the First Battalion had received a lot of gunfire. They had heavy casualties, and we furnished litter bearers for them. By August 10, we reached Mount Camelot, and on the twelfth, we were fired on by machine guns at Mount Cuculo. The enemy withdrew. One man was killed. On the thirteenth we moved to Floresta. Bridges were blown, and the roads were heavily mined. We captured five Germans. On the fourteenth, we moved toward Montalbano where we took one prisoner. On the fifteenth, we received orders to remain in our bivouac. Motor patrols were sent out for stray Germans. It was all over in Sicily.

During this campaign, although we did have our supply problem licked, it was probably tougher on the men than the Sedjeanne, owing to the extreme rugged areas of the country. We hiked long distances each day, and the men were generally exhausted. However, we did eat every day.

When our forces in Italy were having such a terrible time at Anzio, we were alerted to back them up. By September 8, 1943, a toehold was established in Italy, and we boarded a ship and headed west. *Great!* we thought. *We are headed for the U.S.* When we passed the Azore Islands, we turned north and realized that we were headed for "Jolly Old England." When we got there, everyone got a pass or two, and then we plunged full bore into training for the invasion of Europe. We got a little tired of hearing the British say, "Don't you Yanks know there is a war on?" We knew all right.

By this time in the war, Charley had not slept in a bed for over a year. In his diary he wrote, "My hips are calloused from lying on the ground. My knees have rheumatism, and I never seem to get enough sleep. Most of the boys have the GIs (gastrointestinal disorder) most of the time, and we are all suspected of having amoebic dysentery. They better get us home soon, or we will all be in the hospital!"

> Letter Home from Sicily (to a friend and published in the *Cottonwood County Citizen*)
>
> Received your very welcome letter a few days ago but owing to battle circumstances could not answer it at that time, so will try to answer it now that we have everything under control. Yes, we are in Sicily. People here are very glad to see the Americans and greet us with open arms. However, they are expecting us to feed them as they cannot grow enough food to feed themselves. This is going to be another problem for the US to conquer, but they will do it.
>
> We had some pretty rough going over the mountains but now are getting a much needed rest. The country is very nice and almost every kind of nut and fruit and vegetable grows here. One of the most interesting sights is Mt. Etna which is an active volcano. Smoke can be seen pouring out of it for several miles.
>
> No, there is not a thing you can send me except lots of letters; they are the things I need the most. We nearly always have enough to eat even if it is not very appetizing. With the nuts and wild fruits we pick up, we get along very nicely. I am afraid I am considerably thinner than when I was home, but I am still feeling pretty good so cannot kick too much. Guess it is time for me to sign off. Keep those letters coming. Charley.

During this time between the campaigns of Sicily and France, Charley received the Distinguished Service Cross from General Patton on October 26, 1943. Characteristically, he did not mention this in his memoirs or his diary. I will never know if this was because he was conflicted about the award or because he never liked to talk about himself and his accomplishments. During the years when I was growing up and until the 1980s, I never heard him talk about the war, saw his medals, or knew that he was considered a hero.

General George S. Patton giving Charles S. Willsher the Distinguished Service Cross in August 1943

SEVEN

England

November 1943

After the African campaign and the trip to Sicily, Charley boarded a ship at Palermo on November 8 and left Sicily on the tenth. The destination was England so that the troops could prepare for the invasion of France. After passing the Rock of Gibraltar on November 15, and the Bay of Bristol on November 24, they landed on Thanksgiving Day in 1943 and were stationed there until the Normandy Invasion in June of 1944.

On the way to England a lot of money changed hands. There were games in every compartment and even on deck. I suppose that most of the money that started in the hands of many ended up in the pockets of just a few. I knew a guy in K Company who once was a dealer in Las Vegas who sent home lots of money each month.

We landed in Southampton on Thanksgiving Day, were trucked to Winchester, and moved into barracks that the Black Watch, a famous British regiment, had recently occupied.

The barracks were heated by small coal stoves, and soon nearly everyone had a cold; some even had to go to the hospital. We had lived on the ground for nearly eighteen months and never suffered from colds, but as soon as we were inside and sleeping on cots, everyone got sick.

Training started at once: close order drill, long hikes, speed hikes, and commando training. I remember those speed hikes. Our battalion set out to establish a record that others could not match. One day we started out on a ten-mile speed hike, combat loaded of course, and from the time we left the gate and until we returned was one hour and forty-seven minutes. Needless to say we had the long-legged guys in the front and us little guys were in the rear. I had to run nearly every step of the way. I could think, but I did not have enough breath to cuss.

It was cold and wet in England, and all of us men who had been overseas the longest got furloughs of seven days starting on December 16. Another sergeant from our company and I spent our leave in London. We rented a room in a private hotel, just off Trafalgar Square, not far from Hyde Park and Piccadilly Circus. The other sergeant could play the piano by ear, and when we would walk into a pub, he would wander over to the piano and start playing. Soon the top of the piano was lined with mugs of beer. The beer was flat because it had no hops in it, and I thought it a poor substitute for American beer. I would make one mug last for the evening while I played darts, the great British pastime.

London was getting bombed very often in those days, and when the sirens sounded, most of the people would spend their nights in the subways. If we were asleep in our rooms, we would not move, for we knew we would be back in the thick of things before long. We figured that it didn't make any difference if we got hit by a bullet on the battlefield or a bomb in London, so we just had a good time.

On Christmas, we showed some kids a good time.

When we were stationed at Winchester, we were reviewed by Prime Minister Churchill and General Eisenhower. General Montgomery also came to talk to us one day. He was so short that he stood on the hood of a jeep so we could see him. We received some replacements directly from the States, and were built up to battle strength again.

We traveled south to Bournemouth and resumed hard training. Our company was moved into an old hotel that had been stripped for army use. It was right on the beach and a British anti-aircraft outfit was within fifty feet of us.

Whenever the bombers were coming over, the guns would start way down on the beach, and soon the ones outside would just about break your eardrums. The new replacements would run for the air raid shelters, but the rest of us would stay in our sacks where we were dry and warm. They thought we were crazy, but we knew what was coming, and we were not about to give up our comforts.

We knew that the invasion was close at hand. The whole half of southern England was filled with troops and vehicles. You could drive past mile after mile of half-tracks, tanks, trucks of all kinds, field hospitals, and all the other things that were soon going to cross the English Channel.

> Letter Home to Former Employers at Lewis and Lewis Drugs, Dec. 2, 1943
>
> I am somewhere in England. Nothing I can write about except that I am well and did receive your box. Thanks very much and Merry Christmas. I will write later. Your boy, Charley.

EIGHT

France and Normandy

June 1944

We were alerted on June 5 that we would be crossing the channel on the sixth. We spent the day cleaning our guns and equipment and writing letters. On the sixth very early in the morning, hundreds of planes were in the air headed across the channel toward Normandy (1).

We loaded on British ships and were fed a breakfast of liver that had a green, slimy gravy on it. Needless to say, a lot of us had nothing but coffee. There were hundreds of boats in the channel, and we had to wait our turn. The initial plan of the invasion in our sector was as follows: The Fourth Division was to land on the Utah Beach and establish the beach area. The Eighty-second Airborne was to land inland, and glider troops were to secure the river areas. Utah beach was practically flat, but the Germans had built a wall for about ten thousand yards, which was heavily fortified. At the Omaha Beach, the First and Twenty-ninth divisions were engaged.

There was no room initially for our division to land until the enemy had been displaced a bit. Upon our landing, we were organized to move through the other division's areas and move out to the Cotentin Peninsula. Our Second Battalion had crossed the Douve River and run into heavy resistance, and we were to join up with them. This we did just at dusk. In the meantime, the Eighty-second Airborne had moved forward and crossed the river to the south. Then the race was on in an effort to cut the Cherbourg Peninsula. The division swept south toward Saint-Lô-d'Ourville. The Ninth had gained twelve and one-half miles in two days.

The *New York Times* said about our achievement,

> Omar Bradley had done it again. Slipping stronger units past the lines of their tiring comrades, he once more smashed unexpectedly through the Germans to cut off Cherbourg, just as he broke through to doom Bizerte, a little over a year ago. And he used the same outfit—the battle tested Ninth Division—to strike the decisive blow . . . the blow that broke the Nazi's back below Cherbourg was a clever one and aroused real enthusiasm.

The *Associated Press* reported,

> American troops headed by the Ninth Division blasted a seven mile wide path across the neck of the Cherbourg Peninsula Sunday, putting a strangle hold on 25,000 to 30,000 Germans in and around the prized port of Cherbourg and then slashed the Nazi Seventy-seventh Division to pieces in a bloody massacre when the enemy frantically tried to break out. A terrific punch by the veteran Ninth Division—rolling twelve and one-half miles in two days for the invasion's fastest gain—drove clear across the peninsula and secured the seacoast between Cape Carteret, eighteen miles southwest of Cherbourg and St. Lo-D'Ourville.

After we had cut the peninsula, we turned toward the channel and moved to the tip of Cap De La Hague. For our work in clearing out the German troops, the Sixtieth was awarded the Croix de Guerre (2) by the French government.

Then we turned to the east toward the rest of France where the going was rough. The territory we had to travel was hedgerow (3) country where small fields had thick dirt embankments, and trees and brush growing out of them. The Germans had dug deep trenches behind the hedgerows and covered them with timbers so it was almost impossible for artillery to get at them. They had machine guns placed so they could fire through the hedgerows, and tanks, covered with bushes, were placed strategically throughout the area. Their snipers would kill off a few of us and then want to surrender. We did not take many prisoners.

A few of my best friends died, some of them in my arms, and some of them all alone with no one near. Some of the newer men went into shock and died without having anything wrong with them. The aid men were too busy with the wounded to care for those in shock.

Two painful and terrible memories from this time do not go away.

I was up in the front and heard bullets coming from the other side of the hedgerow wounding my friends. A full-blooded Indian and one of his buddies, another American Indian, went berserk and charged the machine-gun nest with his bayonet and killed two Germans in the pit.

I stood talking to a dear friend behind a supposed shelter of a thick clump of hedgerow, and suddenly an armor piercing shell came through the hedgerow, fired from a Tiger tank, and it struck my buddy on the side of the head and neck. A huge clot of blood hit me in the face. My friend's death in my arms was particularly hard.

Day after day replacements were received and assigned to various units, so no one unit would become depleted by heavy causalities suffered in the fighting in this kind of country. I would be sent back to regimental headquarters to get men assigned to the various companies of our battalion and then escort them along with company runners to their assigned outfit. Often I had to bring them up after dark, and if we were getting shelled, I would tell them to dig a foxhole (4) and try to get some sleep until I could take them to their companies. Most of them were new arrivals from the States and so darn tired from being pushed around that they would flop on the ground without digging and fall asleep. We lost a lot of guys that way; they never reached the companies they belonged to.

Many of the old-timers in the companies had been wounded up to four and five times, spent a few days or weeks in field hospitals, and then were sent up again. If the new men could make it through the first couple of days of combat, their chances of survival were improved. The old men would teach the new ones the tricks of survival.

Once in a while bulldozers would be used to blast a hole through the hedgerows, but bulldozers were scarce. Tanks behind the hedgerows drew fire like bees to honey. In the long drives, the companies went for several days without letting up. Ammunition was carried by hand. The daily diet was one K ration (5) and a little water. When relieved by one company passing through, the rest period lasted for a few hours, and then we moved forward again.

Chances of getting through that kind of fighting were not very good. I quit thinking about if I would get hit and started wondering about when and how I would be hit. Sometimes when the shelling was really bad, I, along with others, would stick a foot or arm out of our foxhole to see if I could get wounded and go home. Then I would think about my buddies being there, and I didn't want to leave them, so I would crawl back into the relative safety of the foxhole. Once in a while, our cooks and mess sergeant would sneak up under the cover of darkness and give us a hot meal and hot coffee, and for a short while, the world did not seem so bad.

On July 18, we were dug in on the high ground overlooking the St. Lo-Perriers Road. We got word from high command to make no further progress. We stayed there for seven days, constantly getting shelled, mortared, shot at by tanks, and so forth. Then on the twenty-fourth we were told to draw back so there could be a large bombing mission by airplanes. The planes did not come on that date because of the weather, and we had to take the real estate again. More cussing!

Of course, we were waiting for General Patton to build up his armored divisions. Finally, the day of the bombing came. Eighteen-thousand planes, first dive bombers, four motored heavies, mediums, and more dive bombers bombed the area for two hours. The smoke from the bombing blew toward us, and quite a few of our men were wounded or killed. Then our artillery opened up and shelled for an hour or two. At last we started forward. This was the big breakthrough into France and a full scale second front.

The BBC Broadcast on August 1, 1944, said,

> "It's not just by accident that we war correspondents with the First United States Army in Normandy have seen a great deal of the 9th Division. Ever since they have been in the line, the 9th have been where the news of battle is the liveliest. It was the 9th who cut the Cherbourg Peninsula. Then they fought their way up to the northwestern approach to Cherbourg, and kept on fighting after the other divisions were being rested, to clear the Germans of the Cap de la Hague. It was the 9th again, who began this offensive which has carried American armor clean out of the Cherbourg Peninsula beyond Avranches, it was the 9th who bore much of the heaviest infantry fighting and first took the hills south of St. Lo-Pierries, so the that First Armored could go through the gap and begin to drive south and out of the marshland. Today, they are one of the most battle experienced divisions in the American Armies."

In my opinion, one of the most important days of the war with the exception of the June 6 landing on Normandy was on July 25. That was the date that had been chosen for the big breakthrough from the hedgerow country to northern France. As mentioned before, we had stopped our advance at the St. Lo-Perriers Road so that General Patton's armored divisions could be deployed and his supplies could be built up. The Ninth, Fourth, and the Thirtieth Divisions were directed to break through after a huge bombing mission. In the back of us were two armored and one infantry divisions, to be followed up by a second wave. This operation was given the name of Cobra (6). Other First Army units were told to hold fast initially and then within a few days sweep into the heart of France.

We withdrew from our forward positions for the second time, about eight hundred yards or so, to a bomb safety line. Immediately behind the troops were some thirty battalions of medium and heavy artillery. Our front lines had been marked with the standard strips so that the bombers would know where our men were. Everyone was supposed to remain in his foxhole. This was the first really big land-air operation of the war.

A little before ten a.m. we could hear the planes coming. First, there were about 350 medium dive bombers that carried five hundred pound bombs. They started bombing a strip along the road that had been marked by the artillery with colored smoke shells. The German Flak Guns were firing at the planes when the heavy bombers came in and bombed an area about five miles wide and two miles deep. There were over fifteen hundred Liberators and Flying Fortresses (7) in this bombing. Then came four hundred medium bombers.

The wind had changed, and the great cloud of smoke in front of us was slowly drifting back to us. Many of the bombers dropped their loads into the smoke, and it was coming down on our troops. Over six hundred casualties, including Lieutenant General McNair, in our Forty-seventh Regiment and the 120th Infantry of the Thirtieth Division, were killed that day. The Third Battalion of the Forty-seventh lost so many men and officers that it was necessary to replace it with a battalion from the Thirty-ninth that was held in reserve.

The bombers left, and the infantry moved forward to their objectives. We were dazed and in shock, but the Germans were in worse shape. What a day! It was July 25, and the beginning of the end.

In the evening of the big breakthrough, I was wounded again, this time from flak coming from enemy planes. I was hit by a piece of shrapnel in the right leg, which took out a chunk of bone and came out the front of my knee. I thought someone with a big baseball bat had hit me, and I flew several feet into the air. I was carried off to the battalion aid station, given a shot or two, and put on a jeep to be transported along with some others to a medical evacuation hospital.

It was probably around nine p.m. when we reached the hospital, and a doctor who was a major worked on me. He had an extremely nervous nurse who kept saying she could not put up with any more gore that day. Needless to say, the major ate her out a little. They gave me a shot, and I started to count backward from one hundred. I think I got to ninety-eight before I was out like a light.

When I woke up, I was on a stretcher on the ground beside a C-47 airplane, which was being loaded to fly back to England. I was in a body cast from my chest down, both legs together so I could not move. It was not long before we were in the air, and then after a while, we landed at an airfield near Bristol, England.

From there we were transported to a hospital run by Americans. The first thing they did was remove the body cast, which was killing me. What a relief. Then they operated on me again, cleaned me up, weighed me, and found that I only weighed 118 pounds from extended fighting. They put me into a cast from my hip to my foot and wheeled me to a ward where there must have been at least sixty other wounded men. Some of them were real bad, and some, like me, not too serious. The ones who could be up on crutches, like myself, tried to help the nurses and ward boys by shaving and washing the ones who could not take care of themselves.

There was one kid directly across from my cot who had weights on both arms and legs and was in extreme pain most of the time. He was only eighteen and had never been far from home. He was wounded on his first day of combat. He was only on our ward about three days before he was shipped back to the States. He could not keep from crying, and the other fellows and I would try to encourage him.

Another fellow next to my bed had stepped on a land mine and had a horrible wound with about half of his foot missing. He had been there a few days, and his wound was smelling so bad that it permeated the whole ward. He was operated on and I suppose was sent back to the States.

I was in this ward for about three weeks, and then I was sent to a rehabilitation ward. Here we exercised, which included a walk downhill to the dining hall in a big building one block away. On the second day in the dining hall, I saw someone across the table who looked familiar. It was someone I knew, who at one time had lived west of my hometown. He had been wounded in the arm. We met occasionally and talked.

Then my leg cast was taken off. A trooper from the Eighty-second Airborne on a cot next to me had about the same kind of wound I had, and his cast was removed at the same time. The next day, the ward doctor, a baby doctor in civilian life who was a grouchy character no one liked because of his rough treatment of the men, came by our beds. He told the other trooper and me to lie down on our bellies on our cots. The trooper's wound was on his left leg, and mine was on the right leg. The doctor stood between our cots, grabbed our ankles, and bent our legs back over our backs as far as they would go. It really hurt, and both of us were cussing again. The nurses put in a formal complaint about the doctor, and he was removed from our ward. Soon we were exercising, and though I was limping quite badly, I was getting back in shape and would soon join my outfit.

In a letter to Cliff and Vern Lewis on October 19, 1944, Charley wrote from the Seventy-fourth General Hospital,

> As you can see, I am still in the hospital although my leg is slowly getting better, and I am able to get about on it quite nicely. I have been working in an office in the rehabilitation ward, trying to get myself and others back in shape. It's not my type of work but serves to pass the time, and it keeps me pretty busy, which is good for me.
>
> They want to keep me here as part of the cadre, but I can't bring myself to their point of view. It's all right now while I can't get about so well, but after I get the full use of my leg, I want to go back to my outfit. I earned my stripes the hard way in a darn tough outfit and feel that is where I belong, not in a noncombat outfit even though it would be a soft job and a break for me. It's all a matter of pride, of course, and even though the infantry life is tough, it's my job, and I think you will agree with me. I've seen enough of this war, but still that is where I belong and where I want to go, even though my chances are getting slimmer every time.
>
> The news, as usual, is optimistic, and things seem to be drawing slowly to a climax. I'm hoping for an early conclusion, but you know these 'Jerries'." ("Jerries" was a shortened form of "Germans" that wasn't really any shorter but was a bit easier to say. It was difficult to say "Gers" so it just came out "Jerries"). They are pretty tough customers and are capable of holding out for quite a time yet. My "boys" are still in the thick of it. I hear from them quite often, but they are getting awfully tired. I wish I could be with them, and when the "great day" comes, if anyone has reason to celebrate, those boys do. We have been in this war an awfully

> long time, and although there aren't many of the old fellows left, we do give that outfit the feeling of pride and prestige that is lacking in some of the newer divisions. We all want to see the finish with our outfit.

On November 29, 1944, an article was published in the *Cottonwood County Citizen* about Charley's wound and hospitalization.

In British Hospital

A U.S. Army General Hospital, England—Wounded a third time when shrapnel from a German shell struck his right leg near St. Lo France, First Sergeant Charles S. Willsher, 25, is recovering at this hospital. He holds the Distinguished Service Cross for extraordinary bravery.

Waiting for the day when he can return to combat, Sgt. Willsher is assisting in the hospital's rehabilitation center where wounded soldiers follow a routine of exercises and training during their final convalescing.

Sergeant Willsher was wounded during the fighting in Africa and again in Sicily. He moved into France with his infantry unit shortly after D-Day. His last injuries occurred while he was working at a command post during a heavy German artillery barrage.

He was evacuated to England by plane after receiving emergency treatment at several medical units near the front.

Sergeant Willsher is the son of Mrs. Minnie Willsher. He has been awarded the Purple Heart with two Oak Leaf Clusters for his combat injuries.

NINE

Ardennes

September 1944

The Germans were retreating, but there was still plenty of rough fighting. My outfit would start off the day by getting on trucks, running into trouble, going on foot until the Germans withdrew, then getting back on the trucks or tanks until we met more resistance. We would fire fight for a few hours and then move on again.

We came at last to the ground that had been fought over in WWI. Across the Seine River at Melun, over the Marne at Meaux, near Chateau Thierry, we bivouacked near Bellau Woods. Then we crossed the Aisne River, the Belgian border at the edge of the Forest of St. Mihiel, and kept the Germans retreating until they reached the edge of the Ardennes Forest and the Meuse River. There they withdrew across the river and made a stand.

The Second Battalion got across the river under heavy fire, advanced for a way and then was cut off from the rest of the regiment. All day they fought to hang on to what they had gained, but lost a lot of men. Quite a few of them were missing in action, taken prisoner, killed, or wounded. The total casualty list showed thirty-five officers and 299 men.

This was on September 4. The next morning the Third Battalion affected a crossing and secured a bridgehead in the vicinity of Blaimont, Belgium. The assault elements of the Third had suffered heavy casualties during the crossing, but they kept going. They had bazookas (1) to fight tanks and infantry in the town of Blaimont, and the town changed hands four times in five hours. They finally drove off the tanks and the flame throwers and held the town.

Leaving one company to hold the town, they went on and reached the town of Hastiere at dusk. They launched an attack at dark and met heavy resistance, but they forced the Germans out and secured a site for a bridge. The Germans struck back with heavy artillery fire and mortars to regain the bridgehead. The infantry hung tough with many firefights, hand-to-hand fighting, and grenade duels. The bridgehead and high ground secured by the Third Battalion enabled the corps engineers to construct a bridge over which the whole division transportation flowed.

The Sixtieth sent patrols through the Siegfried Line and started toward the bloody fighting of the Hurtgen Forest. The first German town to be taken by the Allied forces was Rotgen. It was taken by troops of the Ninth Division and from the Forty-seventh Regiment.

The Sixtieth and the Thirty-ninth had moved into the Hurtgen Forest. We had to get control of the Roer Dams. On October 6, the battle for the dams began. The Roer River was a natural line of defense, and several dams were used for flood control. As long as the Germans had control of them, they could flood the land over which our armies would have to operate.

The Sixtieth met heavy resistance and fire of all types. On the very first day of the Battle of the Hurtgen Forest (2), there were heavy casualties in all battalions. The Germans had heavily mined the area, and the fire breaks in the forests were the only places our tanks could operate. But the Germans had fire lines directly on all those areas. Every tree in the ten square miles of the forest was badly torn by artillery shells and mortar fire, and the burning shrapnel came raining down on our troops. Shell fragments, rifle fire, and machine gun fire seemed to come from every direction. Sometimes it came from our own men who were totally confused. The first sergeant of our company wandered around the middle of the field looking for his wife, saying, "Where are you, Alice, where are you?" We dragged him to a battalion aid station to be restrained and hauled away.

There were many soldiers at the battalion aid station lying on stretchers with no wounds, shaking, and dying of shock because all the battalion aid station workers were busy with the wounded. While we were there, a GI from a rear element came up to visit his brother. We had to tell him his brother was killed two days before. These are more of the memories that haunt my sleeping hours.

It was pitch-black at night, and rain and mud made it more miserable. Day after day reinforcements were poured in to replace the many wounded. Finally, we had gained enough territory to make the Germans withdraw a little and we could neutralize some of the fortifications. An all-out attack began about December 10. On December 16, the Sixtieth and a few others crossed the Roer. Around this time the Battle of the Bulge (3) started.

The Hurtgen Forest had levied a terrific toll in manpower, and the Sixtieth had to be relieved. We went to Camp Elsenborn with a schedule of snow, rain, replacements, hikes, training, and the Buzz Bombs. The Germans were fighting at Antwerp and Liege, but the majority of them were falling short and landing in the Elsenborn area. For us, it was comparatively safe. The Bulge was going on, and we were in and out, north and south, pulling back, and reinforcing others, and attacking at points along the line between Duren and Schlieden.

Finally the Bulge was over, and we were directed to attack Konzen. Lots of the fellows had frozen feet and faces with frostbite. They were often in firefight that required pulling a trigger with fingers that couldn't feel. Toward the end of January, the Sixtieth relieved the

Forty-seventh in the vicinity of Monschau, not too far from Cologne. We outflanked the enemy in Konzen and Ingenbroich, and they were captured the next day by the Seventy-eighth Division. We went on to a position that commanded the German's only avenue of escape to the east. An entire German command post was captured with little fighting. We went on to town after town.

Fighting in towns generally followed the same pattern. Fighting in the town of Dreiborn is an example. In the approach march, the soldiers would be strung out on each side of the road, lying in the ditch each time the scouts stopped to investigate something. We were tired after fighting and moving on foot for weeks on end. One time we fought for fifty-six days without rest. We slept on the ground and were wet most of the time. We were always tense, ate only cold rations, saw our friends die or get wounded, and we never got enough rest. We seldom had a raincoat, and because it rained or snowed so much, we never seemed to have dry clothing. We prayed that when we got into the next town we would not have to leave for a while.

Most of the towns were fortified with 20 mm guns. They were guns that would hit the hard ground and then explode. As we entered the town in daylight, one column of men on each side of the street, we had to look out for the guys across the street, and they had to look out for us.

During the nighttime it was worse.

With the capture of Dreiborn, the high ground and the road net in the vicinity of Herhahn were placed within reach. The capture of this terrain would cause the collapse of the enemy positions west of the Roer River. The road net was taken, and the troops went into Herhahn.

The Germans counterattacked and retook the town, but some tanks were brought up, and we secured the town once more. Then the Germans had to clear the west side of the river. They abandoned large amounts of light, medium, and heavy artillery, along with AA guns. We moved ahead to the high ground overlooking the dams so the Germans could not blow them up and flood the Roer River Basin. Then we moved on in fierce fighting until we reached the Rhine.

The Ninth Armored went across at Remagen. The Forty-seventh Infantry combat team was the first infantry to battle across the Rhine. The Sixtieth took the high ground called Flak Hill, and we stayed there for three days of rain, German shells, and our own shrapnel from anti-aircraft guns, which were shooting at German planes trying to bomb the bridge. The Sixtieth finally broke out and flanked the Germans, and then there was room for the Seventy-eighth and Ninty-ninth Infantry Division to move in on the flanks of the Ninth. Then we cut the Cologne-Frankfurt Autobahn and took several more towns. The Seventh Armored began a series of long dashes into the heartland. Other elements of the First Army rolled over the Germans, and we were sent to hold the last possible escape route out of the Ruhr pocket. There were the SS Troopers (4) trying to get out of the pocket. Soon we were pinched out by other Allied troops.

The Ninth Division's last great mission was to reduce the Harz Mountain's pocket of resistance. There were the storm troopers, the SS who had holed up in the Harz Mountains and were going to fight to the last man.

First, we stopped at Nordhausen (5), which had been taken by the Third Armored and the 104th Infantry. Here were the living and the dead lying side by side.

Nordhausen was one of the more notorious concentration camps. The living were too starved to move their limbs, and the dead were unburied or half-buried. One group that could not walk had been working underground. They had not seen daylight for over three months.

Nordhausen had a long drawn-out system. They could crowd prisoners into a courtyard where there was a raised platform, and there the condemned were hanged. One by one, the unfortunates were hung while their families, wives, husbands, and children watched knowing that their time was coming. All of the male citizens of Nordhausen were forced to dig graves and bury the victims. Then all the citizens were made to march by the open graves and see the horrible sight. We could not do much.

The division jumped into the attack upon the Harz stronghold on April 4. At the end of the first day, the division had 899 prisoners, a field hospital, an ammunition factory, and a signal depot. The division's movement was a play to reach the Ninth Army to the north and to eliminate the Germans by joining with the First Division, which was coming from the west. On April 15, we moved forward and captured 1,065 prisoners and five German hospitals. Finally, we were in a position to move to the north and meet up with the army.

On April 17, the Forty-Seventh captured a castle where the archives of the German Ministry of Foreign Affairs were hidden. So important was this capture of the archives that fifty C-47 airplanes were flown in to carry the massive amount of files to safety. Included in the files was the entire library of the Berlin Academy of Arts.

There were lots of rough encounters on the seventeenth, and the day ended with the capture of 2,320 more enemy fighters.

April 18 started with the Sixtieth having a firefight with a force of twelve self-propelled guns and soon developed into a chase. We overran four hospitals and two aircraft factories. The rest of the division had joined up with the Fourth Cavalry group. Together they were motorized to a great extent and barreled through town after town.

The count of prisoners for the day mounted to 2,901. You can tell by the amount of prisoners we were taking that the Germans knew the situation was lost. However, there were still the SS troops in the Harz Mountains.

The biggest factor in eliminating the final resistance was a Task Force X. The Cavalry and the Thirty-ninth Combat Team joined with us and worked as a team. In its brief activation from April 18-24, they sealed the Harz pocket and evacuated a total of fourteen thousand prisoners in one day. They also captured all the field trains of the Ninth Panzer Division and the headquarters and supply groups of the German Eleventh Army. In the six days of its existence, the task group captured 19,147 soldiers, captured or put out of commission 475 hostile vehicles, destroyed thirty aircraft on the ground, and cleared thirty-two towns of the enemy. Other elements of the Ninth Division captured 8,644 prisoners on April 20. There were still pockets of small groups of Germans fighting, but the heart had gone out of them.

The German civilians knew the Russians were coming, and they bent over backward to treat the Americans nice.

The Ninth took over the positions of the Third Armored Division and moved to the junction of the Elbe and Mulde Rivers. There was a bridge there that had not been destroyed, and thousands of slave laborers and a few German troops were rushing to get across it before the Russians caught up with them. They thought that the Americans would treat them better. The orders came down from high command to let no one cross but Allied troops. It soon looked like Times Square on New Year's Eve. Hundreds of German civilians, German troops, and the poor slave laborers tried to surrender to the Americans before it was too late.

On April 27, we sent out patrols and contacted elements of the Russian army.

On May 2, a Russian major and some Russian troops rode up to the bridge and officially relieved us. That was our last outpost of the war.

We went into training immediately, close order drill, retreat formations, and so forth. The Russians used to come and look at us.

On May 7, the following message was received: "At 0001 on May 9, all hostilities in Europe will CEASE. Signed, General Eisenhower."

Paris Liberation in 1945

After the German surrender, Charley was sent home. Because of the length of his service, he was one of the first wave of servicemen to be discharged on September 15, 1945. He had fought three long years in seven campaigns. Of the original 120 men with whom he was shipped overseas, only twenty came home with him.

In an interview with the *Cottonwood County Citizen* in 1984, Charley summarized his feelings about his war experience in this way:

> We always had the confidence that we would win the war. We knew we couldn't come out of it without winning. The support we got from the home front was good. But it was really the leaders who kept us going—and the loyalty of the buddies. Some were wounded four or five times, but didn't want to leave their buddies behind. I wouldn't want to go through it again. We had a few good times, but many miserable ones. We knew someone had to be there, but it was a terrible thing. I am proud of the accomplishments of the men of the Ninth Division. We did many hard tasks and had our share of heroes, but did not get much publicity.

Charley returned home in the fall of 1945 a changed man. He did not receive a hero's welcome. In a speech he gave several years later, he said, "I can't recall that the veterans of WWII got much of a celebration when they returned home. I guess an outfit or two marched in New York and San Francisco. A few people shook my hand." He had written to several people telling them that he was coming home soon, but no one knew specifically when he was coming until he arrived. He was able to catch a train to Worthington, Minnesota, from Camp McCoy in Wisconsin where he was discharged and then hitchhiked the rest of the way home. His mother and sister were happy to see him, as well as his friends in the community, but characteristically no one showed much emotion, nor did the town celebrate.

While WWII had ended, the war my father's mind and body would wage for the rest of his life was just beginning.

At home with sister, Amy, and mother, Minnie

PART III

The Boom Years
1946-1964

Before the Baby Boom, there was a period of approximately twenty years in which having children was difficult because of the effects of the Great Depression and World War II. The Baby Boom reflected the sudden removal of economic and social restraints that kept people from starting families. While austerity and restraint were the norms during the stress of the war years, after the war, couples reunited and returned to traditional roles. Returning (mostly male) soldiers re-entered the workforce; many women left wartime work to concentrate on child-bearing and child-rearing. Marriage became again a cultural and career norm for most women, and the result was an increase in the birth rate. In the United States alone, approximately 75.8 million babies were born between the years of 1946 and 1964 according to the U.S. Census Bureau.

In the years after the war, couples who could not afford families during the Great Depression made up for lost time; the mood was now optimistic. During the war unemployment ended and the economy greatly expanded; afterwards the country experienced vigorous economic growth until the 1970s. The G.I. Bill enabled record numbers of people to finish high school and attend college. This led to an increase in stock of skills and yielded higher incomes to families.

The boom continued in the economic glow of the fifties, but dampened its rate during the recession of 1958. One theory about the end of the baby boom is that it petered out as the biological capacity of boomer parents took its course. The advent of the birth control pill in 1960 in the U.S. also contributed to the slowing birth rate, as previous contraceptive methods were less popular or reliable.

Wikipedia, the free encyclopedia

Throughout the rest of the book, there are many references to various authors and resources. Refer to "Nonmilitary Notes and References" at the end of the book for specific citation documentation.

TEN

Coming Home

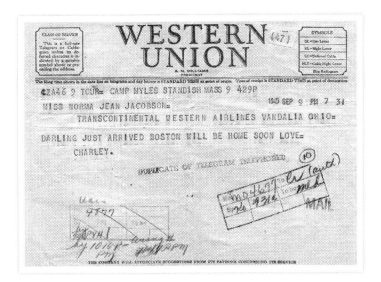

One of the first things that Charley did after reaching American shores was to visit his sweetheart in Vandalia, Ohio. Filled with the euphoria of being home, soldiers were told that it was now their duty to repopulate America. "Go back home, get married, raise a family, and build the American dream." The women who during the war were told to take over a man's job were told after the war to "give up your job, get married, raise a family, and help your husbands build the American dream." Both men and women fulfilled this ideal, and a generation of baby boomers was the result.

We tend to remember the 1950s in small-town America as an age of innocence and morality, of mothers staying home with their children while fathers earned an income that fully supported the family, of unlocked doors, of neighbors helping neighbors, of rock and roll, sock hops, green stamps, of families sitting around the television together watching "Father Knows Best," and "Leave it to Beaver," of everyone dressing up if they were going to be seen in public, of courtesy and honesty, of Sundays being off-limits to commercialism, of children playing freely outside, and many more artifacts, customs, and values. Of course, this was all true. It was like that.

But there was also a dark side to family life, a story largely untold. It is this dark side, American life after WWII where PTSD ruled, that I want to address. I don't know how many families were affected by PTSD, or "battle fatigue" as it was called at the time. There is no exact record for the numbers of people affected. The National Center for Post-Traumatic Stress Disorder estimates that one of every twenty World War II veterans suffered symptoms such as bad dreams, irritability, and flashbacks (1). According to the Veterans' Benefits Administration, by the end of the fiscal year 2008, over twenty-four thousand veterans from WWII were still receiving PTSD compensation (2).

One reason for inexact records was that PTSD was not a diagnosis until 1980. There was recognition that there were after-effects of war, but the assumption was that once a soldier was removed from combat, his trauma would disappear. The WWII veteran was rarely studied in terms of his or her psychological functioning after the war (3). This changed after the Vietnam War had ended, and it became impossible to ignore the fact that combat war changed people, psychologically and physically.

Another reason was that because battle fatigue carried such a stigma, veterans and their families did not want to talk about the veteran's suffering. Silence reigned.

The thinking of the time was that individuals were to blame for character disorders. If a veteran admitted to having some problems, this could affect future employment in and out of the military. If the problems were severe enough to warrant hospitalization, a variety of treatment options were available that included shock treatments either by insulin or electricity. In many cases, lobotomies were performed (4). There was good reason to remain silent.

I suspect that most, if not all, combat veterans who returned home brought some form of PTSD into their families, and each family, like ours, had to learn how to cope, with no one to teach them the fine points.

One clue that this was the case is that in 1946 the divorce rate skyrocketed (5). Marriages after the war greatly increased, as did the number of divorces shortly thereafter. The postwar divorce rate was at its all-time high in 1946 at a time in our history when one party had to assign blame to the other in order to obtain a divorce. Some of the accusations made at this time were adultery, desertion, habitual drunkenness, and cruel and inhumane treatment, all of which were some of the possible behaviors associated with PTSD according to researchers who studied how PTSD affected relationships. Of course these behaviors did not occur solely among veterans' households. However, men who had seen combat in WWII were more likely to divorce than men who had not served. The 1946 record was not surpassed until 1973 when the Vietnam War was raging (6).

Although PTSD was not named or acknowledged immediately after WWII, it existed and adversely influenced thousands of American families. Because it affected generations within families, we are still dealing with the aftermath of WWII and all succeeding wars.

Before I relate the dark side of the aftermath of the war, I would like to bring my mother into the story. The Depression, the war, and its psychological and emotional toll affected her as much as it did my father, although in different ways.

Jean Jacobson, High School Graduation in 1940

ELEVEN

Jeannie

In September of 1922, Norma Jean Jacobson was born on a farm in southwestern Minnesota a few miles away from the town where the Willsher family lived. Her parents were Norman Jacobson (1895-1957), the youngest son of a Norwegian immigrant family, and Vera Davis (1899-2000). They had one child, a son named Lawrence, who was two when Jean was born.

After Norman and Vera were married, they lived with Vera's parents, Charles and Rose Davis, on the Davis farm so that the two families could help each other. Both Jean and Lawrence were born in the farmhouse, and the extended family lived together until the children were nine and eleven years old. Charles and Rose moved to town after retiring from farming around 1931. Norman and Vera moved their family to four more farms in the area before quitting farming in 1944.

Norman's father died when Norman was nine years old. Because his family had to struggle to stay alive, there wasn't much capital to give to the children when they were young or when they reached adulthood. As a result, when Norman grew up and wanted to farm for a living as his father had done, he could not inherit or purchase one.

As the years progressed through times of severe economic hardship, he and Vera rented a series of farms. Every few years, the family moved before spring planting began in hopes that they could improve their living conditions. Moving during the last two to three months of a school session was a hardship for the children but considered necessary for the good of the family.

Jean's memory of "moving days" didn't include any moving van or ease of transport. Instead, several extended family members and hired help contributed to getting all household goods, all the animals, and all the leftover hay, produce, farm supplies, and machinery moved by wagon (or on foot as in the case of the farm animals) on a dirt-rutted road to another location at least ten to twenty miles distant.

Once in the new location, the children had two to three months to adjust to a new teacher and classmates, as well as different academic studies. It wasn't always easy to catch up or to adjust.

Life was especially difficult because of the lack of electricity until Jean was in the fifth grade and lack of indoor plumbing on all their farms. A highlight in Jean's early life was when they moved to a farm that had outdoor lighting, and they could see their way to the outhouse or barn in the middle of the night. The night sounds were no longer terrifying for the children.

Even the milk cows in the barn were affected by brighter light. It took about a week for everyone, including the animals, to adjust to having more light in their daily and nightly routines.

Each day was filled with hard work and the gamble of whether or not they would survive along with their crops and animals. The Great Depression, the grasshopper infestation, and dust storms in the early 1930s that devastated crops and created a gritty household that needed constant cleaning, were challenges that are incomprehensible today. In the summer, a sudden storm or tornado could wipe out a crop and demolish any building. On area farms there was no warning of any catastrophic event because there was no radio, and meteorology was not a reliable form of information. Any warning of doom happened when one looked at the sky and realized that a storm was a few minutes away. A family considered themselves fortunate if they were able to get to the underground storm shelter in time.

And of course there were the Minnesota winters, which seemed to last three fourths of a year. Feeding and watering the animals was a daily task even in drought and blizzard conditions. Digging out of snowstorms that reached rooftops, keeping the animals alive with no electricity or heat in the barn, and keeping warm and fed themselves made staying alive a daunting task. Often Norman and Lawrence had to find their way to the barn to take care of the animals by following a rope that connected the house to the barn. This ensured them that they wouldn't get lost in a blizzard.

These challenges were compounded by the fact that Norman often had bouts with depression that included threats of suicide. Vera would tell Jean to "go to the barn and talk with your dad" in hopes of helping him shift out of his depression. Jean always did so with great reluctance.

She didn't tell me what she said to her dad, but whatever it was, it must have worked, because Norman never committed suicide.

During WWI, Norman was a private in Company H 54, Pioneer Infantry, or soldiers who were cross-trained in combat engineering and infantry tactics. Pioneer regiments included such specialists as mechanics, carpenters, farriers, and masons. They were supposed to work under the direction of engineers to build roads, bridges, gun emplacements, and camps within the sound of the guns. They received standard infantry training so that they could defend themselves if needed. Typically, they were not engaged in combat.

There are no family records of Norman's war experience; we only know that he spent some time in France. We also know that even though America's involvement in WWI lasted for only nineteen months, it was very bloody.

Wave after wave of human beings were matched against cannons, airplanes, poison gases, machine guns, and rapid fire small guns. Large numbers of courageous, but unprotected, human beings could not stand up for long against these machines.

Norman must have experienced seeing horrific sights if not directly participating in them. However, he, like so many others, remained silent about his experiences throughout his life, so we don't know if his depression was a result of his war experiences or from the hardships of the times, or a combination of all of the circumstances in his life. Norman wasn't diagnosed with PTSD (or shell shock, as it was called then), but it is possible that he had it. The Jacobson family thought, like many from this era, that hardships were normal and that one persevered and didn't talk about them.

In order to survive, families lived and worked together. Uncle Einer Jacobson, Norman's brother, lived on the farm and helped the family during the 1930s, as did a number of drifters who moved from farm to farm in order to earn a living. Everyone knew their neighbors and not only helped each other, but also played and celebrated together. Like in the Willsher household, value was placed on multiple generations living and working together for the benefit of all.

There were many fun times for the Jacobson family. My mother remembers trips to Iowa and South Dakota, as well as to neighboring towns to visit relatives and find some relief from the Depression. On most Saturday nights, the Jacobson family would travel to a nearby town to shop, see friends and neighbors, and get caught up on the area news. Weeklong visits with her cousins and other relatives were taken where exciting new adventures awaited, like seeing movies on the backs of buildings while sitting on someone's lawn with a picnic lunch. Trips to northern Iowa to see the Grotto and dance at the Roof Garden at Arnold's Park, an amusement park, and to various county parks in the area for a picnic and fishing, were special treats. Periodically, the family got together with some of their extended family members for a Sunday or a holiday gathering.

These early trips were made in a Model T Ford that the family purchased in the early 1920s. Much of their transportation was done with a team of horses and a wagon, but the trips to town and the surrounding area were executed in style. The speed limit was ten miles an hour, which Jean described as "fast, especially when we were going over the ruts in the dirt roads."

Gravel roads would not come to the area until the 1930s and were considered a vast improvement. A trip to a town twenty or thirty miles away in order to visit with relatives was an all-day event.

There was also homegrown entertainment. Music was important for the family: Vera taught herself to play the piano, and Jean sang, sometimes at home and sometimes on the country school stage, while Lawrence accompanied her with a guitar. Norman often played card games with the children after they had finished chores and homework. During the winters, children who lived on nearby farms frequently got together with Jean and Lawrence to ice skate on a stream or slide down the hills that ran throughout the Jacobson property. Summers were spent outdoors playing in the fields and with the baby animals in the barn.

The atmosphere around her home, even though they lived in tough times, included the companionship of a close family, hope, laughter, and celebratory events. The memory of these good times helped Jean create good times for her daughter after she was married.

Religion in the Jacobson household was not as important as in the Willsher household. Vera had grown up in a family where many of her father's ancestors were Quakers. Norman didn't outwardly practice any religion. When the children were growing up, the family didn't attend a church. I don't know if this was primarily because they lived far from town and it was too difficult to get there, or because they just didn't have any interest in it. Perhaps, with all of the farm chores, they didn't have time. Or perhaps, a church of their liking was not available.

Whatever the reason, religious education was minimal; Jean remembers only one summer when she and Lawrence attended some classes on religion in their country school. The result of this lack of religious indoctrination was that Jean grew up with no concrete religious practices or beliefs.

However, the value of harmonious relationships was deeply ingrained in the family, which was a by-product of their ancestor's Quaker beliefs. Throughout her life, Jean valued peacefulness, like her Quaker ancestors. In her marriage, especially, she often found herself in the role of peacemaker between her husband and daughter.

Jean and Charley met while Jean was in high school. She periodically stayed overnight with one of her cousins who lived in town, and they would go to the drugstore where Charley worked as a soda jerk to get a soda. During the evening, Jean, her cousin Helen, and a few other girls hung out with local boys including Charley at a home next door to Helen's home. Charley and many of his buddies didn't own a car, so entertainment opportunities were scarce. Dating did not take place one-on-one as it does today. Charley and Jean developed a friendship at these gatherings but didn't spend time alone with each other.

Jean told me once that when she met Charley, she was really attracted to how neat and good-looking he was. "He was a good provider," she added, after noting how he had taken care of his family before the war. Indeed, those were characteristics Charley always had. For women of my mother's era, finding a mate who was a good provider was of prime importance since women were not serious contenders in the workforce.

When Jean graduated from high school in 1940, WWII had started, and the country was gearing up for its involvement. The new airline industry sounded very attractive to Jean, so she traveled to Omaha, Nebraska, with another young woman from her high school to attend a training school to prepare herself for working in it. The training school offered jobs for graduates, so after she graduated a few months later, she moved to Dayton, Ohio, where she worked as a teletype operator at Wrightfield Air Base and later at Air Service Command. The hours were long, and she worked at night and had to ride a bus back and forth from home to work, so when an opportunity came to get a job with better hours, she took it.

She moved to Vandalia, Ohio, where she worked for TWA (Trans World Airlines) first as a teletype operator that involved communicating typed messages in Morse Code from an electro-mechanical typewriter to a destination(s) over a variety of communication channels that ranged from a simple electrical connection to the use of radio as the transmission medium. Later, she became a secretary to the assistant station manager.

Her living quarters in both Dayton and Vandalia were simple and congruent with the war effort. In both communities, she lived in a house that had become a wartime boarding house. Houses which had extra rooms were rented out to people who worked for the nearby air industry. Each renter had their own bedroom and shared some of the house including a kitchen with the other occupants. None of the young women had a car but were often able to catch a ride with a coworker or would take a bus or streetcar if needed. They walked most places.

Because they were able to share expenses, they all managed to save a little money for extras even though it was difficult to get many things because of rationing. They helped each other with daily tasks and established the bonds that eventually resulted in lifelong friendships.

Women's Role in WWII

Entering the war drastically changed the United States economy, and the nation immediately demanded more from its men and women. Since women's participation in the war effort was essential for an Allied victory, gender roles were dramatically altered, at least temporarily. While some women joined the new female branches of the military, many of those who stayed at home went to work in factories and filled other traditionally male jobs while their husbands, fathers, boyfriends, brothers, and sons left to fight. Many women who did not fight or work for pay chose to volunteer their time and energies for the war effort.

Although only one-third of Minnesota's adult female population was employed during the war, the two-thirds that were not employed found other ways to assist the war effort. Among many volunteer activities, women offered their services to the Red Cross and the Office of Civilian Defense, providing recreation to the men in canteens and selling war bonds. Women and the Home Front during WWII. At www.mnhs.org (1)

Jeannie, ready for work in Vandalia

Her work, Jean said, was all about "war, war, war!" There was little escape. Nevertheless, she told me once when I was a preteen that her days in Ohio were some of the happiest of her life. She was independent, had fun with her friends and roommates, enjoyed some travel opportunities, made good money for the times, and believed herself to be an important contributing member to the war effort. Her stories included trying out new ethnic foods, dating and dancing, and traveling to Chicago, Washington DC, and New York City alone by air on a free pass. Once in a new city, she explored it with no fear of what could happen to a lone woman in a strange place.

Even though there was a war going on, and rationing was a part of her daily life, life was so improved after the hardships of the Great Depression and Dust Bowl years, and lack of electricity and plumbing, that it seemed like anything was possible. She, like most people, was optimistic about her future. In fact, she painted such a rosy picture of her life during the war that I, as a young girl, decided to have a life like hers was before she married. She inspired me to be independent, make my own life, and have fun along with a career.

Jean, like many young women of her generation, developed friendships with men overseas through letter writing. When Charley enlisted, he asked if she would write to him, and over the war years they corresponded as often as possible. Letters were censored, so there was much unsaid. Jean also corresponded with other men, some relatives, some friends, over the war years, and sometimes she would see them during their leave. When Charley visited her in Ohio during his longest recovery time after being wounded, they spent their first alone time together and decided to get married after the war.

After his leave in the States, Charley returned to Germany and wrote his future in-laws on the thirteenth of May in 1945 from France:

"Dear Folks,

I promised to write you a letter when I arrived back in France, so here goes.

I had a very uneventful trip on the way over, although at times the ocean was fairly rough. I seem to have a pretty strong stomach for I've never been seasick in all of my traveling.

I want to discuss a few things with you, for instance the future. As you know, the Army is starting to discharge the veterans of this war, ones with eighty-five points or more. I happen to be the lucky owner of one hundred and thirteen points due to several factors. For instance, being in the Army for forty months, being overseas for thirty months, being in six major campaigns, being wounded three times, and receiving the Distinguished Service Cross. My chances for discharge seem to very good although it will probably take some time yet.

You, of course, realize that I want to marry your Jeannie as quickly as possible, but we in the Army have a good phrase that I think will apply in this case. It is, "Hurry up and Wait." Although I do want to get married, still I know that it isn't always best to jump into things without looking ahead. I have been planning on taking advantage of the "Soldier's Rights" and going to a vocational school for a short time after my discharge, and then going into business for myself. I know this all sounds pretty indefinite and pretty far in the future but I don't see that I have anything to offer Jeannie as it now stands. I do have a small bankroll from my wages in the Army, but of course not nearly enough to get married on. That's why I don't want to get in a big hurry. Maybe you don't think the same way I do.

I do wish you would state your views on this subject for after all you have a lot of experience and should be able to give me some good advice. Will you do that, please?

This is Mother's Day, and although it will be too late by the time you receive this, I want you to know that you have my best wishes and regards. I hope to hear from you soon. Charley."

On June 12, 1945, he wrote this letter to his future in-laws from Ingelstadt, Germany.

". . . Yesterday I received your letter of June 2. Thanks a million. It helped a lot in straightening out and clarifying my thoughts. I heartily agree with you that I should have something definite to go on, because, as you say, two can't live as cheap as one. And too, I would like to have an income that is at least adequate to take care of our immediate wants.

Since returning to our Company I have been extremely busy, so busy in fact that I have had to let my correspondence with Jeannie slack off a little, and that's bad. We are reorganizing the outfit and training new men to take the old men's place and that of course leaves a million and one details up to the First Sergeant.

Gee, your talk about fishing makes me homesick. I used to be quite a fisherman and a hunter, before this war made a soldier out of me. I hope to be home to enjoy the hunting season this fall, for that is one thing I really like. I had a chance to shoot a deer in a forest near camp a few days ago, but I let one of the new fellows take first shot and he missed.

I am stationed near Munich, one of the most historic cities in the world, and if is at all possible, I intend to go there on pass. It has an awfully interesting tour for soldiers arranged for, and from all reports one shouldn't miss the opportunity of seeing it.

Our living conditions are fairly good at present. We live in German barracks, while guarding prisoners who are cleaning up debris around the area. Showers aren't available every day but it is possible to get one at least once a week and we can go swimming at a small lake every day if desired. Our food has been cut down a little, but it still takes care of us very nicely. I am a good deal thinner than when you saw me, but in fine health and in good tough shape again. We do plenty of hiking and have plenty of exercise every day to keep us in shape . . ."

In Oct. 1945, after Charley had returned to his hometown, he again wrote his future in-laws about his plans.

> " . . . I have out an application with the Bell Telephone Company and am expecting to go to work for them in a week or two. It doesn't pay too much to start with, but will develop into something fairly good as I go along. The Company takes care of their workers, giving them a pension, good working hours, with time and a half for overtime, vacations and such, and is considered a good outfit to work for.
>
> I had intended to go into business with the fellow who was with me the day I spoke to you, but his health isn't very good and I feel it would be too great a risk to start out like that.
>
> Jeannie and I have a little over a thousand dollars saved to start out on. I know that won't go very far, but it will help considerably. We had talked about getting married around Christmas, but nothing has been settled. I still feel that I should have a least a good and steady job before I care to take a chance . . ."

Charley was home a few days when he left for Ohio. Once there, he and Jean made plans to marry in January of 1946.

In later years, when Jean told me about her experience during the war years, she said that she had mixed feelings about the end of the war and the push to return to "normal" life where men were considered the primary breadwinner and women raised the family. During the war years, women's wages were higher than wages before the war, and for the first time society seemed to hold working women in high regard. In July of 1944, employment of American women in the workforce had peaked to 19 million—75% of these women wanted to keep their jobs after the war ended. For Jean, the decision to return to Minnesota to get married was in keeping with the propaganda of the times, but she said, "I felt a lot of turmoil about returning to Minnesota. I really liked my job and my life in Ohio."

Charley and Jean in Ohio

They were married in the home of Jean's parents accompanied by Jean's brother, Lawrence, as best man, and Charley's sister, Amy, as maid of honor. After a small reception, and no honeymoon, they made their home in an upstairs apartment in a house within walking distance to downtown in Charley's hometown. They didn't own a car yet, and they wanted to be able to easily walk to various stores for necessary supplies.

Their new home, like their wedding, was small and simple. They didn't have any extra money for a honeymoon. Charley wanted to afford what they had, and his starting income from the telephone company was modest. Like many in their generation, they placed value on the legality of the ceremony itself and life afterward, and not on having a big, splashy wedding. They spent money that they had; to go into debt for a wedding was not a desire or an option. And to expect others to pay for their wedding was incomprehensible to them. Most area families were adjusting to life after war and did not have extra money to spend on extravagant weddings.

Shortly after their wedding, Charley was called out of town for a week to deal with the aftermath of a snowstorm. Jean began adjusting to life as a young married woman. She did not work outside of her home yet but did all she could to make life comfortable for the two of them.

Both Charley's and Jean's values were a product of their upbringing and culture. Both valued a hard-work ethic and family life. Both wanted to make a better future for themselves than what they had experienced as children. Both were hopeful that in the years after the war a bright future was possible.

Neither Charley nor Jean had any thought about how the war had affected them and how their different experiences of the war would color their future together. Nor did they have a sense of how their personalities would impact their immediate relationship and their family.

Until the time of Jean's marriage, her personality had been formed by her family, cultural values, and the hardships of the times, as well as the changes being made in our nation's history.

She grew up thinking that men were the leaders and decision makers in a family, that women supported men and sacrificed for the sake of the children, that life was hard, and perseverance was necessary for achievement. Because money was scarce, a woman should know how to be thrifty and save for a rainy day. She should also know how to sew, cook, and clean so that money would not be spent unnecessarily. Above all, women should not speak up or stand out in any way. Instead, their job was to keep the family harmonious and to play the role of homemaker and child nurturer. The way to achieve a harmonious household was to follow the leadership of the man of the house. He was the primary provider, and a woman did all she could to make home life easier for him. Making everyone happy within a relationship was a virtue. Marriage, according to the beliefs of the time, should last a lifetime, and if it didn't, there was a stigma against the divorced for the rest of their lives.

For my mother and the other women in her life, communication with others was often superficial, indirect, and was intended to help create harmony and happy relationships. To ask a personal question might embarrass the other person, so personal questions were not asked.

Instead, talk between friends or family was about various townspeople, food and recipes, what one was sewing or crafting, what the children were doing, and about the weather and how one felt about it. Special interest was given to the family a person was related to. "Martha? I don't think I know her family. Who was her father/mother?" Requests of another person were not made, so another person could not know what an individual really thought or desired. One person did not interfere in the life of another or know too much about family situations.

Above all, a woman did not stand up for herself. Instead, she constructed a facade of normalcy, harmony, happiness, and good living. No one discussed inside or outside the family how they really felt, what they really needed, or what they were experiencing in the family. Anything that was unpleasant or controversial became a family secret, deeply buried in the psyche of the family. "Don't talk, don't trust, don't feel!" was the communication standard of my parent's generation. Some subjects like whether one was adopted or not, what one's religious and political beliefs were, family problems, topics related to one's wealth and health, especially women's health and bodies, sex, and profanity, were strictly taboo, especially in front of children.

These values framed Jean's relationships well into her adulthood and middle-aged years. They helped her survive in a tumultuous marriage, but they limited her opportunities and personal growth. In fact, she lived for Dad and me for so many years that she lost her own sense of self. After marriage, she no longer considered her own needs and desires to be important, and thought that someone else's opinion, especially male opinions, to be more trustworthy than her own. Jean continually strived to make connections in relationships and create familial harmony in spite of very difficult circumstances. She just wanted everyone to be happy. Unfortunately, this desire cost her some of her own happiness.

While women repressed a great deal, they were also optimistic and self-confident about their values and place in life as a result of participating in the war effort. After the war, both of these impulses, the suppression of feminine power and the need to push for something better for their daughters, played out in my mother's life and in the lives of many women of her generation in a profound way. My mother's repression of her needs as a result of living with Dad's PTSD led to a loss of self, independence, and self-esteem during her marriage. It took another generation, mine, to begin to turn that around.

Charley and Jeannie married in January 1946

TWELVE

Family Life

Charley and Janelle in 1947

> *Families are one path to knowing God. Our family situations allow us to experience some of the highest spiritual principles, including forgiveness and love. Many families, like mine, have situations that seem unforgiveable, and hurtful. We have a choice in how we handle this: estrangement or forgiveness. If we choose forgiveness, we find that at last we understand love and our lives are blessed. If we choose hatred and estrangement, and any of the lower emotions, we will never find love.*

In 1946 approximately four hundred thousand babies were born in the United States. Like many in their generation, Charley and Jean took to heart their responsibility to repopulate America, and in

November of 1946, I was born and named Janelle, after a war buddy. Shortly thereafter, they bought their first house and moved to the north part of town. This new home was further from the shops but still within walking distance. Within a year, they were able to purchase their first car. They felt like they had realized the American dream. The house and car were modest, but all theirs, and they busily set about remodeling and furnishing their new home.

My mother, Jean, stayed home with me until I was four years old and started kindergarten; then she began accepting small jobs around the community to bring in some extra dollars. Her first jobs were part-time work at a furniture store and at a doctor's office. Since babysitters cost money, she often brought me with her to work, gave me a coloring book, and let me quietly entertain myself while she worked. When she started to work at a local veterinarian's clinic, I went with her with a book in hand. When I was in high school and could look after myself, Mom got full-time employment at a savings and loan institution. The additional money for the family came in handy for a few extras and savings for my college education.

Living in a small town had its advantages. Since everyone knew each other, leniency was given to workers if their family situation was known. Few women could afford or wanted to have a babysitter take care of their children. In previous generations, extended families often lived together, and children were looked after by grandparents if needed. Charley and Jean's generation was the first to be solely responsible for raising the children. Day-care centers were nonexistent. Raising a child was considered the mother's job. As a result, children accompanied their mothers everywhere.

Dad took on the responsibility of a new family with the same courage that helped him through the war. He started working at Northwestern Bell Telephone Company near the end of 1945 and continued there for thirty-six years until his retirement in 1980. During the late forties and early fifties, the telephone company had four basic sections: office, traffic, and inside and outside plant men. Dad first worked as an outside plant man and drove an army-green telephone truck to go on call to repair wires and switches in a forty to fifty mile radius of town.

Frequently, in the middle of the night, he was called out to work on the lines that had been downed by storms. Mom and I often accompanied him in these late-night adventures. In later years, he adapted to new technology and spent more time in the telephone office troubleshooting.

There were some days when Mom had to work and couldn't take me along. Dad sometimes filled the babysitter gap and took me with him in the truck when he went troubleshooting. Often there would be fresh pheasant road kill along the way, and Dad brought it home to clean and eat. These trips in the truck were relatively pleasant for me because they included the adventure of the unexpected, and lessons on the terrain and small towns of the area. In the summer, they also included learning about the local wildlife that we saw everywhere: swans swimming on the river, meadowlarks, orioles, deer, Canadian geese, eagles, and many, many more birds, mammals, and wildflowers that were an everyday sight. I will never forget the smell of the river and fresh green plants and the songs of the birds as they made their way from one tree to another. Dad enjoyed being outdoors and would tell me stories about how he and the River Rats explored the area around the Des Moines River. His love for the county we lived in was contagious and filled me with the desire to be an adventurer too.

During his early working years, Dad was a young father who had dreams for his daughter. He taught me to read at an early age by having me read by his side while he pointed out the words from the *Jungle*

Book by Rudyard Kipling. He told me that he was going to enjoy what we read together and not read "little kids books" to me. This was a strategy that paid off: I could read well before I started kindergarten at the age of four. Since many of the books that he read to me were animal stories, I developed a keen interest in animals of all kinds, which fostered my fascination with the natural world in later years.

Charley teaching Janelle about books

Dad made certain that I was stimulated intellectually. Every visit to the new supermarket in town was accompanied with the purchase of a children's book for me, and every Friday night for years, he and I went to the public library and brought home a load of books after having spent a dime for a bag of popcorn at the popcorn stand on the north side of the downtown square. We each had enough books to read one or more a day for a week.

He often told me of the books that he had read in his childhood and encouraged me to read them. *The Girl of the Limberlost, Anne of Green Gables, Little Women*, and the *Wizard of Oz* series became some of my favorites. Reading and enjoying his recommendations forged a bond between us that lasted well into my adulthood. Our love of books gave us a topic for conversation throughout the rest of his life when we had nothing else to talk about. I could always ask, "What are you reading, Dad?"

He also encouraged me to read books that he had not read by giving me books for gifts. The Bobbsey Twins and Nancy Drew series of books lined the bookshelves in my bedroom, and their adventures became some of my favorite stories.

Through books, Dad taught me to take care of myself, to reach for my highest goals, to entertain myself, and become a lifelong self-learner, lessons that he had learned through his love of reading. He also gave me an important tool for escape, enrichment for my imagination, and possible dreams about my future.

I learned that a very different life existed outside my small world, which led to a desire to experience other people and places. I wanted to become an adventurer and explore the world. Thoughts of hopping aboard a train and traveling the country like a hobo became a definite goal until I reached puberty and decided I wanted to become a dress designer. I also wanted to be at ease with all kinds of people throughout the world. I believed that in order to reach that goal, I needed to be well read, so I established an agenda for myself to read every book that was considered a classic. No one told me that I couldn't reach my goals.

Dad also taught me to be able to create and repair things. He wanted me to be strong and self-sufficient. When I was very little, I went with him to the basement where he had a tool shop and watched him do his carpentry work. He provided smaller versions of his tools for me and taught me how to hammer and use a hand saw and screwdriver. Again, I was expected to learn from the adult version of tools and not a toy or child version. He treated me like I was a small adult. I remember feeling proud about that.

He was creative and skilled in carpentry and enjoyed many hours of conceiving and executing new projects: two garages, a backyard fireplace and fence, an outdoor screen porch, a basement recreation room, improvements in our attic and basement, and some of my bedroom furniture.

He often included me in the grunt work. He had grown up with the ethic of children doing their share of work around the house, and he taught that same ethic to me. I was expected to help both Mom and Dad in their various chores, especially the ones they liked the least. I remember feeling proud about each new skill I mastered even though I may have grumbled a bit about doing some of them. Polishing the silver, ironing the underwear, and washing the car were nonfavorites of mine too!

Dad's projects included repair work for his family and friends, all of whom benefited from his neatness and organization. Dad became so skilled that it seemed to me as though he could fix anything. When I look back on all the time he spent building and repairing, I wonder how much of his constructive and helpful effort grew out of a compulsion to erase the destruction of his war memories or perhaps to atone for the killing that he had witnessed and conducted. Certainly, the physical exercise alone must have been therapeutic.

When I graduated from college, he gave me a tool chest, which I still treasure. Tools meant a lot to Dad; he kept them clean and organized and took great pleasure in buying, using, and displaying them. By giving me tools as a gift, he was telling me I could be creative and build and mend my own life too. Throughout my adult years whenever I bring out my tool chest to repair or create something, I think about Dad and the wonderful gift he gave me.

Dad always had dreams for his family and worked hard to provide for Mom and me. His early love of adventure found expression in vacations each year so that we could see some of the world beyond our home. During the early fifties, newly constructed highways and the national park system were advertised as great places to experience. Dad had the typical two weeks of vacation enjoyed by laborers of his time, and he spent a lot of time beforehand thinking about and preparing for our vacation. He especially loved the mountains, and we spent a few vacations in Wyoming, Montana, Idaho, and Colorado exploring the wilderness. We also spent some time at the Black Hills in South Dakota and in northern Minnesota where we stayed at a lake resort and saw some of what our home state had to offer. During these times of relaxation, Dad appreciated the beauty around him and unwound a bit from the stress of his life. All year long he looked forward to this two-week break from work.

There were some fun times on weekends too. Often we would spend Sunday afternoon and evening with my grandmother and grandfather who lived in a neighboring town, or with my aunts, uncles, and cousins. Playing canasta, a card game, and listening to the radio together, or watching television when my grandparents finally installed one in their living room, were favorite pastimes. We also went bullhead fishing (bullheads were a delicacy in our house) at nearby lakes, and on some Sundays we took an afternoon drive around the countryside with my Aunt Amy and Uncle Orv.

During the summer months, Dad taught me and other neighborhood children to play some of the outdoor games he had played as a child. I loved excelling at kick-the-can and other imaginative games. From sunup to sundown during the summer months, I played outdoors with no rules and restrictions other than "Don't cross the highway." (A few blocks from our home, a highway cut through town dividing the town into halves.) I gained physical strength and was proud that I was almost as good as the top neighborhood boy at running and being able to hit a softball. We kids thrived on deciding when and what we wanted to play and when to stop, on being able to make up our own rules, and on having the town become our backyard. We learned to know the alleys, trees, garages, bedrooms, basements, and all the places to hide in our friend's homes. There were no safety issues as all the mothers in the town looked out after the roaming children. We were all physically fit and enjoyed giving our imaginations ample opportunity for creativity. At noon and six o'clock in the afternoon, a town whistle let the children know that they should return home for a meal. At sunset during summertime the children came inside for a bath and sleep.

In many ways it was an idyllic life for children. I remember with great gratitude the endless games and creativity, the times spent lying on the grass imagining stories about the clouds drifting overhead, and the freedom to be a kid. In the winter, as soon as school was finished for the day, the neighbor kids would gather indoors for creative games or would spend time outdoors, ice skating, sledding, making snow angels, or playing king-on-the mountain. I grew up feeling safe in my environment and knowing I could take care of myself and solve my own problems. My imagination had a lot of room to grow, and I thrived by living in a kid's world without adult interference, adult rules, adult fears, adult schedules, and adult expectations about performance. In that respect, I had a very fortunate childhood.

Dad worked hard to provide for my mother and me a life that mirrored his image of the American dream. He also worked hard to provide for my college education. Even though he couldn't complete that for himself and follow his own dream, he helped me to follow mine.

When I look back and see how he sacrificed his own dreams to go to college for the good of his family during the Depression, and how he took on a leadership role in WWII in order to save his men from annihilation, but brought upon himself his own inner torture as a result, and then how he again sacrificed some of his own dreams for the good of his postwar family, I will always be grateful for my dad and the lessons, skills, and opportunities he gave me. Truly, I stand on the shoulders of a great man—a man who had unrealized dreams, but who kept on persevering. A man who tried to teach me to have the same ideals of helping others and being selfless in return.

My dad paid an incredible price for me to realize my dreams. I always have wondered if I made his cost worth it? I doubt it.

The positive characteristics my dad had, which I have noted above, were not always part of my understanding of him. In fact, I spent the first four decades of my lifetime fearing my dad and having mixed emotions of anger, hate, guilt about anger and hate, shame and embarrassment directed toward him. I also loved him and wanted to be with him, but this emotion was complicated by the other emotions mentioned above. Until I had a transformative experience while in my forties, I could not see my dad's life in a positive way. I could not see how he had helped me and others to grow and live our lives more positively. I could not see his contributions. I could only see his anger, destructiveness, and odd, antisocial characteristics.

Because my dad throughout his postwar years was plagued with nightmares, insomnia, ulcers, pain from his war wounds, headaches, anger, depression, and threats of suicide, he was difficult for my mother and I to live with. We were frequently the victims of his distress and learned to tread lightly when we were around him. None of us really knew what the cause of the trouble in our family was. Post-traumatic stress disorder were unknown words. As the years passed, the after-effects of the war did not lessen for Dad. Finally, in the 1980s he went to a veteran's hospital in the Twin Cities for three months of treatment because his depression was so severe. He was advised to start talking about his experiences because his doctors thought that was the only way to get over them. He did so and wrote the account of his memories told here.

He also started talking to educational and youth groups and was a guest speaker at several local community organizations including being a guest speaker for a Veteran's Day celebration.

For the first time, his fellow community members and family, including my mother and I, learned of his experiences in the war. We did not learn how to deal with our newfound knowledge.

In an article in the *Cottonwood County Citizen* written in 1991, a fellow townsperson paid tribute to Charley in this way:

> Hero worship is a rare condition that happens in the human being. It is one of several characteristics found only in man. Appreciation of the beauty of a sunset or a flower is limited to us humans. So if you are going to enjoy a great life, there ought to be room for a hero—such a man is Charley Willsher. Since childhood he has had the stuffing knocked out of him time after time and still come back for more. Though he weighed only one hundred and thirty five pounds, he lettered in three sports. Though mild of manner and still small of stature, he became the most highly decorated veteran in Cottonwood County—not by Charley's counting, but by others who do those kinds of things.
>
> There is a much told story of a small town boy who worked in the drug store as a Soda Jerk, joined the Army, became a hero,

> returned home to marry his childhood sweetheart and lived happily ever after. You must add one more thing to Charley's life—he still suffers the physical toll that war can take—headaches. They are apparently untreatable, so he lives with them, still flashing a great smile that will brighten everyone's day.
>
> What war at its meanest was unable to accomplish, time in its indomitable march is succeeding, fighting to knock out an opponent who refuses to be subdued. There are little signs, like selective memory favoring those events of the war while clouding those less pressing things like names and dates. Agility has slowed a bit and vision is no longer 20/20. He is no longer able to do his own income tax, but he wants to.
>
> For all this, there is still a heroic quality about this man.

My dad's war experience not only led to his lifelong inner conflict, but also to conflict in our family. He could never completely reconcile what he had done and seen in the war with returning to civilian and domestic life. Was he a sinner for having killed? Could he be worth forgiveness if he had committed the ultimate sin of taking the lives of others? Or was he a hero like his fellow citizens claimed? He never felt like a hero. What was the truth about who he was? I don't believe that Dad ever found a satisfactory answer to this question.

In the years that followed his war experience, this inner conflict became the source of much misery in our family. How my mother and I responded to my father's behavior compounded his invisible wounds. We all searched for answers to questions about how to deal with the role that war played in our lives. We didn't begin to find any answers until the 1980s.

THIRTEEN

Post-Traumatic Stress Disorder

Post-traumatic stress disorder (PTSD) has been included in the *Diagnostic and Statistical Manual* (DSM IV-TR) of the American Psychiatric Association for over three decades. A summary of that definition is that PTSD is a reaction to a psychologically traumatic event outside the range of normal experience. Manifestations of PTSD include recurrent and intrusive dreams and recollections of the experience, emotional blunting, social withdrawal, exceptional difficulty or reluctance in initiating or maintaining intimate relationships, and sleep disturbances. These symptoms can in turn lead to serious difficulties in readjusting to civilian life resulting in alcoholism, divorce, and unemployment. The symptoms persist for months or years after the trauma, often emerging after a long delay (1).

According to Medscape Education Psychiatry & Mental Health, an online resource, PTSD can occur when a person has been exposed to a traumatic event in which the person experienced, witnessed, or was confronted with an event that was potentially life-threatening to self or others, and to which the person responded with intense fear, helplessness, or horror. Symptoms include re-experiencing the event (e.g., intrusive memories or nightmares), avoiding stimuli associated with the trauma, numbing of general responsiveness, and hyperarousal. The majority of people who experience a traumatic event will have some of these symptoms within days or weeks after the event, but PTSD is not diagnosed until symptoms last at least thirty days. Although symptoms usually begin within three months of a traumatic event, onset can be delayed for months or longer. PTSD can become chronic in up to 40% of cases and can persist throughout a person's lifetime (2).

In the last two centuries, what we now call PTSD also had the various names of "railway spine," "stress syndrome," "soldier's heart," "shell shock," "battle fatigue," and "traumatic war neurosis." Various authors and mental health professionals suggest that the symptoms may also include the following: reexperience, such as flashbacks and nightmares; avoidance of stimuli associated with the trauma; and increased arousal, such as difficulty falling or staying asleep, anger, and hyper vigilance. The symptoms last more than six months and cause significant impairment in social, occupational, or other important areas of functioning (e.g. problems with work and relationships). The symptoms may even get worse as time goes on.

In a 1988 study examining the relationship between PTSD and a soldier's having killed, Jeanne and Steven Stellman at Columbia University found that the soldiers who killed suffered far higher incidences of divorce, marital problems, tranquilizer use, alcoholism, joblessness, heart disease, high blood pressure, and ulcers (3).

Some of the more common symptoms that combat war veterans may experience to a greater or lesser degree are the following, gathered from a variety of resources. Not all veterans will experience all of the symptoms.

- Bad dreams and/or night sweats
- Insomnia
- Flashbacks, or feeling like the scary event is happening again
- Scary thoughts that can't be controlled
- Staying away from places and things that remind the victim of what happened
- Feeling depressed, worried, anxious, guilty, or sad

- Feeling alone and different from others
- Lack of intimacy, isolating self from family members
- Social isolation
- Feeling on edge or hyper vigilance
- Angry outbursts, rage
- Cruelty to animals and/or others of lesser status
- Thoughts of hurting self or others and/or thoughts of suicide
- Startle responses
- Avoidance of crowds
- Need to be in control
- Self-medication and numbing
- Sense of loss of soul and/or personal or moral integrity
- Self-involvement

Jonathan Shay, MD, PhD, in his book *Achilles in Vietnam: Combat Trauma and the Undoing of Character* summarizes the symptoms of PTSD as follows:

- Loss of authority over mental function—especially memory and trustworthy perception
- Persistent mobilization of the body and mind for lethal danger, with the potential for explosive violence
- Persistence and activation of combat survival skills in civilian life
- Chronic health problems stemming from chronic mobilization of the body for danger
- Persistent expectation of betrayal and exploitation; destruction of the capacity for social trust
- Persistent preoccupation with both the enemy and the veteran's own military /governmental authorities
- Alcohol and drug abuse

- Suicidality, despair, isolation, and meaninglessness (4)

These symptoms of PTSD listed above are primarily psychological in nature and are the result of a stress and anxiety disorder. Ed Tick, after much experience in treating veterans, concluded that PTSD found among combat war veterans also included a spiritual component. In his book *War and the Soul,* Tick states that PTSD is always the result of the way war invades, wounds, and transforms our spirit. After experiencing the horrors of combat war, veterans know they come back to civilian life changed. They are expected to put the war behind them and rejoin the life they had before going to war. This is impossible for the veteran to do. "When the survivor cannot leave war's expectation, values and losses behind, it becomes the eternal present. This frozen war consciousness is the condition called post-traumatic-stress-disorder" (5).

Tick also states that combat war veterans when returning home from war often experience an identity disorder; killing and witnessing atrocity have disfigured their souls, an aspect of combat trauma far different from the PTSD civilians may experience. The inner self is damaged and needs healing through finding a new identity and spiritual rebirth. "PTSD is not best understood or treated as a stress disorder, as it is now characterized. Rather, it is best understood as an identity disorder and soul wound, affecting the personality at the deepest levels" (6).

After reading my dad's memoir, I realized that he had experienced the kind of trauma that few people ever experience. Perhaps only combat war veterans experience the severity of trauma that my dad experienced. The days, months, and years that a soldier is subjected to traumatic events intensifies the severity of the trauma, making recovery that much more difficult.

Richard Gabriel, a former intelligence officer in the Pentagon's Directorate of Foreign Intelligence, and an expert on combat psychiatry, states in his book *Military Psychiatry: A Comparative Perspective*, "In every war in which American soldiers have fought in this century, (the 20th century) the chances of becoming a psychiatric casualty—of being debilitated for some period of time as a consequence of the stresses of military life—were greater than the chances of being killed by enemy fire . . . War has become too stressful for even the strongest among us to stand for very long." Every person in modern war experiences some degree of psychological, moral, or spiritual breakdown (7).

According to Lt. Col. David Grossman, an expert in the field of the psychology of killing or killology, states in his book *On Killing: The Psychological Cost of Learning to Kill in War and Society,* more than 504,000 men were lost during WWII because of psychiatric collapse. This is enough to man fifty divisions. At one point during WWII, psychiatric casualties were being discharged from the army faster than new recruits were being drafted in (8).

R. L. Swank and W. E. Marchand's WWII study on psychological stress and combat neurosis determined that "after sixty days of continuous combat, 98% of all surviving soldiers will have become psychiatric casualties of one sort or another. The common trait among the 2% who are able to endure sustained combat: a predisposition toward 'aggressive psychopathic personalities'" (9).

This means that 2% of the male population, if pushed or given a legitimate reason, will kill without regret or remorse. This does not mean that 2% of all veterans are psychopathic killers!

What were the factors that resulted in soldiers becoming a psychiatric casualty? Fear of death and injury, resistance to overt aggressive confrontation, exhaustion, hate, horror, and the irreconcilable task of balancing those with the need to kill and the stress of looking their potential killers in the face "eventually drives the soldier so deeply into the mire of guilt and horror that he tips over the brink into that region that we call insanity."(10)

While Dad was not clinically insane, he did suffer from severe PTSD. Now I wonder what prevented him from becoming insane after what he experienced. I will never know.

Some of the circumstances that led to his PTSD include the following:

- Killing three men with a bayonet
- Losing friends who violently died in his arms
- Seeing other soldiers' violence and killing behavior
- Seeing other soldiers go berserk
- Being expected to not have feelings
- Extreme physical hardship for months at a time
- Having fear of being killed at any moment in a three-year time span
- Surviving being wounded and almost killed by drowning, gunfire, and other events
- Seeing the horror of Nordhausen Concentration Camp
- Experiencing the killing of American soldiers by American soldiers
- Being under the orders of someone else and not having control over his life and decisions or locations
- Losing men in his unit in noncombat situations and realizing this was part of being in the army
- Seeing American and Allied troops sacrifice themselves for the good of their cause
- Being wounded and mistreated while wounded

- Hearing the sounds of war which were often close, deafening, and constant
- Being in charge of bringing new recruits to their companies and see them be killed before they were "safe" with their companies
- Experiencing the magnitude of war that was in conflict with his prior experience, worldview, and religious beliefs

Participating in extensive combat, killing enemy soldiers at close range with a bayonet, and holding his buddy in his arms as he died from close-range enemy small-arms fire I think would be trauma enough to put him over the top on extreme trauma charts. His ability to function at all after the war seems like a miracle.

In a letter written to me around 1990, Dad stated that killing was the primary event that caused his nightmares and other symptoms of PTSD. He didn't refer to his experience at Nordhausen Concentration Camp at all in this letter. Nor has he ever talked about it. I thought this odd, especially since I remembered the pictures he had taken there, and had a personal glimpse into the horror that he had witnessed. How could he not be affected by what he had seen? I was profoundly affected as a child when I didn't even understand what I was seeing!

During the writing of this book, I became acquainted with the 2011 publication of *Gated Grief: The Daughter of a GI Concentration Camp Liberator Discovers a Legacy of Trauma,* by Leila Levinson.

Levinson discusses how her father, a doctor in WWII, was affected by his experience at Nordhausen where he had been assigned to take care of survivors. "My father saw the death throes of his people's genocide . . . the countless rows of disfigured, unrecognizably human bodies; the walking corpses covered with lice begging for a cigarette or a drop of water; the barracks saturated with excrement, the tunnels in the mountains from which the walking dead emerged, after having excavated tunnels with no more than pickaxes." Levinson concludes that her father, who after seeing this horror had a nervous breakdown and was sent to the Riviera for some R&R, then remained silent about his experience for years afterward. She states, "Unless tended to and resolved, part of the personality splits off, taking with it the awful memories and intolerable emotions so that the individual can continue to function" (11).

Later in Levinson's book she quotes other veterans who also experienced the horrors of being a liberator of the concentration camps in Germany. One said, "I lost my faith. How could God exist if this could happen?" God took on another meaning for him, becoming only a personal conscience to do what is morally right, rather than a Supreme Being.

After the war, my dad lost his faith as well. It is easy to believe that his experience at Nordhausen could have caused this, if not his entire war experience. My guess is that loss of faith was accompanied with guilt, since he had grown up in such a religious household, and this also led to his silence.

The above may be an explanation for why my dad was silent about his Nordhausen experience and how it affected him. Another explanation could be that Nordhausen was a different level of trauma altogether. The men whom Levinson interviewed said the camps made "the rest of the war pale in comparison," which is an amazing statement. They said that at least in combat, the soldier has rules of engagement; the fight is somewhat even sided, followed some sort of code of war. The victims of the camp had no chance whatsoever.

A third explanation could be that Dad simply could not bring himself to expose other people to the horror it evoked.

Whatever his reasons were for not talking about Nordhausen, I will never know. I can only guess at how it might have affected him through the words of other men who were there and could manage to talk about it.

Silence reigned and cost Dad dearly. Not only did it result in misinterpretation of his behavior and consequent relationship problems, it also found expression in various physical illnesses and aberrant behaviors that caused him further relationship problems. Dad was put into a "damned if he did, and damned if he didn't" situation. He could not protect others or himself with his silence.

The only recognition of his trauma and injuries was articulated in his disability compensation issued by the Veteran's Administration Center at Fort Snelling: For scars and a shrapnel wound in the right leg, he was considered 10% disabled and received $21 monthly for life. A concussion with headaches, nervous condition, hypertension, nerve deafness, and residuals of gastrectomy were noted but not considered disabling, so Dad received no compensation for these effects. Nor did he receive any compensation for the psychological and spiritual trauma he experienced. His doctor did recognize that he had serious effects from his experiences in the war, but this recognition was verbal only. No ongoing psychological, spiritual, or relational treatment was recommended or available.

As I stated previously, I did not always know about my dad's war experiences. As a young girl, I knew that my dad had been in WWII and that he worked at the Northwestern Bell Telephone Company as a lineman and seemed to be stressed most of the time. I knew that he had a hard time to settle down and talk with anyone, or to express his emotions. I knew that he had a stomach ulcer because he complained a lot about stomach pains, and we only ate bland, white food at mealtimes. I saw that he liked to retreat from others by reading, watching TV, or doing carpentry work. I knew that he was silent most of the time and then would end the silence by erupting in rage. I believed that he liked and respected boys and men more than girls and women, and that I could never measure up to his expectations. He seemed emotionally absent from my life in any meaningful way. I believed that he didn't love me or my mother.

Mother and I lived in constant fear of one of his outbursts. As I grew older, it was best for me if I avoided him as much as possible. I was frightened about the possibility of having children in the future because I thought Dad would be a terrible influence on them, and I was reluctant to bring friends of both sexes home to meet him. When I was around Dad, I constantly drummed my fingers on any hard surface nearby. I realized I had a nervous disorder and didn't know what to do about that. I asked a school counselor to help me, but my plea was ignored. I wanted my mother to divorce my dad for both of our sakes. When she didn't do this, I focused on escaping home as soon as possible. I thought going to college and then living in another state far away would solve my dad dilemma. I found out in later life that a geographic fix for one's problems doesn't really work because we take our mental processes with us. Unfortunately, at this time in my life, I didn't have the capacity to empathize or forgive, nor did I have the wisdom or counseling of a compassionate adult to guide me.

My inner conflict with Dad lasted until I was forty. During the time I was growing up, I was aware, as my family was aware, that our lives were not like the ideal family that was being pictured on television in the popular shows of "Father Knows Best" and "Leave it to Beaver." This comparison of real life to televised life contributed to our problem. I saw my family as lacking an unnamed something and was angry and embarrassed about the lack. A generation earlier, families were lacking but didn't know they were lacking . . . they were like everyone else in their neighborhoods. They thought of themselves as normal. I looked at our family and saw it as abnormal. I felt powerless to do anything about that except escape.

As a young girl, I escaped by reading and playing outdoors as much as possible. As a teenager, I escaped by reading and being involved in a number of extracurricular activities at school, and when I graduated, and physical escape seemed near, I celebrated by packing the next day for college. Even though college would not start for three months, I spent time every day going over the items in my suitcases and dreaming about the day when I would leave home. After college, I escaped to Oregon where I made my life and began to heal my trauma. (The west coast was as far away from home as I could go and still be in the mainland United States.)

What exactly did I need to escape? The following anecdotes are some of the experiences in our family that were the result of living with Dad's PTSD. Of course, not every family who lives with PTSD will have the same experiences. But some of our family experiences may be similar to other family's experiences. Sometimes it is helpful to read or listen to another's experiences so that one doesn't feel so alone. Sometimes it is helpful to have another name some experiences as problematic so that one can understand one's own experiences better. Many times when I have listened to the story of another and have found my own story in their story, I bring to consciousness something that had been buried or not fully understood. Understanding can lead to compassion and healing. Until we bring unconscious material to the light, we can't heal from the past. I hope you will find the experiences written here to be helpful in your own healing journey.

Most of the symptoms of PTSD listed at the beginning of this chapter were very real in our family, and they existed to one degree or another for decades.

When I first began to write about these experiences, I realized that each symptom could not be adequately explained by recalling a single event. Often there was an overlap of symptoms. Sometimes, one symptom seemed to cause another symptom. For example, a flashback was not simply a flashback in a vacuum. Instead a flashback might lead to other situations that became problematic and would cause other trauma in the family. Sometimes multiple symptoms were in play together.

Therefore, I haven't listed the experiences as they occurred in a sequential time frame, or as they related to a particular symptom even though I recognize that this might make understanding easier. Instead, I have related a variety of incidents as they pertain to each symptom and have tried to show how the symptoms relate to each other. All of these remembrances are intended to add clarification to the symptom, and not intended to vilify my parents or victimize myself.

Because the incidents happened in a family setting, I also include my family's reactions in order to show the impact of events on the emotions and subsequent actions of the family. Of course, other family's reactions to PTSD inspired events will not necessarily look like ours. Again, the intent is to offer clarification and to illustrate how an entire family goes to war with the soldier, and how the dynamics of a family are altered upon the return to civilian life after combat.

This is why I believe that entire nuclear and possibly extended families of combat veterans need treatment after living with PTSD for a while. As a culture, we recognize that alcoholism and substance abuse are disorders that require whole family treatment. Often the kinds of consequences of living with a person with PTSD and with a person who has a debilitating addiction are similar. It seems obvious that the whole family should be part of the treatment.

I recognize that some of the incidents described here taken alone may not be a classic example of PTSD related events. Sometimes it is difficult to say what is caused by exposure to trauma, and what is an example of cultural or personality influences on behavior. Certainly, personality and cultural influences have an effect on how one responds to trauma. I believe that the interplay of culture and personality on traumatic events creates an unique individual response to stimuli. Every PTSD family may have different anecdotes, with more or less dysfunction included, but similar patterns.

I also recognize that some of the incidents described here may be more or less traumatic than what may have happened in other households. I was not the victim of severe beatings, sexual molestation, or incest for instance. Some of my friends were. I do remember, however, wondering for a long time if I hadn't been such a victim and wiped the memory from my mind, because I had some of the same symptoms of survivors of severe sexual and physical abuse as these same friends. Any abuse is too much abuse.

In my journey of discovering what PTSD is and how it affected my family, I ran across several different descriptions of circumstances related by others that described how PTSD was problematic in their families. Frequently, I discovered that I had experienced the same circumstances but would never have paired it with PTSD. For example, my Dad's need to be ahead of everyone when he was on the road would not by itself seem like an example of PTSD being out-pictured in a family. And I am not saying that all speeding behavior is a result of PTSD. However, when I read about this symptom occurring in another family, I understood more about my Dad's behavior than I had before. I began to reflect on why my dad speeded rather than on how unsafe I felt when he speeded. I now believe that his speeding was a safety issue for him related to his war experience. Being ahead of everyone else would insure safety. Understanding and compassion was the result, rather than anger and fear.

My hope is that when others read of the circumstances described here, they will realize and understand some of their own experiences better. When several people have similar experiences and record them, then a new body of knowledge and understanding is born. The more we learn about PTSD and its symptoms and effects on the individual and the family, the more we will be able to successfully treat it.

Cruelty and Intolerance

Underlying many of Dad's symptoms was cruelty. Through both words and actions, he demonstrated little regard for other people's psyches or treasures. I can't say that this tendency is directly related to PTSD: it could also be the culmination of his upbringing and tendency to put others down in order to build himself up. His need to build himself up, however, escalated after the war because he had such a damaged self-image.

How do I know this since I wasn't in his life before the war? In hearing the talk about him from my relatives and Dad's friends and acquaintances, I gathered that he was quite personable, outgoing, and friendly before the war. I do remember hearing some accounts of mischief making when he was a boy, but he never seemed intentionally cruel to other people. I have read some of his letters written before and during the war, and they are markedly different from how he expressed himself after the war.

My mother was the primary victim of his cruelty. Often his words directed to her were belittling. He either called her stupid or implied it, and found numerous occasions and ways to put her down, privately and in front of others, including me.

I hated him for doing this and wondered why she didn't stand up for herself. I began to think of her as weak and spineless, and I vowed to myself that someday I would look after her myself, and the two of us would go through life without him. I was very motivated to become a strong woman so that I could take care of myself and my mother. I did not have an understanding yet about why she didn't speak up to defend herself. Nor did I have the ability to see through his words and know what the truth was about his mental condition. And I certainly didn't understand that I was being set up to take on the role of the enabler in a dysfunctional family.

Unfortunately, through his words I began to see her as he did, which led to conflict between my mother and me since sometimes words came out of my mouth that were belittling as well. I felt shame when I did this, anger at both my dad and mother, and fear about my anger. Since my mother was my sex and my biggest ally, it was dangerous to annoy her. I needed her to be on my side to protect me.

Fortunately, she was able to love me in spite of my words. She seemed to attribute my obnoxiousness to teenage rebellion and always forgave me. It wasn't so easy for her to forgive Dad. Neither of us understood the contagion of name-calling and demeaning behavior. We proved in our family that the often-heard childhood saying of "sticks and stones may hurt your bones, but words will never harm you!" was not true. Words hurt as much as actions. Sometimes more.

I never knew if Dad felt shame about belittling us. He never apologized. He, however, absented himself from us for a while and sometimes would attempt kindness or give us a gift when we saw him next. My guess is that he did feel shame and struggled with his own self-image and self-hatred but didn't know how to make amends. He was a prisoner of the cultural masculine image of male toughness that was so predominant in those times. The words "I'm sorry!" were not in his vocabulary.

Since I identified with my mother as a female and naturally aligned with her in her victim role, I thought he also belittled me when he called my mother stupid. This led to a desire to prove to myself and to him that I was not stupid and therefore worthy of his love. Nothing that I achieved in high school, college, or life, however, ever earned me any praise or recognition for my efforts or abilities from Dad. A need to achieve and to be praised and recognized grew out of this psychological hole that took years of therapy to heal. I longed to hear Dad say, "You are wonderful. You are beautiful. You can achieve anything. You are so smart. I am so proud of you." Instead there was notice of my weaknesses or, worse, silence. I understood this to mean that I hadn't quite done enough or lived up to my dad's expectations of what was admirable or even acceptable. I labored on to rack up more achievements. Of course the gift in this kind of experience is that I pushed myself to succeed at things that I may not have tried otherwise. I am grateful that I have done all that I have done. However, I was not able to look at his lack of praise and see a gift in that until much later in life.

Dad's words directed to me were not quite as belittling as they were to my mother. However, he found other ways to torment me. When I was little, he would grab me and tickle me mercilessly until I started screaming to get away. I remember seeing a shocked look on his face as if he was surprised that he had gone past the limits of what was fun. The look he gave me also suggested that I was not tough like a boy, and that was why I couldn't stand the torment. At these times he called me a crybaby and walked away in disgust. I decided I would be tough and began to practice repressing my emotions.

Often I would be called a "bad little girl" by both my dad and his mother. If I dropped a piece of paper on the floor while I was cutting out paper dolls, I was bad. If I didn't eat everything on my plate, I was bad because there were children in China who were starving. If I made a mess of any kind, if I didn't follow the rules lodged in Dad's head, or if I misbehaved in any way, I was bad.

As a result, I began to believe in my core that I was bad, unworthy, undeserving, and unlovable. I started a mild form of self-mutilation at a very early age and went to great lengths to cover it up. I prevented wound healing by picking at scabs and used enormous amounts of handkerchiefs to soak up the blood. (Kleenex tissues were not yet a staple in every household.) Then I buried the handkerchiefs in the garden in our backyard.

When my mother commented on the shortage of handkerchiefs, I would go to the garden and dig them up to find, much to my amazement, that the evidence of blood was gone. For some reason, I never had to explain the dirt on the handkerchiefs. Secrecy ruled.

Self-harm is listed in the *Diagnostic and Statistical Manual of Mental Disorders* (DSM-IV-TR) as a symptom of borderline personality disorder. However, patients with other diagnoses may also self-harm, including those with depression, anxiety disorders, substance abuse, eating disorders, post-traumatic stress disorder, schizophrenia, and several personality disorders. Self-harm is also apparent in high-functioning individuals who have no underlying clinical diagnosis. According to the DSM-IV-TR, the motivations for self-harm vary and may be used to fulfill a number of different functions. These functions include self-harm being used as a coping mechanism, which provides temporary relief of intense feelings such as anxiety, depression, stress, emotional numbness, and a sense of failure or self-loathing. Self-harm is often associated with a history of trauma and abuse including emotional abuse, sexual abuse, drug dependence, eating disorders, or mental traits such as low self-esteem or perfectionism. There is also a positive statistical correlation between self-harm and emotional abuse.

In my case, self-harm stemmed from the belief that I was bad and unlovable, and was a symptom of my own self-loathing. By inflicting physical pain on myself, I diminished some of my emotional pain. I never received a clinical diagnosis but felt shame and practiced secrecy and repression to keep my shame hidden from view. Of course, it took years of therapy later in life to undo the self-loathing at my core and to learn other healthier coping mechanisms.

Another aspect of Dad's cruelty besides hurting our psyches was devaluing our treasures. Without asking permission, he threw away some of my mother's most valued possessions. For instance, her father had made Mom a doll's crib that she treasured and kept in a box in a closet. She didn't have any other childhood keepsakes. One day, Dad decided to saw up the doll's crib because "We need more room in the closet! You don't need to keep this junk anymore." Another time, after Mom had worked hard to save enough money so she could order a special mirror that had a magnifying side, Dad took it to his workshop in the basement, drilled a hole in the handle, and hung it up for his own use.

Throughout the years, more items mysteriously disappeared or were discarded in a fit of rage but never discussed. Instead, there would be underlying seething, a buildup of resentment, and a generalized lack of trust for Dad, instead of open conflict resolution or joint decision making. I remember my mother telling me through her tears about items taken or discarded. I became angry at Dad for hurting my mother and was concerned about the safety of my own treasures, especially after the disappearance of a ping-pong table and a board game that we all enjoyed.

He also threw away some of my treasures, the most important of which was Myrtle, the turtle, my first pet, whom I named after Dad's mother's middle name. One afternoon after playing outdoors, I came in and got ready to feed Myrtle. She wasn't in her bowl. I asked Dad where she was, and he said, "I threw the damn turtle over the cliff." (Our house was next to a lot that was considerably lower than ours.) He didn't explain why but just walked away. I was inconsolable in my grief. Later, he spanked me for crying and said, "I'll give you something to cry about!"

To my knowledge there wasn't any reason to destroy Myrtle. We never talked about it again. However, his threat to give me something to cry about became all too common in our household. Frequently, when I cried as a little girl, I would hear that phrase. I quickly learned to shut off or hide my feelings from him. Later I wondered if he threw Myrtle over the cliff because it was named after his mother? I will never know.

There were other pets, birds, and animals that Dad hurt too. He had a BB gun and took potshots at squirrels, birds, neighborhood cats, and other small animals. He also threatened to kill these small animals but didn't follow through. Our pet dog was a little terrier who barked a lot. Whenever this would annoy Dad, which it often did, Ritzy became the brunt of his rage. While he didn't physically hurt Ritzy, his threat to do so terrified me. Every time he acted violently toward any animal, I hated and feared him more.

At the time, I couldn't understand his cruelty. It didn't match up with his interest in nature that I witnessed when riding with him in the country. Now I know that this kind of cruelty is a symptom of a serious lack of self-esteem and latent violence that should warn one to stay away.

In the fifties, that kind of cruelty was not looked upon as being particularly unusual or harmful. Often men and boys in our town would do the same thing. Any small animal or child was a probable target for cruelty by some. Today, the people who do this kind of thing are subject to investigation and are recognized as being a bully or potentially dangerous. In the fifties, this behavior was not talked about. People coped by trying to be invisible rather than by turning the violent person in to authorities. It wasn't until the 1970s when the word *abuse* began to be heard, that children and pets began to receive some protection.

Not only were my mother and myself affected by my dad's lack of respect for personal property, but other people too experienced his weakness to claim as his own something that did not belong to him. One day, for instance, he came home with some binoculars that he had taken from a coworker. They were never returned or talked about. Another time, on a road trip with some friends, Dad stole some agates that he fancied from a western store. He didn't return them. This episode wasn't discussed either.

I was never present when he stole someone else's property and didn't know that he did this until I began writing this book. His stealing was covered up by my mother over the years because she was afraid to confront him.

I don't know if stealing has a connection to any symptoms of PTSD or if there is some other causative factor. What is evident, however, is that Dad had little respect for other people or their belongings. The boundary between what was his and what was someone else's seemed blurred. Perhaps this was due to loss of his personal identity during his war experience . . . he didn't know if he was a good or a bad person because he had killed. Or perhaps he thought that anything was his for the taking, as it was during the war. He told stories about fellow soldier's taking food, clothing, and bedding when needed because the condition of their own was either poor or nonexistent. Whatever the reason he had for stealing, I imagine that he felt badly about himself afterward, and this increased his tendency for depression. After all, stealing was not part of his religious upbringing.

Another example of his cruelty and disregard of other people's lives that had a huge impact on me happened during a conversation we had. During the 1950s, the cold war and the McCarthy era captured everyone's imagination and fear. We talked a lot about it in school and one day were asked by a teacher to find out from our parents what they thought about building a bomb shelter. (At this time in history, families were told that it would be a good idea for each family to have their own bomb shelter.)

When I brought this up with Dad, he said he thought it was a good idea to build one and stock it with supplies for our family. When I asked him about what he would do if any neighbors wanted or needed some of our supplies, he answered, "I would shoot them!"

I was horrified at this response. In my youthful opinion, sharing what we have was my standard of ethical behavior. I could not understand how killing our neighbors in order to survive ourselves would make a better life for ourselves. We would only live for a few more days or weeks with the fact that we had killed. I could see firsthand that thought did not provide quality of life. My dad was probably thinking about survival and his role of family protector. He also was probably thinking about how he had learned to protect his family while in the war—killing others was the way to ensure survival.

I don't know if my shock and horror at his response had any effect on him. I do know that we never built a bomb shelter or stocked up on supplies.

This conversation helped me to determine to live my life differently. I vowed to never harm my neighbors in order to help myself survive. My convictions about the need to deal with people peacefully grew stronger as I struggled to develop in an opposite direction from Dad.

Not only was Dad cruel at times, he also was intolerant of others: he belittled or avoided anyone whom he perceived as different from himself. People of other races and ethnic backgrounds, sexual preferences, and women in general, and people who had college backgrounds were especially degraded, although not typically in their presence. Frequently, Dad would put down other military personnel who were not combat veterans, men and women who were conscientious objectors, people who had been in the air force, people who played golf, listened to the opera or classical music, or who were interested in the arts, or had a higher standard of living. Anyone who was not like him was subject to a put-down. Dad valued the people, like himself, who were combat war veterans in the army. Period.

A few others were tolerated. There was a very clear delineation between people like him and everyone else. As Dad matured, the line between himself and others began to blur somewhat, but he never was totally comfortable around people unlike himself.

The army had taught him well to dehumanize and degrade others who were not like himself in order to survive with his unit or tribe. In fact, the dehumanization of others is taught specifically so that killing can happen. We cannot kill those whom we perceive as like ourselves! He was never able to understand that this strategy that was useful in the army was not so useful in civilian life and led to a lot of fear of others, social isolation, and personal limitations.

The people who were the most difficult for him to tolerate were avoided. For instance, if he felt particularly unlike someone else, he would go out of his way to walk down another street or avoid a particular building or event where the other person was. If we were traveling in another state and an Indian reservation was on the road ahead, he would find another way to get to where he wanted to go, even if that meant spending much more time on the road. If there were some people on the street ahead of where he was walking who were of a different ethnic origin or skin color, he would act fearful and cross the street to avoid them. Keeping constant vigilance about the line between himself and "others," knowing where the others were, and avoiding them became a way of life.

Unfortunately, the acorn does not fall far from the tree, and I learned at a very early age to be critical of others too. Unlike Dad, however, I had opportunities of education and travel to broaden my surroundings and the kinds of people I knew. Gradually, tolerance and empathy became my standard of behavior and thinking, although being critical of others unlike myself is an all-too-familiar behavior. Fortunately, I have an advantage that my dad did not have; I am mindful of my judgments about others and take steps to change my thinking. Dad was unaware that thought patterns could be changed or should be changed if we want to be mentally healthy and happy. He was a victim of his thinking and training until the end of his days.

Nightmares, Insomnia, and Flashbacks

During the 1950s, Dad frequently had nightmares accompanied by night sweats. Over the following decades, nightmares continued to plague his sleeping hours, but the night sweats diminished in frequency. He never talked about his dreams. He just got up, changed his pajamas, walked around the house, and then settled down to read, usually in the living room. Even though he tried to be quiet, we were aware he was prowling around and concluded he was upset. As a result, we had difficulty sleeping too. We wondered, "Why is Dad so upset that he can't sleep? Will he take it out on us in the morning?" When we saw him in the morning, no mention was made of the sleeplessness. We avoided any talk of trouble in our family.

Dad's typical method of coping with his nighttime horrors was to read. His favorite reading material included mystery, adventure, westerns, and particularly war stories. Often, in later years especially, he read the same stories over and over.

After we got a television set in the late 1950s, he watched any program that would distract him from his dreams if he grew tired of reading. War stories were his favorite programs although anything that included violence of some kind would do. Apparently he watched the same kind of programming that he saw in his dreams and belittled the kinds of programming that Mom and I liked to watch.

I often wondered why he read about or watched the same kind of things that gave him nightmares. Was he wanting to learn more about his experience during the war, or wanting to feel connected to a time where he felt more needed and alive? Perhaps he got an adrenalin rush. I also wondered if the reading about the same kind of events triggered more nightmares. I never knew the answer to those questions because Dad never talked about his nightmares. Nightmares, however, were almost a daily occurrence for decades until Alzheimer's claimed his mind.

Insomnia and restlessness at night accompanied the nightmares. Often, it seemed like he spent more time in the night awake than asleep. The result was being tired during the day. When I was living at home, Dad had a lunch hour at noon. He would come home, eat quickly, and then take a nap for the rest of the hour. Often he was in a bad mood when he came home, and if my mother didn't have lunch ready at the stroke of noon, he became even more upset. His anger resulted in either belittling her or in being totally silent. Lunchtime became a nightmare for all of us. Dinnertime, at "5:10 p.m. sharp!" was a repeat of lunch.

Dad's sleeping habits kept him from family interaction. It was difficult to interact with him when he was napping during the day. He also would often fall asleep after the evening meal. When this occurred, I was told to "Be quiet. Your Dad's napping!" I soon learned to escape in a good book or in my bedroom, or play outside or at the home of a friend. Escaping Dad eventually became a priority in my life.

Startle Response, Hypervigilance, and Control Issues

Dad slept so lightly that the slightest whisper of a sound would be heard. This, of course, is survival behavior in the trenches, but not usually necessary in the safety of one's home. As a young girl, I was told to go to my room and turn out the lights at the required hour. Often I was not tired enough to go to sleep and would sneak a flashlight under my bedcovers so that I could read. I was terrified that my dad would find out and punish me. Punishment could involve belittling me, slapping me, shouting at me, and taking my book away—perhaps for good. While the punishment never happened as badly as I imagined, the fear of punishment did not go away.

I based my fear about what could happen on what actually happened in other circumstances such as the following two events.

Dad often had flashbacks or feelings that the scary event is happening again. Sometimes these occurred around my mother and me, and we were the worse for it. When I was around seven years old, Dad and I went to the library one Friday night. When we got home with our load of books, Dad unlocked the front door and turned on a light in the living room. Several large, black beetles were crawling on the floor near us. I screamed. Dad turned instantly and slapped me very hard on the face. In retrospect, I understand that he hit me because of a flashback or startle experience. My scream probably evoked memories of men screaming after being hit in combat. At the time, I hated him because he hit me. I thought he was telling me that something was wrong with me for screaming. I didn't understand what could be wrong. I didn't realize that the slap was motivated by his demons and was not about me. Of course, he didn't tell me what he was experiencing, nor did he apologize. To my mind, he was my dad and supposed to be my protector. Anger festered inside me.

This was the first, but not the last time, I got slapped by Dad. I might have forgiven him sooner if that had been the only time he slapped me. However, throughout my early childhood, there was more than one occasion when bugs scared me. A scream at the sight of crickets hopping all over the basement floor when we had to get to the basement fast because of a threatening tornado earned me another slap in the face. Now I know that a scream was a trigger for him and that he was reacting to a memory that had nothing to do with me. At the time, I learned that my dad (my protector) could turn on me when I needed protecting the most. I repressed my feelings so that I would not be slapped.

Over the years, I learned to put a smile on my face and become a caricature of a "good girl." This stopped when I was in high school and a teacher asked me why I smiled all the time. I started to realize that a smile was not always an appropriate response to an event. I began to work on erasing the constant smile from my face because I wanted to learn how to manage the impressions I gave to others so that I would fit in and appear to be normal and likable.

When I was a preteen, my dad's hyper vigilance often was accompanied with controlling behavior. When he was with Mom and me, his reaction to things we said or did seemed to be instantaneous and without reason. For instance, there was a particular Sunday afternoon when I was eleven and sitting in the living room reading a novel. Mom was starting to do the dishes, and Dad called to me to help her. I said, "I will as soon as I finish this page. I'm almost at the end of a chapter." I fully expected him to be sympathetic to my wanting to finish a chapter because he enjoyed reading too.

Instead, he charged into the living room, picked me up by the hair, and dragged me into the kitchen while yelling at me, "You will do as I say when I say it!" I thought he was totally unreasonable, and my resentment and hate started to bubble over. I repressed it and wiped the dishes.

In later years, I learned that this was probably a behavior that was instilled in the army: obeying instantly. If one didn't obey instantly, a life could be lost. Knowing this helped me to understand his behavior, but at the time it happened, I thought that I was living with a madman. How could I respect a madman?

Another example of this kind of controlling behavior where obedience was expected instantly happened on another Sunday afternoon. Our family often went to my maternal grandparents' home to spend some time visiting and watching television together. I was watching the Clark Gable and Claudette Colbert movie *It Happened One Night* in the living room when Dad said, "Let's go. Get up off the chair. We're leaving."

There were only fifteen minutes left before the end of the movie, and I begged, "Dad, can't I just watch the last fifteen minutes, and then we'll go?"

"No. We are going now!" he said angrily. Again, resentment and hate engulfed me and were repressed. Again, I thought I was living with a madman. I also felt unimportant myself.

Reason told me that to wait for fifteen minutes for an end to a program that I had already spent over an hour watching would not bring about the end of the world. When my desires were consistently overlooked, I began to feel that my wishes and even myself were not valued. My dad's lack of valuing me eventually led to my not valuing me as well. In later years it took many years of therapy to begin to love and value myself.

I don't know that Dad's controlling behavior had a connection to his nightmares, but I suspect that because nightmares were beyond his control, he valued any kind of control over his life that he could muster. Two examples of this were control over what we listened to as a family and control over how we spent time.

Dad liked to repair and build things, and in one of the houses that he and Mom lived in after I left home for college, he put a radio in the bathroom, turned the dial to WCCO, his favorite, and wired the radio to come on when the light was turned on. We had no choice but to listen to WCCO every time we used the bathroom. If we turned the volume up, down, or off, and forgot to change it back to the way he had it when we left the bathroom, we would hear about it.

In the living room, he presided over the television, and in the kitchen the radio station WCCO was also on whenever there was someone in the room. There was always noise in our house. Even when we had company, the television was on, and Dad had half of his attention on the show he was watching. The message was very clear to anyone around him: "You don't matter as much as the TV show."

Television and other constant household noise may have distracted him from his nightmares and reflections, but it was very annoying to me. I saw it as controlling behavior and rebelled against it, although never to his face. I valued social interaction and vowed to myself that in my home when I grew up, I would concentrate on people and not on television. Again, I repressed my feelings and let anger and hate fester.

Many years passed before I saw Dad's radio hookup as an expression of creativity and a desire to improve our home. Of course, making decisions to do something to improve our home were never discussed with my mother or myself. Dad would do what he wanted to do regardless of whether my mother or I liked it. Neither Mom nor I had that privilege.

My mother did her best to be accommodating to any guests, and consequently conversation was directed between my mother and guests while Dad was largely ignored. She became the family member everyone liked, and he became the family member who was tolerated and regarded as a little strange or absent.

Now, when I think about this, I wonder how much this behavior led to the friction between them and to Dad's self-hatred. I imagine that he was aware that other people liked my mother more than him, and this must have led to inner shame and resentment of her.

This may also have led to his use of inappropriate endearing terms he used when he was around waitresses and salespeople. He called nearly every waitress "honey." He knew that this behavior upset both my mother and me, but this knowledge instead of stopping the behavior, seemed to increase it. "Honey" was always said with a phoniness that made me sick.

Never once did my mother or I hear endearing terms directed toward us.

Instead, in our eyes, he was a hypocrite. His behavior in social situations suggested that he was a kind and loving man. He offered to do things for others or said kind things to others that were never duplicated at home. I often wondered who other people were talking about if they said something kind about my dad. And I was angry that others had good experiences with him while I did not.

Dad controlled how we spent time by being ready to go wherever we were going (to a friend's or relative's home for a meal, to church or any other event) at least half an hour to forty-five minutes early. After we arrived early, much to the dismay of an unprepared hostess, we also left too early. Dad would often say in the middle of a conversation after completing a meal, "Well, it is time to go now!" And he would get up from the table and expect Mom and me to follow him out the door. I was deeply embarrassed at this lack of social grace.

Now I understand that there probably was much more going on with my dad at the time that led to this kind of behavior. When it was happening, I just hated him for his expectation that my mother and I would follow him out the door just when, in my opinion, the conversation was getting interesting. Why couldn't we stay even if he wanted to go home? Why did we have to do what he wanted when we clearly didn't want the same thing? I never understood why Dad had to be so early to arrive and so early to leave every occasion. My resentment grew.

Every occasion we attended as a family was accompanied with stress about getting there on time. Dad was always ready to go to the event at least an hour before we would leave. During that hour's waiting time, he would either shout at Mom and me to get ready or give us the silent treatment to let us know his displeasure in our inability to be ready an hour early. We were all stressed and not speaking to each other before we left for the event. In my teenage years, if I could manage to go alone, I did. I told my parents I wanted to walk to get some exercise. Or if I could stay at home, I often chose to do that so that I could "get some homework done." I used to wonder about what I could have accomplished by not spending so much time waiting.

Time, in Dad's head, seemed to run on a clock experienced only by him. Not only was it important to be on time (which meant to him to be early), but also to use time as a marker for events. Breakfast, lunch, and dinner always happened at exactly the same time every day. If there was a delay for any reason, Dad was unhappy, and everyone suffered.

For example, if we were in the car taking a road trip and a town wasn't nearby so that we could stop and eat at the appropriate time, Dad would become withdrawn, silent, or would find some fault with Mom or me and tell us it was our fault that we weren't there yet. "If you hadn't taken so long in getting ready, we would be there by now." His need to run his life by the clock became a problem for all of us.

Another example of Dad's control issues was his driving behavior. He always drove on highways at top speed. If there was a car ahead of us, he passed it. He had to be first in the line of cars and would often take risks to get there. When the speedometer reached seventy or eighty miles an hour, my mother would make a remark about his speed, which resulted in a putdown directed at her. Perhaps, after his war experience, he felt safest when he was ahead of everyone else. We, the passengers, didn't feel safe at all.

Being in control in social situations was also important to Dad. Whenever we went out to dinner with family or friends, he wanted to pay for the entire meal. "Give me the check!" was a part of every restaurant meal conversation regardless of how many people were involved or how large the check was. This behavior may have been a consequence of low esteem trying to build itself up by saying, "Look at me, I can afford this." Or it may simply have been about Dad's need to atone—to do good things for people after having killed.

I don't know his motivation. I do know the discomfort this behavior caused over time with the people who accompanied Mom and Dad at meals. Dad's need to be in charge of the meal and of the transportation to and from the restaurant seemed to diminish any other male or female who offered to pay or drive.

I also felt diminished when I grew old enough to pay my own way. He insisted on paying for me when it was uncomfortable for me to accept. The concepts of "I'll get it this time, and you can get it next time" or "Let's each pay our own way" was not part of his thinking. He was generous, which was a good thing. However, his generosity was accompanied by so much insistence that going out to eat seemed like it ended in a battle with the other person being defeated rather than a pleasant time spent with friends or family. Compromise was not part of Dad's social strategies. On the road and in relationships, he had to be the one in charge.

Later in life when I reflected on these times, I wondered why my mother and I obeyed all of my dad's controlling behavior. The answer is that we were both very intimidated by him.

If my mother confronted him, he threatened to throw up. He could become unstable, unreasonable, and scary very quickly. Often his threat to vomit was followed with a severe headache, which ended with a hypodermic needle and a trip to the hospital, followed by a week of recuperation. We learned to tread lightly and not rock the boat. We also learned to stick together and form a silent alliance against Dad.

Lack of Intimacy and Silence

Another example of how Dad's nightmares had a lasting impact on our lives involves a story my mother told me once about a time when she was pregnant with me and when she and Dad were sleeping. She moved in her sleep, which startled Dad, and he kicked her in the stomach. A startle reflex is very common in combat veterans, but at the time, my mother didn't know this.

Nor did she talk with him about why this happened. She thought it was because she was pregnant and Dad didn't want their baby, or because Dad didn't love her, and some part of her died. After that, she was afraid to move in bed and always slept on her side facing the edge of the bed. She learned to take up as little space as possible and to make as little movement or noise as possible. For the rest of her life, this habit prevailed. My mother after that never wanted to be the center of attention, never wanted to make known her preferences or thoughts, never wanted to stand out in any way. Emotional survival was all about being unseen and unheard.

This event had another effect—one on me. I was born shortly afterward and for the first week or two didn't want to drink my formula. (Children born at this time were not typically breastfed.) My mother was very concerned because I cried a lot, and she didn't know what to do for me. Finally, Dad went to a two-week training period in connection with his work, and I started to suckle. She concluded that the tension in our household was so great that it affected me adversely.

We don't know what would have happened if Dad had not left for a while. Would I have started suckling? Of course we can't prove that my not suckling was connected to the tension in our household, but it seems likely.

Later in life I learned that this event was the origin of my own feelings of not being lovable and safe. I had a distinct sense of my world being scary where anyone could hate me and strike out at me or reject me. This led to a lot of fear about putting myself out into the world. There was a part of me that imagined the worst possible catastrophes happening if I revealed myself.

When I was a young girl, my parents got twin beds and sexual intimacy was very rare, as was touch or any show of affection. When I was in college, they moved to another house where there were three bedrooms, and my parents never again slept in the same bed or bedroom unless they were on vacation or there were no other options.

For decades, I thought this was because both Mom and Dad had grown up in households where affection and sexuality were not easily expressed. Nor were feelings and thoughts about feelings expressed. It wasn't until I read Dr. Tick's book *War and the Soul* that I began to understand that there might be another and maybe even a more compelling reason. Tick states, "Many veterans who have survived hand-to-hand combat talk about the erotic nature of the death struggle. The violence of battle can thus constitute a kind of reverse intimacy. In the aftermath of violence, vets sometimes find they have lost their ability to be intimate in a positive, loving way" (12).

My parents certainly were not intimate in a positive and loving way. I never saw them kiss, hold hands, or hug. I never saw them express verbal affection for the other. I never saw them have a conversation with each other with an intent to solve a problem that did not turn into an opportunity for Dad to belittle Mom. I never saw them have a difference of opinion that was handled in a fair and effective way. Instead, I saw them avoid each other as much as possible while still remaining in the same house. Separate bedrooms, time spent alone doing individual things (sewing, reading) were coping skills developed to ensure survival. Silence and tension, more than closeness and conversation, were the norms in our household.

I learned very early by watching my parents that sexuality needed to be repressed. This idea was reinforced one day when in my early teens I applied makeup for the first time. Mom was away for the afternoon, and I was preparing to leave the house when Dad saw me and my new look. He immediately became enraged, slapped me, and called me a whore. "Go wipe off your face, you whore!" he shouted. All thoughts of my new beautiful image left, and I once more seethed inside while I did as he directed. I left the house and took a long time coming home. When I returned, Dad's way of handling the situation was silence. I learned how to apply makeup secretly or when my dad was not at home.

As I advanced into my teenage years, I discovered that I was attracted to boys but was so shy that I dare not say anything to them, especially if I liked them. Some of this hesitancy was due to the culture of the times where a woman waited for a man to initiate a move. But my shyness was mainly due to feeling paralyzed around boys because I thought so little of myself and had not seen healthy interactions between males and females modeled for me at home.

I didn't know how to act around boys so I buried myself in pamphlets my aunt gave to me to find out about my sexuality and in romantic books to discover how to have a relationship with a male. The instruction of the times was very poor and did not include conversation with a real person. I never learned what I really wanted to know. As a result, I became a dreamer rather than a doer. I fantasized that "if he looked at me, that must mean he loves me." The thought of initiating an interaction myself was incomprehensible to me, as was standing up for myself. I was a victim of the culture of the times and of my environment, and became well prepared for dysfunctional relationships in my adulthood.

Throughout my teenage years, I thought of my dad as an absent father. He was withdrawn into his own world and rarely came out for interaction with Mom and me. I didn't take the initiative to include him in talk about my experiences, triumphs, disappointments, or questions.

My mother didn't keep him informed either. As a result, he was largely ignorant about what was going on in both of our worlds. We felt like Dad was a stranger to us, and he must have felt that way about us. It wasn't until after my divorce in 1986 and subsequent therapy that I realized that to talk with both men and women about these kinds of things strengthened intimacy. But I never knew intimacy with my father. The habit of not informing him about what was happening in our lives persisted until his death. As a result, I never felt that my father knew me. He probably felt the same way about me.

My dad's silence at times was frightening. When he was particularly bothered by an event, he would clench his jaw in silence and remain that way for hours, days, weeks, and sometimes months. His jaw would remain rigid until something triggered an outbreak of rage. My mother and I learned to watch for his clenched jaw, and then we would remain as quiet and unobtrusive as possible. The rage that ended the silence was almost a relief.

Silence used as punishment is particularly cruel. It suggests we are a nonperson, unworthy of recognition or love. Often people prefer any form of discipline over silence because discipline does not make you invisible. I don't know if my dad used silence primarily because he was afraid of what would come out of his mouth, and he was clamping down on his emotions so that he would not be abusive, or if he used silence as a way to control Mom and me. Whatever his motivation, we felt unloved, unworthy, scared, and diminished as people during the times of "silent treatments," as we called them. Sometimes the silent treatments lasted as long as three months. When I was around forty years old, Dad didn't talk to me for two years.

I also don't know if he learned to use silence as a tool from his family or from the military. In some military academies today, silence is a recognized method of stripping an underling of their personhood. Perhaps Dad learned about the power of silence during his war years. Perhaps he was intentional in using silence as a weapon. Whatever his reasons for using silence, my response included seething and resentment, which I was afraid to express. My desire to escape my family was fed by silence.

Often, after a period of silence, Dad would buy something for Mom or me. Perhaps these gifts were meant as an apology for the silence, but since words never accompanied the gifts, it was difficult to know the motivation behind them. Perhaps he meant to say, "I'm sorry for the silence." Or perhaps he just intended to be affectionate. At the time, his gifts were not accepted with gratitude because there was so much resentment about his silence and other actions that belittled and devalued my mother and me.

In later years I learned that Dad's gifts to us were his way of showing affection. If I mowed the lawn or washed the car, Dad, in silence, would put a dollar bill on my dresser. He never said, "Thank you." Or, "You did a great job!" Because I longed to hear the words, I learned to hate the sight of the dollar bill. To me that meant that Dad was "buying my love." It took years of therapy to begin to understand that different people express love in different ways and for me to develop a healthy relationship with money.

Dad's way of showing affection for my mother involved always doing what he could afford to make her life easy. She never lacked for any appliance she desired or help in keeping the home clean and organized. She, like me, however, yearned to hear affectionate words or feel a hug. At the time, I disrespected her because she accepted goods and stayed in a relationship that seemed to have no love. I equated this with legal prostitution. It took me several years of education and therapy to overcome this lack of respect for my mother and, later, for myself when I realized I was doing the same thing in my marriage.

Although Dad could not easily express affection and love for his family, he did experience deep love for his fellow soldiers. Because they shared the same unit, nationality, and cause, as well as the same threat to their lives, a bonding occurred that surpassed any bonds that Dad experienced after the war. Many believe that the greatest honor one person can give another is to be willing to die for them, and that kind of honor was reciprocated and experienced in war.

Dad's face would light up when he received a letter or phone call from one of his buddies. He sometimes mentioned how much he cared for a few friends who had died in his arms. Vacation times spent with his buddies were highlights in his life.

My mother and I never quite measured up to be as worthy of love as Dad's war buddies. That can be understood with hindsight, but during my teenage years, I was pained to think that "if only I had been a boy, Dad would love me." I knew that he expressed great reverence and affection for his buddies, and that my mother and I never received that kind of affection. We were "girls" in my dad's eyes and not as worthy of love.

Several times Dad would attempt to make me do "boy things" like shoot a gun, run like a boy, hit a softball like a boy, catch a ball like a boy, and he often told me, "Don't cry like a sissy." He made many attempts to toughen me up. At the time I saw these as attempts to make me like a boy, and I heard "You are not as good as a boy!" underneath the action. When I failed to be interested in shooting a gun, he turned away in disgust and never brought the subject up again. In later years I learned to appreciate that he had tried to teach me some skills that he believed were useful.

Social Isolation and Numbing

Dad not only had difficulty showing affection to us, but also to anyone else. He often chose to not participate in events involving me and school, or in events that included family and friends. A headache was both a fact and an easy excuse. My mother spent a lot of time talking with me, playing games with me, and taking me places, but my father frequently chose to go into the basement to do his carpentry work or spend time reading or sleeping.

Sometimes my mother and I went without Dad to our relatives' homes for a meal or a weekend. We both felt relief because of Dad's absence. I think our relatives felt relief too when Dad wasn't present. We could all relax and be ourselves. There was always a noticeable lack of tension in the air when Dad was absent. We would celebrate by eating food we liked, rather than a meal that catered to Dad's stomach ulcer, and doing things we enjoyed in our own time frame.

Whenever other women were around, Dad would exit. He seemed to be uncomfortable and would say something that was belittling either about women in general or directed to my mother or myself in particular. Since belittling others is one tactic that people use to build themselves up, he probably was attempting to make himself more valuable in his own eyes each time he demeaned us.

This tactic backfired since we learned to exclude him from our conversations with each other and with other people. I am certain that this was as hurtful to him as to us. We didn't know how to talk with him, nor at this time in our lives did we know about PTSD and the events in the war that had resulted in his self-hate. Nor did we have compassion for him during the times that we were made small in his eyes. We all could have used some strategies for building self-love and esteem for others, and some communication strategies that would have helped us to talk constructively with each other.

In looking back, I can see that Dad was largely numbed to life. At times when emotion was expected, it was absent. For example, I don't remember any emotion at all when his mother died in 1955. He remained stoic throughout her illness from cancer, at the time of her death, and at her funeral. He did the things expected of him, but it seemed like he wasn't really present.

When my mother's father died in 1957, Dad again showed no emotion even though he had respected and liked my grandfather.

Most of Dad's days were passed in pain and stoicism. Sometimes, it seemed as though he were resigned to life, that he had to carry out his duty to his family, but there was no joy in that.

In fact, I don't remember Dad ever expressing either grief or much joy. There were a few times in my childhood when he seemed to enjoy himself, but these were so few that they stand out in my memory as an oddity. There was one wintry Sunday afternoon when I was about ten years old, when Mom, Dad, a friend of mine, and I went sliding down a hill in our town. Every winter one particular gravel road would be dedicated to the town's children to use as a sliding hill rather than as a roadway. I remember watching my dad laugh as he slid down the hill on his sled and being so amazed to see him enjoy himself. I also felt relieved because we were having a good day. The part of me that was always afraid of Dad lightened for a few hours.

When I grew older, I often wondered why some of the things that Dad had enjoyed with friends before the war were no longer a part of his life. When he was in high school, for instance, he was a football hero. Some of his class friends continued to refer to his prowess as a football player decades later. Yet he never attended a football game or watched one on TV after the war.

The same thing was true for baseball. Dad and his friends used to play and enjoy baseball as young men. After the war, a few of the River Rats returned to town, and some of them continued to go to games and watch them on TV. Dad never accompanied them or expressed any interest in either football, baseball, or spending time enjoying a sporting activity with old friends.

Another earlier interest was in hunting, again with the River Rats. After the war, Dad never wanted to hunt, even though he had a rifle and the friends to accompany him. In one of his letters home while he was in the war, he referred to looking forward to returning home so he could go hunting again. After his experience in killing, could he not kill again?

Was this change of interests a normal change that we all experience as we grow older, or was it due to his social isolation, or change of personality as a result of having PTSD? I don't know the answers, but I do think it odd and sad that Dad chose to be by himself, rather than engage in activities that he once so enjoyed with what became his lifelong friends.

Threats of Suicide

During my high school years when Dad was in so much pain, he often made statements like, "Maybe I should just kill myself." A gun was in the house that Dad had brought back from the war, and it would have been easy for him to do so. After he threatened to kill Mom and me too, Mom took the gun from the house and gave it to my grandmother for safekeeping. (Later in life, this gun was given back to Dad, and he eventually gave it to some friends. That was a good day for our family's peace of mind and for Dad's recovery! Not having a gun in our house made us all feel much safer.)

At the time, both Mom and I were very fearful of Dad, and our fear drew us together. We became each other's best friends and confidants. It was comforting for each of us to have someone solidly in our corner, but in later years I learned that this response on our part was not particularly healthy for us or for our individual relationships with Dad. We spent many hours talking about what to do about Dad, and of course in the 1960s, there were no clear answers. I begged Mom to get a divorce, but she refused, saying that "I don't know how

I could support myself and you if I got a divorce." In her worldview she felt that she did not have the capability to get a good enough job to support us. I don't know if she did or didn't. I do remember being disappointed that she didn't try. And for many years I secretly blamed myself for being the cause of my mother's unhappiness. I reasoned that if it wasn't for me, she would divorce Dad and be happier.

The relationship that Mom and I developed at this time was not a particularly healthy one. No daughter should be asked to be her mother's confidant, especially when the subject being talked about was her Dad. Together, to some extent we demonized him, which helped us to feel stronger and more righteous. We were doing the same thing that he did—demonizing others to build ourselves up. As a result, none of us felt good about ourselves or each other. The fact that it seemed to take the two of us to demonize my dad suggests how powerless we thought we were. My dad loomed large in my mind as someone to fear. He became the person I feared most in my life.

I am certain our talks were noticed by Dad. I don't know if he overheard them. But he must have felt ostracized and unwelcomed by us. Of course this led to his further isolation and self-condemnation. And each of us had a harder time to relate to him individually. I got to the point where I did not want to be in a room alone with him, and I planned my times in the house so that being alone with Dad seldom happened. Talking with him became so uncomfortable and so rare that I can only remember one occasion from my high school years where we had a conversation that did not end in a fight and seemed to be like what a father—daughter conversation should be. The nature of the talk was what to do when a date asked me to drink alcohol. Dad, as I recall, gave me some good advice that I remembered and treasured since it was so rare.

Loss of Soul and Personal Integrity

"Generational consequences abound with the wars of today, especially for the soldiers, veterans and families, for they have been spiritually wounded."
—Scott. E. Lee

"PTSD . . . is not best understood as a stress disorder. Rather, it is best understood as an identity disorder and soul wound, affecting the personality at the deepest levels."
—Edward Tick, PhD, in *War and the Soul* (13)

What is soul loss?

Sandra Ingerman in her book *Soul Retrieval: Mending the Fragmented Self* refers to soul as vital essence, the principle of life, or that part of ourselves distinct from the physical. She claims that a loss of vital essence is attributed to the soul being frightened away by such traumas as incest, abuse, loss of a loved one, surgery, accident, illness, miscarriage, abortion, addiction, or the stress of combat (14). A part of our vital essence separates from us in order to survive the experience by escaping the full impact of the pain.

According to Ingerman, patients who experience soul loss may call it by another name. They may feel deadened, numbed, fragmented, dissociated, or spaced out as a result of some shock. They may observe something with their mind, but they don't connect emotionally. Sometimes they have a gap in their memory or are severely depressed. They might also experience some form of an illness or even coma. Most yearn for a reconnection to self and to others. Many try to fulfill that need with drugs or alcohol. Dad seemed to experience most of these indications of soul loss, only his method of fulfilling the need for wholeness was to use prescription drugs.

Typically, psychotherapeutic techniques do not work with the missing parts of a person or with the spiritual self. Instead, work is done with the existing or physical aspects of a person. So how is one able to heal or become whole? One method that has existed for centuries and in all indigenous cultures is through shamanism. The shaman ventures into the spirit world and brings back what is missing.

A well-respected expert in healing trauma, Peter A. Levine, PhD, in his book *Waking the Tiger: Healing Trauma* states, "Throughout recorded and oral history, it has been the task of the shaman, or tribal healer, to help restore balance and health in individuals and communities where it has been disrupted. In contrast to Western medicine, which has taken its time in recognizing the debilitating impacts of trauma, shamanistic cultures view illness and trauma as a problem for the entire community, not just for the individual or individuals who manifest the symptoms. Consequently, people in these societies seek healing as much for the good of the whole as for themselves." Levine then continues to say that "The welcoming support of friends, relatives, families, or tribal members, is needed to coax the spirit back into the traumatized body. This event is often ritualized and experienced as a group celebration. Shamanism recognizes that deep interconnection, support, and social cohesion are necessary requirements in the healing of trauma" (15).

Since I am not a shaman, my intention here is not to tell of the process in which one retrieves the soul. If this need resonates with you, there are many resources available. Instead, I want to merely point out that the idea of soul loss is common, and the therapy for it is available, but not through many traditional resources. Tick, in his work with veterans, is one therapist who attempts to help clients restore wholeness. It is my hope that because the need is great, there will be many different possibilities for holistic help for restoring the soul in the future. Often, various Native American cultures provide this kind of help. Traditionally, they have been effective in healing the soul of their warriors after battle.

While Dad never stated outright that he had lost his soul, there were many indications that he thought he was bereft of whatever it takes to be a worthwhile person. His common reference to and about himself was "I'm just an old fart!" His listener might laugh with him, but it was clear to anyone listening at a deeper level that Dad really disliked himself and thought that some part of himself was missing. He never wanted to be the center of attention and always was self-denigrating. He also was numbed to life and emotions, as stated earlier. When in his presence, I felt like he wasn't there. Some part of him was unavailable to all who knew him, including himself.

Dr. Tick in *War and the Soul* has another explanation of soul loss. "In war, chaos overwhelms compassion, violence replaces cooperation, instinct replaces rationality, gut dominates mind. When drenched in these conditions, the soul is disfigured and can become lost for life. What is called soul loss is an extreme psycho-spiritual condition beyond what psychologists commonly call dissociation. It is far more than psychic numbing or separation of mind from body. It is a removal of the center of the experience from the living body without completely snapping the connection. In the presence of overwhelming life threatening violence, the soul—the true self-flees. The center of experience shifts; the body takes the impact of the trauma but does not register it as deeply as before. With body and soul separated, a person is trapped in a limbo where past and present intermingle without differentiation or continuity. Nothing feels right until body and soul rejoin" (16).

The phrase "where past and present intermingle without differentiation or continuity" applied to Dad in at least two different ways. As already illustrated, he repeatedly confused past and present by reacting to a present event as though he were still at war. And throughout his life as I knew it, it seemed as if time had stopped, and he never grew to embrace the various decades and learn the values, customs, language changes, and artifacts of each of them. He responded to life as though he were still in the war or in the early 1950s. Frequently, adapting to something new was very difficult, if not impossible for him. This probably contributed to his sense of not belonging.

One example of this was how he referred to me. After I left home, he seemed to forget my name, or not call me by the right name. During my adulthood, I moved from using my full name, Janelle, to Jan, then back to Janelle when I was forty years old. When I called myself Jan from about the age of seventeen to forty, he could not get used to Jan and still called me Janelle.

This was understandable; many parents or close friends and relatives have a hard time to adjust to a name change such as this. However, what amazed me was that when I changed my name back to Janelle at forty, he started calling me Jan. I used to wonder if he knew who I was or if he knew anything about me. Dad always seemed to be out of touch with basic information regarding me and what was happening in my life and career. Not only did Dad not know what to call me, he seemed to not know what I did for a living. When I was an adult and teaching, he could never explain to others what my career was or where or what I was teaching when introducing me to a friend. (I was a teacher and taught English, speech, and drama classes in a high school and later taught communication classes in several different colleges and universities.)

Another indication of soul loss was a spiritual crisis born out of killing. In war, the collective will replaces the individual will. The military runs on a hierarchy of power and discipline. In basic training, the soldier learns to do everything the army way, and brutal combat damages or destroys will as soldiers are forced to act in ways that oppose their civilized identities and religious perspectives.

When Dad killed some German soldiers with a bayonet, he broke his moral and spiritual code in order to survive and lead his fellow soldiers to safety. He was never able to forgive himself for this deed. His blood guilt and remorse ate him up inside and contributed to his stomach ulcers, numbness, flashbacks, depression, and other symptoms of PTSD. If he had not killed, he would have been shamed by the blood guilt of his fallen comrades, and the fact that he hadn't lived up to his profession, nation, and cause of the U.S. Army. Dad was caught in a double-bind situation: He was damned if he did and damned if he didn't. This spiritual crisis had no resolution. It was impossible to do "right" in this situation.

His inner self never again had a sense of being a good man or an evil one. If he had done evil in the killing of another, what did that make him? He was in mental and spiritual limbo for the rest of his life.

Dr. Tick reflects on the many veterans who face this dilemma of doing evil in order for good to be done: "To our internal self-image it does not matter that we had no choice; we are still haunted by the awareness that by killing we have committed the greatest wrong. The soul freezes on this moral crisis point. It says: I killed my own. Or I killed whom I should not have killed and that is murder. I have become foul and cannot get clean again. 'What you do, you become,' as the saying goes." After the soul had been pushed to the breaking point, it is very difficult for the individual to ever believe in his own goodness and worth again. This moral pain and harm to the soul is a root cause of

PTSD (17). If the veteran does not address the moral issues in therapy, it is impossible to heal even though there may be many medications prescribed.

Many therapists today are uncomfortable with the idea of soul loss and do not know how to help veterans retrieve their soul and sense of innate goodness. How can a veteran feel safe going to therapy when many therapists are uncomfortable with soul loss?

One of the effects of loss of soul is to feel numbed or without feeling. Dad experienced this for the rest of his life. His capacity to enjoy, laugh, appreciate, have fun, or be lighthearted was hugely diminished. His capacity to grieve seemed destroyed. He never said a word or shed a tear when his sister died in 1997. She was his only remaining birth family relative, and they had been very close earlier in life. Both of us sat by her side in silence for three days while she lay dying, and Dad didn't show any emotion at all while my face turned into a river of tears. To call his face and posture rocklike is to understate it. When I tried to talk with him about the things that needed doing at the time of Amy's death, he had very little response. It was as if he was not available. His stoicism shocked me. Of all the people and situations that I would have expected to make an emotional impact on Dad, the death of his sister was at the top of the list.

In looking back, it seems that his numbness was a supreme effort to not think about death, aging, and his own mortality. Perhaps her death brought back memories of all who had gone before, how he had taken some lives, or how he had not made peace with himself and with God.

Tick states that "survivors cannot find peace unless they make peace with the legions of dead with whom they may have any kind of relationship—as relative, friend, comrade in arms, former enemy, or even as their killer. Relations with the missing and the dead, and with death itself, are at the core of the soul wound we call post-traumatic-stress-disorder" (18).

Perhaps another indication of soul loss was Dad's lack of interest in religion. After his return home from war, Dad did not go to church regularly for decades. Even though he had grown up in a religious household, religion had no draw for him. He felt that he was not forgivable for what he had done, so going to church would just confront him with that fact. It was easier to not go.

His sister, Amy, was very religious. When I was a child, my aunt and uncle took me to church with them and saw to it that I had a religious background. I sang in the church choir during high school and eventually attended a church-affiliated college. I never knew what Dad thought about this. He must have felt some pressure from the family to attend church, and as years went by, he did attend Christmas and Easter services if he didn't have a headache. Did he think of himself as a failure for not being more religious? Did he think of his religion as a failure in helping him? I will never know. In his later years he did attend church more frequently and even became an usher. Perhaps he reached some kind of peace about his role in the war. Or perhaps he thought that some kind of peace was possible if he did good works and went to church. He didn't tell us.

One result of soul loss is a sense of not belonging. Dad throughout much of his early adult life felt that he wasn't a loved and valuable member of our family, of his community, or of his church. He also believed that the best part of him was gone. He was not whole or healthy in mind, body, or spirit.

After he was admitted to the veteran's home in his eighties, Dad, when he saw us, would ask to go home. Of course at one level, this was understood to mean that he would like to go back to his house where he had lived so many years. I always wondered, though, if *home* didn't also have a metaphorical meaning. Could he mean *home* in the spiritual sense, as in "I want to go home to Jesus, or to God"? Or maybe *home* meant that he wanted to return to home inside himself, where he was restored to wholeness. However home is interpreted, it was clear that it meant some kind of wholeness or completeness, something that was lacking at the time. The something that was missing needed to be restored.

Physical Illnesses

Besides all of the psychological effects of trauma that Dad experienced, there were significant physical problems as well. Since he had been wounded during the war in his knee and ear, the pain from these shrapnel wounds continued to bother him for the rest of his life. He sometimes walked with a slight limp or complained about how his knee hurt. His hearing ability decreased over the years, and he eventually succumbed to wearing a hearing aid. These were minor problems, however, compared to the illnesses that came in succession over the rest of his years. When it seemed as though one illness would be either medicated sufficiently or removed through an operation, another would appear in a different part of his body. His first major illness was ulcers.

Soon after coming home from WWII, Dad started complaining about how his stomach hurt. Various kinds of food seemed to aggravate the problem. After seeing a physician, he was diagnosed with stomach ulcers.

During the 1950s it was believed that ulcers were caused by stress, spicy foods, and alcohol. Dad was told to eat bland foods, drink lots of milk to coat his stomach, and to de-stress himself. To him, that meant taking a lot of naps. Most of our meals consisted of white food: potatoes, white meat, overcooked vegetables, white bread, and milk-based soups. His regimen did not result in lessening his pain, so in the early 1960s he underwent surgery and had more than 60% of his stomach removed. This was followed by more diet restrictions and directions that ruled our meal times.

I will never forget the day just before his surgery when Mom told me that "you better talk to your dad and make up the bad blood between you. He might not live past the surgery, and you will regret it if you don't." I remember thinking, *Why doesn't he make it up with me? He is the father! Why am I asked to do the adult thing here?* (Perhaps she thought it appropriate to ask me to play the adult role since her mother had asked her to talk to her dad when he was threatening suicide.) Again, anger seethed inside me and was buried.

I tried to talk with him and seemed to get nowhere. By that time in our lives, Dad was so numbed that it seemed like very little could get through to him. He also was probably very preoccupied with the upcoming surgery and couldn't deal with his emotional daughter clumsily trying to reconcile fifteen years of grievances.

Besides the pain in his stomach, he had severe headaches. I don't know what triggered his headaches, but he had them monthly. A typical episode happening while Dad was working involved his calling Mom at her work and telling her he had a headache. She would pick him up and take him to the hospital where he received a hypodermic injection. By the time she got him home, he was ready to pass out and would lie down and sleep for a long period of time.

Typically, it took several days to recover completely. He was fortunate that his employers did not give up on him since he missed almost a week of work monthly for several years. He was on daily medication for his headaches, so when he awoke, he would take his medication. Decades into this scenario, his doctor discovered that he was taking inappropriate medication, and this is why it took him so long to recover from his hypodermic injections. When the medication changed, the headaches became less severe.

As Dad got older, other problems started to surface. He had high blood pressure and in the 1980s had heart bypass surgery with five bypasses. A few years later, he had surgery for prostate cancer. As the years progressed, his hearing decreased, and his eyesight deteriorated. After he turned eighty years old, he developed Alzheimer's disease.

Throughout his life, Dad took a lot of medication for his various conditions. He always hoped that the drugs or surgery would heal him. Of course, they never did. They never addressed the root of Dad's problem: his WWII experience and the memories of death and destruction that haunted him.

I remember thinking when I was a teenager that Dad used his medication for other purposes besides treating a specific physical problem. He seemed to benefit by using illness as an excuse to not do something when he didn't know how to say no. Often illness was a convenient excuse to not participate in an event or be around other people. When he was sick, he got sympathy, and Mom and I catered to his needs and did everything we could to be quiet and not get in his way. Other people often said, "Poor Charley," and he seemed to thrive on their sympathy.

Even though I was very young at the time, I began to understand that illness can serve us psychologically. When my dad couldn't face something, an illness would provide an excuse for not facing it. I tested out my theory one day when I particularly did not want to go to school. I thought myself sick and later that day developed a "real" cold. This provided the opportunity to avoid school and get the sympathy I wanted. When I realized what I had done, I decided to find ways other than being sick to get what I wanted. I also began to respect the power of the mind to control the body. And I began to disrespect my dad even more for not finding ways to get what he wanted instead of being sick. My tolerance of his illnesses waned, which further alienated us.

Another effect of taking medication was that he also seemed to become more numb. He would sleep for hours and act like a zombie when he awoke. Now I know that this is a common reaction to taking painkillers. However, besides numbing our pain, they also numb our Self. I believe that Dad became addicted to them and relied on them to heal him when no other help was available. Pills became my dad's daily companion and hoped-for savior for the rest of his life.

Of course Dad had legitimate physical, psychological, and spiritual pain. Only the physical pain was addressed. Unfortunately, Dad thought of doctors, as many people of his time did, as "healers." Doctors were expected to heal all wounds with the right medication and/or surgery. When healing didn't happen, either a new doctor was obtained or more medication was prescribed. I always thought it amazing that as soon as there was one operation on my dad that another pain and problem were found and needed to be addressed. I intuitively knew that what caused Dad's problems was not completely physical and that healing could not happen until the cause of the problem was addressed, which of course, it never was. He chased after physical solutions to spiritual and psychological problems until Alzheimer's disease claimed his mind in his last years.

If only there had been a therapeutic process in place to help us cope and heal. But there was none. The relatives we reached out to could not help. The doctors could not help. My high school counselor could not help. Our family need existed, but the kind of supportive services for veterans that we needed were not in place yet. Instead, there was some medical help, but denial that there was a need for psychological and spiritual help. We did the best we could in these circumstances. I am very saddened to think that the best we could do probably contributed to more pain for my dad.

FOURTEEN

Secondary Post-Traumatic Stress Disorder

All of the effects of combat trauma discussed here so far relate primarily to my dad. I also attempted to depict how his behavior affected our family and in turn how our reactive behavior may have further traumatized him. Of course, when any veteran experiences symptoms of PTSD, the family is affected as well. None of us live in a vacuum. Sometimes the effects on the family can be what is becoming known as secondary or transgenerational PTSD.

Secondary PTSD is not a disorder that is recognized by the *Diagnostic and Statistical Manual of Mental Disorders* (as of the fourth edition). However, as a daughter of a veteran who had PTSD, I have noticed that both my mother and I obtained symptoms that mirror some of my dad's symptoms. I have had more than a few "aha moments" when I've realized the extent of some of our unhealthy beliefs and behaviors that stemmed from living with a combat war veteran who had PTSD.

As I started to do some research regarding current family coping strategies within families who experience PTSD after I started writing this book, I found the term secondary post-traumatic stress disorder on the website of www.FamilyOfaVet.com. After reading about it, I was struck with how similar my mother's and my experiences were to those of other veterans' families. The articles on this website make a cogent case for the idea that families of veterans experience trauma too as a result of living with a vet who has PTSD. Much as a child of a smoker inhales the smoke of a cigarette that the parent is smoking and will be adversely affected by it, the people around a person with PTSD will be adversely affected by his or her behavior. According to this website, some examples of secondary PTSD include the following:

Spouses and Secondary PTSD

- Becoming the caretaker of the vet. This includes watching for people or circumstances that might "set him off." The spouse tries to ensure that everything stays in line—that nothing aggravates or upsets the vet—that everything is "perfect."
- Being screamed at or berated despite efforts to keep things perfect.
- Losing a sense of self.
- Being abandoned emotionally and sexually by the spouse who has PTSD.
- Feeling depressed, angry, resentful, impatient, etc. (1).

Other sites list suicidal thoughts and feelings, substance abuse, feelings of alienation and isolation, feelings of mistrust and betrayal, anger and irritability, or severe impairment in daily functioning as common experiences for the spouse of a combat veteran who has PTSD.

My mother certainly, over the years, has exhibited many of these behaviors. She often lied for him so that others would not know the extent of his situation, she tried to make our home life perfect by working hard at keeping the house in immaculate order and squeaky clean, and making sure that meals (and everything else) were on time so that he would not get in a rage or have one of his headaches, she repressed her feelings when she was demeaned in spite of her best efforts, she lived for Dad and me and lost her sense of self, and she was abandoned emotionally and sexually by my dad. Examples of these reactions to his behavior were illustrated in the previous chapter. The culminating effect of these experiences of abuse was numbness.

Instead of acting out or depending on some type of substance abuse for relief, Mom repressed her feelings and indeed her life in order to cope. After being told she was stupid and unworthy for years, she came to believe that about herself. She stopped making any decisions because they were always wrong, and she stopped having opinions or preferences. Her response to "What would you like?" is still "I don't care. Anything is OK with me. What do you want?" Her worst fear was to do or say something controversial or even different from someone else. She lost her ability to think for and express herself except through her beautiful handwork.

Another example of numbness was reflected in her lack of desire to make any changes. She doesn't like to read and has never pursued learning through reading. One result is that she never seemed to embrace change in the decades after the 1960s when I left home. The changing music, language, politics, technology, traditions, beliefs about gender equality, diversity in people, kinds of entertainment, economic changes, various kinds of goods and services—all seemed to bypass her. She lived her married life from the perspective of a young woman of the 1950s and '60s in small-town America. When asked about why she hadn't made any particular change, she said, "Because that was the way I grew up." Learning new information or skills, using the current idioms and technology, learning to know people different from herself, speaking up privately or publically, embracing any of the feminists' values regarding equality—all put her into retreat mode.

By the time she was around fifty, Mom had lost her initiative. She never suggested doing a particular activity, asking a pertinent question of an authority figure, having a different opinion than what she heard her friends express. She seldom spoke up on her own behalf by asking for what she needed or wanted. If she was curious about the activity of a neighbor, she would call a friend of the neighbor to find out what was happening rather than to ask the neighbor directly. Rather than confront life, she spent most of her days in her home working on crafts.

Numbness was also reflected in her everyday behavior: she seldom acted exuberantly. Raising her voice (even in the presence of a person who was hard of hearing), getting excited, singing so that she could be heard, dancing or moving quickly, laughing wholeheartedly, taking exception to anything that was happening around her—these are all behaviors that seemed dumb to her. When watching children play spontaneously or laugh with abandon, she often criticized them by saying, "That's stupid" or "They need to be disciplined."

In later years, she rarely showed any emotion—not even at the time of Dad's death. Instead, she refrained from sitting with him during the last days of his life and, to my knowledge, has never shed a tear over his death. At the time of his funeral, she did what was required of her, and on the day after his burial, she packed up all of his remaining clothing and sent them off for recycling. Since then, she has rarely talked about him or the times, good or bad, they spent together. When asked if she misses him, her response typically is "I don't think about those days."

Her life has been lived in a neutral tone devoid of many imprints of her personality. After her marriage, the Jean who was an adventurer and went traveling by herself, who sang to the accompaniment of her brother's guitar playing on stage in her high school, who had the gumption to leave home, travel to another state to receive the education to take on a wartime job and then to move to yet another state alone to fulfill that job was lost forever. Did she lose her soul too? She never experienced the kind of trauma that Dad did but certainly experienced a loss of self.

All my life I have missed that Jean. It seems, in some ways, the war experience of my father robbed me of both my parents.

Children and Secondary PTSD

According to Jennifer L. Price, Ph.D. in an article entitled "When a Child's Parent has PTSD" located on the US Department of Veterans Affairs website, children of combat veterans who have PTSD may also exhibit PTSD symptoms.

"A parent's PTSD symptoms are directly linked to their child's responses. Children usually respond in certain ways:

- a child might feel and behave just like their parent as a way of trying to connect with the parent. The child might show many of the same symptoms as the parent with PTSD.
- a child may take on the adult role to fill in for the parent with PTSD. The child acts too grown-up for his or her age.
- some children get little emotional help. This results in problems at school, depression, anxiety (worry, fear), and relationship problems later in life."

In addition, children may exhibit social and behavior problems, and emotional problems. When a parent is experiencing flashbacks, nightmares, or some other symptoms of PTSD, children may not understand what is happening or why it is happening. They may worry about their parent or worry that the parent cannot take care of them. They may also believe that their parent does not care about them if the parent avoids them (2). That was certainly true in my case. I could not believe that my Dad loved me.

I have already written much about how my dad's PTSD affected me including the following:

- Nervousness exhibited by finger tapping and fingernail biting
- Repressed anger and depression
- Self-loathing, shame, and guilt
- Hatred and avoidance of my dad
- Self-mutilation
- Desire to become my mother's protector and keeper
- Inability to have healthy relationships with the opposite sex
- Inability to make a commitment in relationships
- Inability to have healthy boundaries
- Secrecy

In addition, I experienced nightmares when I was very little. Soon after I saw the pictures of emaciated bodies in the pictures of Nordhausen Concentration Camp, I started to fear going to bed at night because I was certain that I was going to be attacked and killed during the night.

The dreams I had were so vivid that I can recall them today. My belief was that if any part of my body like a hand or a leg hung out over the edge of the bed, I would die a violent death. My mother bought some clamps that she used on the bedcovers to ensure that all my body parts remained in the bed.

I can't prove that my nightmares were connected to Dad's PTSD, but it seems likely, especially since the origin of the dreams was so close to the time when I first saw the horrific pictures from Nordhausen. Perhaps emotional contagion was happening in our family, and I was experiencing in my dreams similar situations to my dad's nightmares.

Another example of the kinds of effects that I experienced as a result of my dad's PTSD was a form of hypervigilance. Like so many children who experience abuse at the hands of a parent, I became hyperaware of my environment. It was like having special radar to check out the mood of Dad so I could go into hiding if he were near. This hypersensitivity was helpful in some ways, and costly in other ways. It helped me to protect myself but also kept me guarded in some situations where I didn't need to be. Trust in others, especially males, didn't come easily.

I didn't experience all these effects at the same time. Nor were any of them so severe that they became completely debilitating. Sometimes personality and cultural traditions interfaced with the symptoms and compounded them. For example, my early inability to have a healthy relationship with the opposite sex was partially due to the traditional beliefs that women were supposed to be submissive to men as well as having that modeled for me in a dysfunctional and sometimes violent way because of PTSD. However, all of these effects of PTSD have provided major learning curves throughout my life as I have sought to heal my wounds of war.

As a result of each of these symptoms acting out in my life, I have experienced greater empathy and understanding for others. In that way, each symptom has been a gift.

I have found that some of these wounds have shown up at various times in my early life, and others have taken decades to emerge. For instance, as a young girl and woman, I was thin and healthy, primarily because I was so active. As an older woman, I discovered that some weight issues I had were related to my self-image developed from my war wounds.

There certainly are a lot of reasons for weight gain, and I believe that war wounds or other trauma is one of them. It is one way individuals have to rebel and take control. In my case, I thought that weight gain would keep me safe by helping me to avoid problematic relationships with men. I reasoned, if I was no longer beautiful or attractive, men would no longer bother me. After a few dysfunctional relationships, I thought this rationale was entirely credible. I was wrong, of course. All men are not only attracted by physical beauty, although that helps. Of course, it didn't keep me safe at all, since over the years it contributed to various health problems.

Besides the obvious effects on spouses and children, I also believe that other people with close relationships to the combat veteran can suffer consequences. Friends and relatives of the veteran are also fair game. For instance, as I look back on the relationship between my dad and his sister, Amy, I believe that his war experience impacted her desire to live a very religious life. I believe that she knew, better than anyone, what he had been like in his youth, and she saw what killing had done to his psyche. A promise of salvation drew her to the church, and doing good deeds for others became a way of life.

In the 1950s, Amy and Dad were very close. As the years rolled by, and she saw the consequences of his experiences on his behavior and family, she tried to make things easier and to take up the slack, especially with me. Her home was my refuge when things became really tough. Of course, Dad realized this, and he must have felt some guilt and shame. These emotions found expression in his belittling her and her husband, and sometimes they received the same kind of silent treatment that Mom and I did. Since our two families didn't discuss emotions, over the years less and less time was spent together while resentment grew. In later years, there seemed to be more of a sense of obligation to spend time together during a holiday than a joyful family event. All times spent together seemed to be more about things not said than said. A holiday became a family duty rather than an occasion for family fun and celebration. Often Dad would distance himself from the others in the living room by picking up a book or turning on the television, and Amy would fall asleep. I believe that all the family members involved felt a loss of connection and joy.

Amy's husband, my Uncle Orv, was also in WWII where he had seen action in the Pacific for a longer time period than Dad was in the war. I have no personal knowledge of his experience—he was always silent too, and we, his family, failed to ask questions. However, in later years, after researching his war history, I found that he had been in the Fifth Infantry primarily stationed in Australia and East India where he had ordered supplies for his unit. I remember my dad having some disdain for my uncle because my dad claimed that "he never saw any action."

What Orv really experienced was unknown to us as a family. But the contagion of my dad's disdain was felt by all and contributed to further family alienation.

Over the years, Amy relied on religion and her home-based printing business to escape from family trauma. Both of these activities took up more and more of her time so that it was hard to get her to do anything else or to spend time with anyone else. When she was at church or printing, she was not having to deal with family issues. She too seemed in many respects to have become numb to life and joy. Most things in life were seen as her duty, and she shut out joy, music, free time, play, vacations, and interactions with friends and family. It is clear to me now that somehow she was greatly impacted, not only by the culture of the times where it was proper to remain silent, but also by the war experience of those closest to her. She chose another way to numb herself than my mother did. We had no understanding of what had happened or the tools to help us recover as a family. The hole in my heart grew larger.

My father's PTSD also affected my maternal grandmother. She was not immune to his critical comments, and she knew something of the abuse that happened, especially after Mom gave her Dad's gun to keep. She always tried to keep the harmony and to sympathize with my mother and me. Since my grandparent's home was at times a refuge for my mother and me, my dad probably felt guilty about our need to seek that refuge and some shame in my grandmother's presence. Of course, nothing was ever said to address the problem.

While I was growing up, my grandparents lived thirty miles away from us. Even though we saw them frequently, we did not see them as often as my aunt and uncle. Consequently, my grandparents probably experienced less war wounds at the hand of my dad than the rest of us.

In later years, however, my grandmother and parents lived in the same town. The relationship my grandmother had with my dad was friendly but emotionally distant. She, like my mother, tried to keep the peace by giving into his needs even though they might be opposite her own. He was the one in charge, and she went along with whatever was taking place.

None of us knew how to help my dad or how to help ourselves. We were all victims of war.

We, as family members, were not the only victims of Dad's war experience. I am saddened to realize that my experiences as a child deeply impacted my beliefs and behaviors so that many others in my life have been impacted too. PTSD is not just the combat veteran's problem but is like a contagious virus that impacts the family, friends, future generations, and the culture in general. PTSD is a societal problem that insidiously affects us all until we decide to stop going to war or begin to individually assume the responsibility to heal.

By the time I reached adolescence, I was obsessed with the desire to escape. I knew that our lives were unhealthy. I just didn't have any psychological understanding of it or solutions for it. In order to attain a proper perspective, I had to escape my roots. I had to be able to stand outside my box in order to evaluate what was inside. I had to reinvent myself.

PART IV

Escape
1964-1984

FIFTEEN

Escaping my Roots

By the time I entered high school, I was ready to escape. After watching relatives and friends get pregnant and then married while still in their teens, I was convinced that I did not want to go down that path of escape. I knew I was not ready to make a marriage commitment or to have a child. Fortunately, I was not drawn into any relationship that involved sexual intimacy, especially since birth control measures did not yet exist in my world.

Higher education was the answer for me, and I threw myself into all the studies and activities in high school that I thought would help me reach my goal to go to college. I not only wanted to escape my dad and my abusive surroundings, I wanted to escape my economic class, lifestyle, and white Midwestern life. During this time, the civil rights movement was gaining momentum, and I was very aware of how the Midwest lacked diversity. Everywhere I looked, I only saw homogenous white people. I wanted to find out what it would be like to live in an environment that was more culturally diverse.

During my early high school years Dr. Martin Luther King Jr. came to Mankato, Minnesota, to speak to people who were sympathetic to the civil rights movement. A friend and her family asked me to accompany them to the meeting. Dr. King was the first black person I saw in person. I was so struck with his message and the practice of nonviolence that I decided to become a nonviolent person myself, even though I wasn't fully aware of what that meant. Until then, I had only known about war as a way to settle differences. In fact, history classes seemed only to contain a long list of wars. Was war inevitable? I didn't want to believe it was. Learning about nonviolence and an entire movement devoted to that philosophy gave me hope for the future.

At the same time that I was learning about the civil rights movement in real life, I was also learning about the transcendentalists in history and English classes in high school. Henry David Thoreau and his writings about civil disobedience and environmentalism completely intrigued me, and I was inspired to learn about Mahatma Gandhi and the downfall of colonialism through nonviolent means. I wanted to learn more and become actively engaged in practicing nonviolence. I somehow knew that the practice of nonviolence was an antidote to the problems my family faced. I wanted to develop those skills and lifestyle. It was the only way I could imagine a better life than a life filled with war and its aftermath.

The practice of nonviolence became a theme in my life. Through the years, I was drawn to anything that promoted nonviolence. As a child I remember watching the movie *Friendly Persuasion*, the story of an Indiana Quaker farm family during the civil war, my first exposure to Quakerism. At that time I didn't know that many of my ancestors were Quakers but was so drawn to two of the Quaker beliefs: "We seek a world free of war and the threat of war" and "We seek a society with equity and justice for all." I longed for that kind of world.

I didn't have an opportunity to practice Quakerism at that time because there weren't any Quakers in the communities around me, but I do remember being hopeful about knowing about groups of people who believed in nonviolence. Much later I would learn more about the practice of nonviolence in a therapeutic setting and in communication styles and attempt to consciously bring nonviolence into my personal behavioral repertoire. Although I didn't realize it until recently, I was following some of my Quaker ancestors' beliefs in nonviolence. They seemed to be deeply embedded in my soul.

In high school I was determined to completely reinvent myself. To me that meant to be as unlike my family as possible. Whatever my parents were, I wanted to be the opposite. I thought that the process of reinventing myself would keep me occupied and away from Dad, and provide an opportunity for escape. I did all I could think of to better myself.

I took a psychology class, which was very innovative for the times; the instructor used a college textbook, and I devoured it. The "A" I received for the class convinced me that I could survive in college. I joined the speech and debate club even though I was terrified of speaking. Shyness was a limitation that I knew I had to overcome, and I forced myself to give speeches and learn how to debate. After winning some debates, I slowly began to develop some confidence along with an ability to think more critically and do research. I even began to enjoy myself while in front of a group of people. I loved drama and poetry and often lost myself in reading or acting out someone else's words. Since I was out of touch with my own emotions, borrowing someone else's emotions and life experiences for a while allowed me to experiment with possibilities and express emotions that at the time I could not identify in myself. I went to several speech contests where I did interpretive readings and acted in local high school plays. All of these events helped me to build confidence and to hone skills in communication that I reasoned would be useful in college and later life. They also helped me recognize that doing things I feared helped me to overcome my fear and consequently broadened my life.

Fortunately, I had a few teachers who were dedicated to helping kids like me develop skills. Many an hour and many a night were spent practicing with teachers who would say, "Now, say it (or do it) this way." Not only were these teachers inspirational and motivational for me, but also, later in life, they were a role model when I became a teacher. Their dedication and caring helped me survive and thrive.

I knew that to realize my goal of getting out of my surroundings, I had to push myself in ways that were uncomfortable but would help me converse with others and get along socially and academically in the world beyond my home town. I decided to read every book my English teacher advised and then read most of the books in the public library. (It was a small library!) In the summertime I was more ambitious and decided to read the complete works of Shakespeare along with many classics. I wanted to be well read, conversant, and comfortable with others. I idealized college and college graduates, and did all I could within the limitations of my school and family to prepare myself for "moving up" in life.

My Aunt Amy and Uncle Orv were very supportive of my efforts to better myself. They saw to it that I learned to know and appreciate classical music by taking me to local concert association events. Seeing my first opera, Mozart's *The Marriage of Figaro*, and hearing the African-American contralto who was one of the most celebrated singers of the twentieth century, Marian Anderson, sing on the stage in the local high school were highlights. Orv, especially, loved music and had many classical albums, which he played whenever I visited (which was often). They also bought me my own record player and later a stereo so that I could have my own music collection. Music of all kinds became favorite presents from them.

When I was a teenager, they encouraged me to sing in the church choir. During my high school years, I stood next to Amy in the alto section singing my heart out and absorbing the religious beliefs of the church and my family. With their help and inspiration, I learned to transcend my environment. Aesthetics and the arts were instrumental in motivating me and showing me possibilities that existed in the world. They were also healing to my wounded spirit. Through art, music, drama, and literature, I learned not only to express myself and a variety of emotions, I gained hope and inspiration for a better life.

I was very fortunate to have the kinds of school activities and support that I did in my early life. Not all kids did. (Nor do they today. In an era of budget cuts, the kinds of programs that provide so much support for kids like me are the first to go. This is a tragedy that many people do not even begin to comprehend. The arts and creative programs are often considered fluff. In fact, they provide not only an opportunity to learn confidence and new skills, but they are much more likely to translate into lifelong practices than sports. And more importantly, research today is showing that the arts play a critical role in brain development and in healing. Veterans are using the arts in their therapeutic process to good effect. The arts enrich lives in ways we do not even comprehend or can measure.)

Even though my home life was stressful, it provided an impetus to grow. I learned the skills at home that helped me to become independent. I learned academic skills and received the encouragement at school to create a different kind of life for myself. And the support and love I received from Amy and Orv helped me to feel good enough about myself to believe I could escape and build a better life, and also exposed me to ideas, events, and cultural opportunities that were lacking in my home. All that was needed from me was the willingness and courage to carry out my dreams.

In retrospect, I believe that while in high school I intuitively was seeking answers to my family's problems. Psychology was a new course of study, and I eagerly read everything I could to better understand my family. I didn't find much that was helpful but was fascinated enough to want to pursue psychological studies later in life. I also realized that communication in our family was extremely poor. At the time, relationship skills and interpersonal communication skills and theory were not part of high school or college curricula. Even so, I wanted to perfect my own communication skills as much as possible. I reasoned that if I could be a better communicator, I would be able to have happier relationships in life and with my dad. I didn't fully understand at the time the concept of "it takes two to communicate!" If the other person doesn't want to cooperate in communication, or doesn't have the necessary skills, there is no positive interaction.

The more I read and prepared myself, the more I saw that our family life was not like other families. I never read or heard about any father who acted like mine did. Now I realize that there were thousands of families who hid their troubles like my family did. As an adult, some of my friends' trauma stories came to light, and I was shocked when I realized that I had not been alone in my ordeal as a teenager. Several years after high school graduation, I heard stories about a friend who had been regularly whipped until the welts on her back bled, and another who had been the victim of sexual and physical abuse, and countless others who had experienced emotional and verbal abuse. One close friend's dad committed suicide when we were in high school, but I didn't know this until many years later. All these stories were told by the children from families of WWII combat veterans where, in retrospect, we know that PTSD raged, but the victims were silent until they were safe enough in their adulthood to reveal their story. Many, like me, are just beginning to reveal their story now, fifty-plus years later.

Because I didn't hear these stories as a teenager, I became convinced that our family was abnormal, and I was ashamed and embarrassed about my parents. By the time I was a junior and senior in high school, I mastered the art of avoidance by spending most of my home time in my bedroom doing homework and talking on the phone. I spent long hours at school being involved in extracurricular activities, and on weekends I went on speech trips, rehearsed for plays, and spent time with friends. I even arranged with my Aunt Amy to have my noon meals during the school week with her because I couldn't handle being around my dad and the tension in our home. Since she lived across the street from the school, it was very convenient for me to go there rather than walk the eight blocks to my home.

While my "outer me" excelled in my activities and school, there was an "inner me" that was deeply troubled. At home, I would drum my fingers constantly on any surface when Dad was around, I picked at my fingernails, and had other symptoms of agitation and nervousness. I also tried to be very silent and "Minnesota nice." I worked hard at being perfect, which included a two-hour time period of getting ready for any activity outside my home. Wrinkles and lint were not tolerated on clothing, and ironing and standing up until I left the house were rituals. If I looked perfect and acted perfect, perhaps others (and especially my dad) would love me, I thought. Probably the biggest symptom was my shyness and shame about my background. I was motivated to keep that hidden and to wear a mask of confidence. I felt like a fraud. Most of all, I longed for the issues in my family to be resolved and for us to be a normal and loving family.

Neither one of my parents supported my decision to attend college at first . . . no one in either of their families had ever completed college, and they thought it wasn't necessary for a girl. Their goal for me was to get married to a local person, live near them, and live a life like theirs. I saw their life as "living in a rut" with no opportunities, growth, or adventures, and I did not want to repeat it. I also wanted to escape living near Dad. By the time I reached my junior year in high school, they started to support my decision when they saw how determined I was. I also believe that my mother's remembrance of her own independence when she worked for TWA in Ohio helped her to help me escape. My dad was probably glad to see me go. Since he and I did not see eye to eye on most matters, he must have felt some relief at my not being in the household. He didn't show any emotion, however, nor did he talk with me about leaving home.

I graduated from high school in 1964 and three months later left for college in Iowa. My choice of a college was partially dependent on how far from my hometown I could get with my parent's approval and financial support. One hundred and twenty miles was their limit.

During the next four years, I continued my reinvention project. I told everyone to call me Jan because I associated Janelle with my home life. I also made an effort to be more social than I had been in high school. Since my dad was not around on a daily basis anymore, I felt freer to have a social life and establish friendships. I also traveled with my new friends to their homes and learned that other families were healthier than mine. I wanted to make a future for myself that did not include the kinds of things that I felt ashamed about in my past.

I still had a close connection to my mother but seldom heard from Dad. Telephone conversations with him consisted of "Are you OK?" and "Do you need anything?" And then he would hang up. Most of the time he did not even get on the phone, nor did he write many letters as my mother did. In fact, I remember only receiving four letters from him during my college years. I kept them because they were so rare, and I was so hungry for communication with him. I began to feel freer of my connection with him and at the same time grieved not having a "regular" dad who showed me he cared.

I also continued to do my best to avoid the possibility of being alone with him. For instance, when father-daughter events were held, I didn't mention them to him. I did invite my mother to mother-daughter events though. At the time, I told myself that I didn't care what my dad thought about this. Now I am sorry for any pain that I may have caused him. I threw myself into my education academically and socially in an effort to dissociate from my parents and background, and seldom went home to visit. In the back of my mind, the thought of my parents and all of what I was trying to escape lingered like a festering sore.

By the time I was a senior, I "fell in love" with a veteran who had recently entered college after being in combat in Vietnam. After several months, we became engaged and planned to move to California after I graduated. As my graduation date grew near, I realized that he drank a lot and that the drinking bouts were increasing, although I was never present when he drank. Often he would call me around midnight when he was closing the McDonald's where he worked, and it was evident that he had been drinking. He also seemed to have numerous other problems. I thought that my love could solve all his problems and that eventually we would be like my fantasy of a happily married couple.

Fortunately for me, we saw a counselor who advised me to break up with my fiancé until he had received therapeutic help for his drinking problem. He told me, "You cannot solve your fiancé's problems. Nor can your love!" I was devastated, but some part of me recognized the truth in that, and I broke off the relationship. (Probably the part of me that knew my love could not heal my dad.)

However, at the time, I didn't draw any connecting links between my experience with Dad and with my fiancé. I still didn't know that being a veteran of combat war could result in PTSD and that my fiancé had some similar symptoms to my dad. I didn't know that we seek to heal our wounds in our relationships and consequently are drawn to be in relationships that are similar to past relationships until we heal. I didn't know that we are likely to repeat the problems in our secondary relationships that existed in our primary family relationships and that this repetition continues until they are resolved. Instead, I thought that the fact that my fiancé was also a veteran would bring me closer to Dad. (Dad would love me because I was married to a vet.) I also didn't receive any therapy for myself. I learned, however, at least for a while, that I could not solve anyone else's problem. This was a lesson that I repeated several times throughout my life.

I followed the advice of the counselor, graduated, and a few weeks later moved to Oregon with a friend who also wanted to escape the Midwest. We didn't have a plan for what we would do or where we would live when we got there; we just had a lot of confidence that we would be okay and find some kind of job.

My mother was sad to see me go and at the same time was happy that I was achieving independence. She probably wished she could go too. My dad didn't have anything to say about my moving to Oregon other than "good-bye." His good-bye to me, in retrospect, was similar to his mother's good-bye when he left for WWII.

After packing up my friend's car with the few possessions we each had, we took off for Oregon filled with the excitement and anticipation of embarking on a new life. We spent three days on the road and arrived in Oregon on a Saturday night. On Sunday, we headed for the coast and the thrill of being on a beach that stretched as far as we could see. I still remember being awestruck by seeing the ocean for the first time, running down the beach into the water, only to be shocked by how cold it was. My image of "California surfing" was not how it was on Oregon beaches! On Monday we found a place to live in the basement of an elderly couple's home. And on Tuesday we started looking for a summer job. It took a few weeks for each of us to find one, and we were down to our last seven collective dollars before we found one, but we were determined that we would not call our parents for help, nor would we consider returning to the Midwest.

The summer jobs tided us over until I found a teaching job, and my friend started graduate school.

The next several years were filled with the adventures of starting a high school teaching career and graduate school, establishing friendships (some of which became lifelong), learning about my newly adopted state and exploring every corner of it, doing some traveling to other states and countries, and growing up. I fell in love with Oregon, had a lot of fun, and enjoyed my life and teaching career immensely. I was able to put my creativity to work by initiating a variety of classes and school programs like Minority Week (common terminology for the times) where students were released from their ordinary classes for a week in order to attend a wide assortment of multicultural events. I also became involved in community theater and wrote and directed a couple of reader's theater presentations for the high school where I taught.

One of these presentations was called "War." It was 1972, and the United States was in the Vietnam war. My heart ached because so many of the young people I worked with were planning on participating in the war. I wanted to give them another perspective so put together a reader's theater presentation that depicted other viewpoints about war besides the glorified ones. I secretly hoped that my students would rethink their goals. A few did. Many did not. Each time a student told me that he was heading off to war after graduation, I cried.

Part of my own high school experience that I found so valuable was being involved in speech and drama activities, and three years after starting to teach, I became the school's forensics' director and gave back what I had been taught. Working with students in the way my teachers had worked with me was so rewarding! Best of all, I was completely independent of my parents and took immense pride in that. Finally, I was living a life that was congruent with my dreams and ambitions.

Thoughts of my family faded into the background until the weekly phone call with my mother or the yearly visit to Minnesota. During these phone calls or visits, I was troubled about my relationship with Dad but didn't know how to deal with it so ignored it as best I could. After each annual visit to Minnesota, I would return to Oregon depressed and angry, and would throw myself back into my Oregon life. I noted to myself that I took about a month or more to "recover" from my Minnesota visits and started to dread making them. I noticed that when I was in the company of my family, all the old fears and behaviors would arise, and I would feel and act like my child self, instead of the adult self I was in Oregon. Only the desire to keep my relationship with my mother motivated me to make the journey.

By that time, the estrangement with my dad was so deep that I told myself it would be OK with me if I never saw him again. I even fantasized about the possibility of how I would sever any relationship with my father if my mother died first. There were a few times when Dad and I talked for a couple minutes on the phone, but most of the time my knowledge about what was going on with Dad came from my mother. She told of her work, and a few trips they had taken, and other things they did with friends. Once in a while, when the burden was too great for her, she would share some story about what Dad had done that was especially hurtful to her, or how he was ill, or in the hospital again with his headaches or some other illness or surgical event. I left every conversation with a secret yearning for things to be different. A hole was in my heart where a father should have been.

Early in the 1970s I met the man who became my husband. I dated a lot both in college and after moving to Oregon. Unconsciously, I was trying to fill in the hole created by the absence of my father's affection. I imagined myself to be "in love" many times before I met my ex-husband. Four years after meeting him, I married a man who also had a war story.

SIXTEEN

Marriage

> *When World War II ended in 1945 six million European Jews were dead, killed in the Holocaust. More than one million of the victims were children. Driven by a racist ideology that viewed Jews as "parasitic vermin" worthy only of eradication, the Nazis implemented genocide on an unprecedented scale. All of Europe's Jews were slated for destruction: the sick and the healthy, the rich and the poor, the religiously orthodox and converts to Christianity, the aged and the young, even infants. Thousands of Jewish children survived this brutal carnage, however, many because they were hidden. With identities disguised, and often physically concealed from the outside world, these youngsters faced constant fear, dilemmas, and danger. Theirs was a life in shadows, where a careless remark, a denunciation, or the murmurings of inquisitive neighbors could lead to discovery and death.*
>
> http://www.ushmm.org/museum/exhibit/online/hiddenchildren/insideX/

My ex-husband was born in a Jewish family who lived in the Netherlands at the beginning of WWII. His mother and father were taken to a concentration camp when my ex-husband, age two or three at the time, and his only older brother, age six or seven, were saved by some neighbors who asked two separate Dutch families to take the boys into their home. After brief reflection, the two families agreed. The brothers didn't see each other again for the duration of the war.

During the time when my ex-husband was adjusting to living with his new family, Nazis occupied the family dairy farm and threatened the lives of all the family members. I will never forget the story my ex-mother-in-law told me about herself, her husband, and their teenage birth daughter. "Because we were blond, we had to be very careful so that we were not all seen together with our newly adopted little boy because he had dark hair. One of us could go with him somewhere, but we couldn't go as a family anywhere. If we did, the Nazis would know immediately that our baby boy was not a birth son, and all of our lives would be threatened. We had to make up new family names and stories for everyone in order to stay alive."

This was probably very difficult for a little boy to understand. When his name changed along with his family, he must have questioned, "Who am I?" He must also have thought himself to be a throwaway to be taken away from his birth family so abruptly, and later, he must have known that he was a threat to the lives of the family who had adopted him. All of his early experiences left a wound so big that he became afraid of intimacy and trust in relationships in spite of the love and the pride that his adopted family had for him.

Before the war ended in the Netherlands, the Nazis burned their family farm to the ground. My ex-mother-in-law told me how even though that had been a devastating day, she had learned something of great importance from that experience. "Things are not important. People are." She told me about how she used to value possessions, appearances, cleanliness, and rules. "After the fire, nothing was as important as loving our family and spending time with them."

This conversation with my ex-mother-in-law was the only one we ever had about this subject. She didn't tell me the circumstances of their lives during the Nazi occupation of their farm.

After acting in the play *The Diary of Anne Frank* and seeing the movie *The Hiding Place,* about Corrie Ten Boom's experience of saving Jewish families from the Holocaust, I imagined the horror of their experience. I'm certain that my imaginings didn't come close to the reality. What would it take to hide a little boy from people who wanted to kill him when those people lived on your property? I will never know.

After the war, my ex-husband's new family reunited the two brothers and brought them to the United States. My ex-mother-in-law told how the boys remembered each other when they saw each other again, and each boy called the other boy by his birth name. They were told that name was no longer their name and that each boy had a new identity now. That must have been very difficult for two little boys to understand.

I remember feeling so inspired by this story when I first heard it. I thought of my in-laws-to-be as being so kind, generous, tolerant, and courageous that I believe I fell in love with them and their story as much as the man who became my husband. I also began to respect the little bit about my father's war story that I knew at the time regarding his experience at Nordhausen Concentration Camp. I remembered the pictures of emaciated bodies piled in a heap that I had seen early in life and was appalled to think that my ex-husband's parents were subject to such brutality. I was proud that Dad had been a part of the liberation of Germany. My relationship with my ex-husband seemed like destiny to my imaginative mind.

It wasn't until after marriage that I began to realize that my ex-husband was traumatized by the early years of fear of being discovered a Jew and the bombing of his homeland. He was afraid of thunder and lightning storms because they reminded him of the bombing around his home. Because he found it difficult to relate emotionally to people, he made his work the focus of his attention. He moved through his days at a run, literally, and didn't take time for intimate or emotional conversation and relationships, for introspection, or for much relaxation.

We set appointments two weeks in advance to have a conversation, usually about money. His workday started at 6:00 a.m. and didn't end until after 10:00 p.m. most days of the week. More often than not, I would be asleep when he left home in the morning and asleep when he came home at night. Since cell phones didn't exist, we didn't communicate with each other in the day, as many people do now. He came home to sleep and shower and took no interest in household concerns. Because of his schedule, we didn't eat together or do much of anything together except for ten-day vacations twice a year and an occasional get-together with friends on a weekend night or an occasional weekend away from town so we could have privacy. By the time he did stop for relaxation, he was often so tired that he fell asleep in the middle of whatever event we attended or got ill on a vacation. Frequently, our fun times were not very fun or long enough to be satisfying and restorative.

Whenever he was in the room, the radio and/or television was turned on because he couldn't tolerate quiet. The noise and tension level around him was always above my level of comfort, like it had been around my dad when I was a child and young adult. Sometimes the tension would erupt into rage. I feared my ex-husband, like I feared my father. Even though I was never physically abused by my ex-husband, there was an underlying threat that I might be struck in a fit of anger. After I saw him put his fist through a wall at his workplace, I was especially afraid.

Just as my mother had done, throughout my marriage I played the role of the enabler: the person who allows the dysfunction to continue by not speaking up or making appropriate changes. I made excuses for my ex-husband when he could not attend a function because he was working. I maintained the home or contracted with a professional when I needed help. I made an effort to keep up appearances so that anyone looking in would think we had a happy, successful middle class marriage. I handled all of our social needs and responsibilities. Because of the role I played, my ex-husband could continue ignoring his home because everything was taken care of there.

He was so successful at ignoring his home that he didn't know where things were kept. All that was left for him to do was work and bring home the paycheck. As I see it now, this demeaned us both and kept us in a codependent relationship that was mentally and emotionally unhealthy.

At this time PTSD was not recognized as a problem, and my ex-husband was not a veteran. It didn't occur to me until a few years into our marriage that his problems with relationships might be related to his war experiences. After losing a family and his identity at such a young age, and later losing his home twice (once through burning and another time through emigration), and being constantly under siege of the war bombs, and fearful of being caught would be enough to cause anyone PTSD. He, like my dad, must have questioned, "Who am I?" He, like my dad, was compulsively neat, was very reticent about talking about himself and engaging deeply with others, and he liked to be in charge. He never felt very safe or trustful of others. He refused to talk about his childhood or his war experiences. Life and memory for him seemed to start in the United States. He had no interest in learning anything about his life in the Netherlands, his Jewish background, or his birth family even though he had opportunities to do so.

When I married him, I thought he was vastly different from my dad. He was far more comfortable in social situations, was college educated, and seemed to care about other people and animals. He had a terrific memory and could recall phone numbers, children's and animal's names, and other details of people he met. This quality endeared him to most.

The fact that he seemed opposite from my dad was highly attractive to me. However, as time passed, I began to recognize that, once again, I was in a primary relationship with a man who was emotionally unavailable to me. Once again, I knew of no satisfactory therapeutic process that could help us cope with our problems, although I tried to find one. He was not interested in any therapeutic process, or in discussing or improving our relationship. At the time, I thought that was because he was not interested in having a relationship with me. Now, I suspect that his lack of interest in therapy had more to do with what he would discover about himself than it had to do about his feelings about me.

I also suspect that any therapy we would have received would have been one-sided. I was so intent on changing him to fit my dream of what a husband should be like that I didn't see my own problems. I didn't realize that because my dad had not been emotionally available for me, that I was seeking in my husband someone who would heal my heart and be everything that my Dad wasn't. Unfortunately, I didn't know that I had to heal my own heart—no one else can do it for us. My ex-husband could not possibly live up to what I wanted from him. As a result of our family dynamics, he probably received the message loud and clear that he wasn't good enough for me and decided to not take part in a therapeutic process where he would have been the villain. In retrospect, that seems perfectly reasonable. It takes two to communicate, after all. I just hadn't faced up yet to my own dysfunction. All I saw was his. I am not so sure that the therapeutic processes of the time could have dealt with our issues since this happened before PTSD was a diagnosis.

I was aware, however, that some of my ex-husband's problems resulted in dysfunctional behavior that was socially acceptable, workaholism. He tried to cope with his internal demons by using socially acceptable behaviors but did not deal with the cause of the problem, his war experience in Europe. Of course, dealing with socially acceptable addictions are much more difficult than dealing with addictions that are recognized as individual and societal problems. It is almost impossible to get supportive and therapeutic help for socially acceptable addictions. Few people notice that working compulsively is not mentally or emotionally healthy. There was no place to turn to for help.

For many years I felt victimized, and my self-esteem was extremely low. While I didn't exactly believe that I was at fault for causing my ex-husband to work so much, I grew to think that he didn't love me because he was absent most of the time. I reasoned that we choose to spend time with those we love, and family is our first priority. I could not believe that I was loved when I realized that I was not a first priority or even a second priority in my ex-husband's life. Instead, I thought of myself as being a hotel manager and prostitute because I was accepting a nice house, a steady income and affluence, and community prestige in the place of love and affection. I remembered having the same thoughts about my mother earlier. My self-respect diminished like my respect for my mother had diminished when I was growing up.

I grew increasingly unhappy and became obsessed with finding an answer to our problems. Unlike my mother, I found others to talk with, including a therapist. But no answers seemed to come. I remember being told to make myself more sexually attractive in order to make my husband want to spend time with me. The belief at that time was that if a woman wrapped herself in saran wrap and met her husband at the door with a big kiss, he would never leave her side. I couldn't quite buy into that theory or bring myself to adopt that practice in an effort to manipulate him. I was also told that I should work on myself instead of trying to fix someone else, but I had no concept of what that meant. Therapeutic help seemed nonexistent.

Also, unlike my mother, I sought answers in the culture and education of the 1970s, which was changing dramatically. Besides teaching high school during these years, I returned to college to earn a master's degree and work on obtaining a PhD. The fields of communication and women's history were highly attractive to me, and I started to learn that women had contributed to history in very different and significant ways than men. Women's history was not a long list of wars but instead included a long list of social improvements. I began to take pride in being a woman.

I also learned that it was desirable to be assertive, to speak up with appropriate communication skills. There was a difference between aggression and assertion; aggression was violent or coercive in tone and was not respectful of others, while assertion regarded the other as an equal and was cooperative in tone. I realized that I had never been assertive. I was a product of my culture where passivity and manipulation were considered to be the ways that a woman properly communicated.

I started to practice being assertive with my ex-husband, to ask for my needs to be met, only to be refused over and over again. I felt like I was doing all that I could do and that my ex-husband was not meeting me halfway. We evidently did not want the same things in our marriage. Since I was growing to value equality in marriage and didn't feel like my ex-husband thought of me as an equal, I could see no future in our relationship. But I didn't want to give up.

One night my ex-husband came home very late after having been out drinking with friends. While he was not a habitual drinker, he did enjoy a night out with his college buddies after a football game between his alma mater and an Oregon team. He stumbled into the house and made his way into the guest bathroom where he vomited and passed out. At the end of what I could endure, I started screaming, "I hate you, I hate you!" and fell onto our bed in shock about what I could no longer ignore, the depth of my anger about our marriage, about my life, and about my dad and myself. I laid awake shaken as I confronted the real feelings that I had.

That night I realized that I had been in a reactive trance until then. I had, like my mother, tried to put up with behavior that was unloving and demeaning. By putting up with it, I was numbing myself in order to cope, and as a result, I was becoming dishonest with myself and with others. My life was a secret like my parents' life together had been. My mother couldn't tell the story of what her life was like with my dad because he was a war hero. I couldn't tell the story of what my life was like with my ex-husband because he was a prestigious member of the community. That night, I woke up out of my trance and victim thinking, and realized that "I married my dad." Even though I was half a continent away from where I grew up, my life situation was basically the same as my parents. I had not escaped at all. I had just repeated an old pattern. The two most significant men in my life, because of their war wounds, were emotionally unavailable to me and were so self-involved with their own needs and life that they couldn't see or value the needs and life of those around them. They were their first priority, and they expected those around them to think of them as the priority too. My war wounds bought into that scenario, and I was a classic enabler who allowed the dysfunctional pattern to persist.

Furthermore, the pattern being repeated was not just about my relationship with the men in my personal life, it was also about the contrast between my home and professional life. When I was growing up, I was miserable much of the time at home and deeply troubled about my family, but I excelled in school and in my public world. When I was married, the same thing was true. I remember dreading going home because the tension there was so extreme at times. However, life beyond my home was good. I was a graduate teaching assistant and later became an instructor in the university system in Oregon. I also belonged to a few organizations and was active in my community and developed many close friendships that still exist today. In contrast to many people, my public life was my refuge, not my home.

The realization that I had just repeated an old pattern with different people shocked me into an awareness that I had an enormous amount of anger, and it was up to me to heal it. No one else was responsible for my feelings. My anger was not caused by anything other than how I thought and responded to situations. I was literally shocked out of my thinking that I was a victim and realized I was in charge of me and my future. Fixing another would not fix me. I was the only person who could fix me. I had to take an inventory of my own beliefs and emotions and find out why I was in the same kind of relationship that I had grown up in. I needed to transform me so that I could have a happier life. My own healing began when I recognized this and decided that I was worthwhile and needed to begin my own process of healing instead of waiting for other people to change. Escape was not the answer as I had thought earlier. Transformation was.

That event occurred in 1984. The next twenty years were ones of profound change. Outer changes were easy to detect. I moved to four different cities in Oregon and to Tucson, Arizona. Every two years I had a new address and a new opportunity to reinvent myself. My friends and occupations changed, as well as my eating preferences, and social values and practices.

My inner changes, although harder for others to detect, were no less dramatic. My spiritual values, my self-esteem, and all of who I thought I was, changed. I no longer thought of myself as a victim but as a young woman in charge of creating my life to be the best one that

I could imagine. This did not mean material success to me. I didn't care about having stuff or having a certain kind of job or prestige. What mattered the most to me was becoming a compassionate person who could embrace all people with a willingness to understand them and care about their well-being. I wanted to learn how to love, both myself and others. I wanted to bring peace to my inner war.

During this period, I became obsessed with healing myself and was drawn to a number of resources, trainings, and experiences that had a profound healing effect on me. I was fortunate enough to live in an area that had a lot of resources and information that I craved, and for several years I signed up for dozens of workshops and trainings, some of which were facilitated by prestigious people who had a powerful impact on my emotional and spiritual life. As a result, I decided to practice using some of the tools I was learning about in my own start-up business that I called Mind, Body, and Spirit Integration Therapy. This business was portable, and I practiced it in all of the locations I lived in for the next several years. We teach, or practice, what we need to learn!

As a result of my healing experiences during this time, I was able to forgive my dad and let go of all the negative feelings I had for him. We developed a new kind of relationship that to some degree was healing for him too. From the early 1990s onward, we were able to spend time in each other's company where compassion replaced anger. Instead of running away from my dad, I ran toward him. I am so grateful that a healing between us happened before his death.

In 2003 Dad was admitted to a veteran's home because he had developed Alzheimer's disease and could no longer handle being at home. I decided to move back to Minnesota and to live with my mother as her caretaker since she needed my help and support. This move was my most dramatic move in terms of change. I let go of my network of connections, occupation, lifestyle, material goods, culture and cultural opportunities, and beautiful environment, which included easy access to mountains and the ocean, and moved back to the place of my birth. I felt like I had moved to a different culture, much as immigrants to the United States must feel when they first arrive. All of my past forty years spent away from Minnesota faded into the background as I tried to adjust to my new circumstances.

Sometimes the loss of what was once loved and familiar seemed impossible to overcome, but I reminded myself that I was living with my mother for a purpose. That purpose was reconciliation between myself and my family. My dad's admittance to a veteran's home was a reminder to me of our mortality. I didn't have much time left to have an experience of being in a family and attempting to fill the hole in my heart with love and gratitude. The last few years have resulted in the reconciliation with my family that I desired, and I now feel complete with that part of my family experience. My hole has been filled.

In 2006 my dad died. A few months later I found a box in a closet filled with his war memorabilia and the transcript of his memoir shared here. I started reading, and at last I began to understand some of what he had experienced. I was at a place in my own ability to listen to his story that I had not been able to achieve before. I was so moved by his writing and by the fact that most WWII veterans are no longer around to tell their story that I decided to tell his story for him. After talking with some friends about my plan, I decided to include my family's story along with my dad's story. These same friends were very involved in looking at their own family war story and suggested to me that my dad had experienced severe PTSD, and I should look up some information about PTSD and its effects on the individual and the family.

Thus began a major journey into understanding my dad and our entire family, and how we were all victims of war. This understanding has changed my perspective on life, my own and other people's lives as well. PTSD and its effects are so insidious and so pervasive in our culture that I now believe that the majority of us have some aspect of it lurking in the shadows of our lives.

In talks with friends since embarking on this journey of discovering my family through the lens of PTSD, I have discovered that some of their family history can also be explained and understood by seeing how the aftermath of combat war experiences affects families. Not only do I have a newfound understanding and compassion for my own family, other people, through shared storytelling, are finding their own understanding and compassion for their families as well. When one person achieves reconciliation, it is possible for others to achieve it too. When we reach reconciliation, we no longer think solely from the perspective of how the actions of others affected us but how our actions affect others. Our perspective becomes larger, whole, and holistic in nature. We see we are all playing a part in our family story; we are not the victim of someone else's part. We are a family unit playing out our part in a much larger cultural story. It is up to each of us to determine how to play that part.

The next two sections of this book detail some of the experiences I had while on my healing and reconciliation journey. After I started writing my family story in 2008, I realized that when looking back on my life, I could detect some specific kinds of things that helped me to heal. I also realized that my parents had also done their best to heal by making some changes in their lives that were similar to mine. I have included most of what our family has done in order to offer possibilities and inspiration to others.

First, I would like to explain what I mean by healing. It is understood to mean many different things by different people.

PART V

Healing
1984-2003

"The traumatic impact of war and violence inflicts wounds so deep we need to address them with extraordinary attention, resources, and methods."

—Edward Tick, PhD, in *War and the Soul* states,

"The war-wounded soul can be regrown in individuals by nurturing and educating a positive identity that surrounds the war experience with love, compassion, meaning, and forgiveness. When the survivor can accomplish this work, post-traumatic stress disorder as a soul wound evaporates."

—Edward Tick, PhD, in *War and the Soul* (1)

"When we are no longer able to change a situation—we are challenged to change ourselves."

—Victor Frankl, psychologist, author, and Nazi holocaust survivor

"Fortunately, the same immense energies that create symptoms of trauma, when properly engaged and mobilized, can transform the trauma and propel us into new heights of healing, mastery, and even wisdom. Trauma resolved is a great gift, returning us to the natural world of ebb and flow, harmony, love, and compassion. Having spent the last twenty-five years working with people who have been traumatized in almost every conceivable fashion, I believe that we humans have the innate capacity to heal not only ourselves, but our world, from the debilitating effects of trauma."

—*Waking the Tiger: Healing Trauma*, by Peter A. Levine with Ann Frederick (2)

SEVENTEEN

Healing Mind, Body, and Spirit

What does it mean to heal?

Healing is complex and has varied meanings to different people and professions. In my view, there is a difference between curing and healing. Both practices are valuable.

Curing refers to using various means to diagnose and treat a multitude of physical problems. An attempt is made to make the problem disappear. It is thought of as "the enemy," and war is usually made on the enemy by using drugs and/or surgery that hopefully, in the mind of the patient, will serve to annihilate the enemy. There is no attempt to consider the whole person when one is being treated or cured, or in finding a causative factor that isn't physical. Interest is in only the part of the physical body that is malfunctioning. When the enemy can no longer be seen, felt, or experienced, one is well. While this method works and saves lives, it does not consider the whole person, nor does it work all of the time. However, most people are satisfied with this kind of symptomatic relief.

Treating is part of the curing protocol and usually is considered to be the process by which drugs and/or surgery are applied. The treatment may be as simple as applying an antiseptic to a cut and topping it with a bandage, or as complex as radiation therapy for cancer patients.

Sometimes treatments work to eliminate the physical problem; sometimes they work to make the disease more tolerable. For example, if someone is dying from cancer and in severe pain, the patient may receive morphine, but without any expectation of getting better.

Some problems are cured without treatment, such as a simple cut that eventually turns to a scab while the skin recovers. When the scab disappears, the problem is over. Our bodies have divine intelligence that knows how to heal. We often say that the cut has healed when we no longer see the scab. Healing can happen without the addition of drugs or surgery or any other manipulation.

The way that I am using the word *healing* here, on the other hand, involves an entirely different mindset where everything in life is seen as an opportunity to grow physically, mentally, and spiritually. Instead of a war model where we destroy or get rid of parts of ourselves, healing involves a wholeness model where body, mind, and spirit are brought together. There is no place for an enemy in the healing process. Instead, all parts of our physical, emotional, mental, and spiritual being are thought to be continually striving for the good of the person. There is intelligence in every part of us, and it can be accessed and brought to conscious awareness. If we bring love and gratitude to a part that we think has caused a problem for us, we can thank it for having served us and let it go, peacefully. For example, once I understood the gift or service of a problem whether it was physical or emotional, the emotional pain of it disappeared and usually the physical pain, if there was any, did also. Healing is a gift from God and is always certain.

By observing my dad, I learned many lessons, not the least of which was how our bodies and physical problems provide communication to us about what might be going on emotionally and spiritually. How we think is at the core of every illness.

Bruce Lipton, PhD, an internationally recognized cell biologist who pioneered studies at Stanford University's School of Medicine, in his groundbreaking book *The Biology of Belief,* states, "Our new understanding of the Universe's mechanics shows us how the physical body can be affected by the immaterial mind. Thoughts, the mind's energy, directly influence how the physical brain controls the body's physiology. Thought 'energy' can activate or inhibit the cell's function-producing proteins via the mechanics of constructive and destructive interference." He later states that "harnessing the power of your mind can be more effective than the drugs you have been programmed to believe you need."(3) There are numerous studies demonstrating the truth of that. For instance, we all know that taking a placebo instead of a drug can have a curative effect.

Our subconscious beliefs are more powerful than our conscious ones in affecting our biology. Our conscious mind is creative and can at will think positive thoughts. Our subconscious mind is made up of stimulus-response tapes that come from instincts and learned experiences. According to Lipton, they are habitual and will play the same behavioral responses to life's signals over and over again.

I saw the power of the subconscious frequently in my own life and in my clients' lives when I was a therapist in Oregon and later in Arizona. For example, I had a client who came for her first appointment to relieve lower back pain, which she had experienced for years without ever finding any lasting relief. I had just started to do some massage work with her when she told me that she was remembering a dream she had the previous night. I asked her if she would like to tell me about the dream. As she did so, she started to cry because she realized that the dream was really a memory of her birth. "My mother didn't want me to be born," she sobbed.

When she could listen, I validated her memory by saying, "It might be true that your mother didn't want you to be born right then. We don't know the reason why. Maybe she was on her way to the hospital and wanted you to wait until she got there. However, other people are glad you were born."

When she heard that, her face lit up. She said softly in what sounded like a little girl's voice, "You mean it is all right for me to be here?"

I said, "Yes! A lot of people want you here and are grateful you're here!"

She said, after reflecting a moment, "Yes, that's true. My boyfriend wants me here. And . . ." she went off into her private space with a half smile on her face. I finished with the body work.

Three weeks later she called to tell me that she hadn't experienced back pain since her appointment with me. She also said, "I realized that belief of 'no one wants me here' has impacted my whole life. I didn't want to be here myself. That's why I have had so many car accidents that ultimately hurt my back, and that is why my back pain never went away. I typically would get a massage, and it would help for a day or two, and then the pain would return. But this time, I haven't had any pain for three weeks. I also haven't had any accidents! What's amazing, though, is that I finally decided to get married. I've been dating my boyfriend for seven years and could never make a commitment. Now I can. Thank you."

Months went by before I heard from her again. She continued to be pain free and happier.

As I reflected on what she told me, I realized that the profound wish to "not be here" had transferred from mother to daughter and over the years had morphed into a generalized feeling of reluctance to being alive. Various means, like having accidents, were used to produce the possibility of exiting the planet. The fact that my client could not make commitments was another illustration of being conflicted about being alive. I thought it remarkable that even though she unconsciously did not want to be here, she remained. Her Higher Self seemed determined to heal, and when she finally was in a safe enough place so that she could access the unconscious beliefs that contributed to her accidents and back problems, she could let them go and change her core beliefs to something more positive.

Thoughts are made up of energy. Energy has to go someplace. When we have negative beliefs that are not expressed, they are suppressed or stored in the body. When they become expressed fully, as in the case described above, they leave a void in the body. Nature doesn't like a vacuum and wants to fill it. Healing happens when that void is filled with positive energy.

If we can tap into the belief that is a causative factor in our physical problems, we can let that belief go and adopt a healthier belief. Positive, life-affirming beliefs are necessary for a healthy life. Negative beliefs that include shame, guilt, anger, resentment, hatred, or any of the lower emotions set us up for a life filled with conflict and physical problems. The body becomes a metaphor for our beliefs and emotions. I could see how Dad's self-hatred resulted in a variety of physical problems including stomach ulcers, and heart and prostrate problems. (I can't stomach my life, I hate myself, I have intimacy issues.)

When we start practicing mindfulness and become a witness to what our bodies are communicating, we can make decisions about whether or not to keep that belief. For example, once I realized that I had overwhelming anger directed at myself and my dad, I could look at the events that triggered that anger and bring forgiveness and compassion to that situation. I immediately felt lighter and relieved when I did so. This in turn impacted my health and well-being in a positive manner.

When in the therapy session described above, my client understood that she didn't know the circumstances around which her mother didn't want her to be born, she could forgive her mother and move on. She adopted another belief, a healthier belief that became her core belief: it's OK for me to be here. People love me and want me here. Her life and her pain changed as a result of bringing her subconscious belief to consciousness, examining it in order to see if it served her, deciding it was not her truth, and letting it go. The energy void that resulted could house a newer and healthier conscious belief. Her subconscious mind and her conscious mind were no longer in conflict with each other.

Lipton summarizes the power of the subconscious mind as follows: "Endowed with the ability to be self-reflective, the self-conscious mind is extremely powerful. It can observe any programmed behavior we are engaged in, evaluate the behavior and consciously decide to change the program. We can actively choose how to respond to most environmental signals and whether we even want to respond at all. The conscious mind's capacity to override the subconscious mind's preprogrammed behaviors is the foundation of free will."(4)

These lessons in the body-mind connection I learned intuitively by watching Dad for many years before I became a therapist. In the 1980s, I started finding scientific and written support for these ideas that seemed so obvious to me. Today there is a wealth of information available that supports the mind-body connection. Much research has been done to show how what we think affects our health and life situations. I invite you, the reader, to explore some of the data if you are not already aware of it.

I believe that reconciliation is part of the process of family healing. As stated earlier, reconciliation means settlement, resolution, compromise, reunion, or bringing together. There is a letting go of one's personal agenda and a trust in God's plan that takes place when one becomes reconciled. There is a reunion with one's higher self and God, and often a reunion with the people in life with whom we have been estranged or separated. There is understanding of the oneness, wholeness, or unity of all humanity. We honor our connectedness with another, and this can be a turning point in a healing process. As we touch another's humanity, we may understand that to do so is the very reason we are on earth at this time. We touch more than a body, mind, and heart. When we look into the face of another, we look into their soul, and it mirrors us back. This is what connects us to universal love, which is the healer of all things.

Thus, healing is not just about the physical body restoring itself to health through Divine Intelligence, but about the mind and spirit becoming whole and undamaged. The body restoring itself to health may or may not occur as a result of healing. In fact, many people are "healed" but not cured symptomatically on the physical level. They may even die.

I first learned this very important lesson from one of my clients. She was a young single mother who had several children ranging in age from two to thirteen. Her ex-husband was in jail, and her elderly mother helped her with the children as much as she was able. I will call the young mother Jane here. Jane called one day and said she was dying from several cancers in her body. She had received all of the usual treatments from her health-care professional, but the cancers had not gone into remission. She was in severe pain and took morphine to alleviate it, which left her in a clouded and sleepy mental state. She knew her days were numbered. She was in tremendous conflict about that because she was concerned about her children's welfare and didn't want to die before they were grown. There was also a part of her that wanted to die. She intuitively knew that it was her time, and because she was experiencing so much pain, she was ready. She had heard about the work I did and thought I might help.

Over the course of a few weeks, I met with her frequently and facilitated a process where she could address her fears safely. I also met with her children and her mother and taught them Reiki, an energy healing technique, so that they could all work together to offer Jane comfort. Jane's pain lessened enough so that she could get off morphine, which was an enormous relief to her. She was able to spend quality days with her family. Her life improved physically, mentally, and spiritually. She forgave those people in her life whom she had blamed and moved from being a victim to finding peace inside herself, with God, and with death. Her last days were ones that would be forever treasured by her family. They were brought closer together as a family than they otherwise would have been if "healing" had not occurred.

The healing process may take much longer than a curing or treating process. Sometimes, the curing or treating process follows a healing process. In the case of Jane, the healing process followed the treating process. But for healing to occur, the mind, body, and spirit must all be engaged although not always at the same time or in the same therapeutic process.

Being in peace and experiencing love are the outcomes of the healing process.

Being treated and cured of a physical illness may or may not be evident. Carolyn Myss beautifully sums up this process by saying in her book *Defy Gravity*, "Healing is not about the illness or crisis that has befallen you. Healing is about your capacity to engage in your own transformation from fear to courage, from holding on to the past to letting go, from living in illusion to embracing truth" (5). Personal change is part of the healing process, and becomes an opportunity to grow in self-awareness and in soul awareness. It is an opportunity to know and embrace the Divine within yourself.

How does one go about the process of healing? There is no prescription that fits all. We each have to find our own way. My journey was different from the journey of either of my parents, although there were some similarities at times. Of course, I do not know the entirety of their healing. I can only guess at some of it. However, through close observation and communication, I believe that they each embarked on their own healing journey, like I did, which resulted in some relief from the pain they each experienced and in some wisdom to share about their journey.

Where does one start the journey? Each person must sincerely want and ask for healing. Then everyone starts from where they are, beginning with the information closest to them, and moving logically, and often organically, to other areas. The opportunities to heal will build on themselves; one aspect will suggest others that relate to it.

What is the goal? Each person's goal is for them to decide. At first, the goal may be a small part of a larger picture as in, "I would like to relieve my back pain." As we progress into our healing process and learn more about the mental and spiritual forces connected to the physical pain, we may change our goal as it becomes appropriate. My ultimate goal was reconciliation with my father and mother. That goal took me down a different path than that of my parents.

Throughout the healing process, individuals awaken to their misconceptions and beliefs that no longer work for them in a constructive way. They then can use their power of choice to make a decision to change. This is true freedom—to determine what is in your highest interest and to decide to embrace that.

Healing is a lifelong journey that, like life, is not a straight path from one place to another.

However, it does seem to include some steps that anyone can follow on their own journey. Of course, not everyone will have the same kinds of experiences along the way. And not all the steps in the journey will be made in the same order; some steps may be experienced simultaneously. Other steps may take longer for one person to accomplish than another. And sometimes, the journey is interrupted before it is complete. Some people find that the risk is too great to heal completely. I have known many individuals who stopped the healing process because they believed it would involve changing or eliminating a relationship or a career and a source of income. Some people may not use all of the steps discussed here while others may even create and experience different or additional steps. My parents did not embark on all the steps that I took. Sometimes we took the same steps. Sometimes we lingered for different lengths of time at a step or we took the steps in a different order. These steps are not mandatory for healing. They were the experiences that my parents and I had that were helpful to us. Because they were helpful, I wish to share them in hopes that they will help others.

As I started to write this chapter and look at the events of my life from the perspective of "steps," I realized that the ideas for healing help that I have included here are not new or my original ideas. In fact, they are age-old spiritual practices that are commonly known and written about by many spiritual seekers throughout the ages. I was amazed to see how I first had the experience, then I understood it from the context of a step rather than set about to follow some steps in order to have the experience. Since there are many people who talk and write about each of these steps, I will not go into a lot of detail about what they each entail. Instead, I will give an example of how the steps were helpful in our healing journeys. You can find much additional information on each of the steps in other resources.

You may also find many other resources that I have not included here. I have only included the practices in the various steps that worked for me. I do not mean to imply that these are the only practices that work. Since much of my process was done in the 1980's and the people and practices that I used may or may not be readily available now to you in the part of the country where you live, you may find it difficult to replicate my process. However, including steps that include physical, mental, and spiritual transformation are important to consider in your healing process if you truly want to change your life. Changing your life includes changing your brain, and these three levels of work are necessary for that to occur.

After a time of reflection on my journey, I realized that there was a logical order to some of these experiences that could be called steps, and other steps occurred in no particular order.

For example, the step regarding appreciating beauty can be done at any time or at all times during the healing process. There had to be a beginning point, but after that the healee could wander in many different directions. The steps also included work on a physical, mental-emotional, and spiritual level. My own ordering of the steps included working on the spiritual level first, then the physical, and finally the emotional. That order is not mandatory. However, all parts of a person need to be addressed at some time throughout the process.

Throughout my own healing process, I have begun to realize that there is more to healing than usually discussed. The process of healing generally includes bringing a traumatic event or unconscious belief to conscious awareness, forgiving the circumstances of the event, the people involved, and yourself in the process, and letting it go. Forgiveness is key. Once one has forgiven themselves, they are able to move on to self-love. After healing has occurred, one frequently moves toward reconciliation with those we have forgiven. Reconciliation is not necessary for healing as I have discussed it, but is necessary for the larger spiritual journey of feeling one with one's self, with others, and with God. When we reach reconciliation, our communication patterns change so that they reflect our transformed selves. We no longer use victim language, for instance, and instead our communication patterns in our relationships generally reflect a positive and self-responsible outlook on life. We are no longer the same person we once were; we become transformed.

Consciously learning about and changing our communication patterns is the most neglected part of a transformational process because we take the ways we communicate for granted. They then become a habit which usually is unconscious, unrecognized and unstudied until we become mindful enough to observe our own habits and decide if they work for us or not. It is one thing to transform ourselves internally; it is another to transform our language and communication strategies to reflect the new person we are becoming. Finding nondestructive ways to talk about our anger or other negative emotions, to problem-solve without involving obstructionism or guilt, to deeply listen to others and to ourselves, and to reflect a healthy self-image and build self-esteem in another are vital strategies to creating healthy relationships with other people in our lives. Our communication reflects who we are and what we believe. As we transform our inner selves, our messages to others need to be transformed as well. As we change from being a victim and a reactor to life circumstances, to a creator of our life, our language and communication patterns must change too.

However the steps depicted below show up in another person's life, I believe the result will be transformative and healing. By the time of my father's death, I was profoundly grateful that I had made the healing journey to reconciliation between us. I hope that you, the reader, will realize as much inner peace and gratitude as I have after your journey.

Steps for Transformation

Step 1: Decide to Change

Every process has a beginning point. Begin by being willing to change and then making a decision to change. Ask for change sincerely and then be willing to accept it. Often willingness to change is a result of "reaching bottom."

Step 2: Take Responsibility

Instead of blaming others or waiting for others to change, take responsibility for making your own changes. Notice where you have some emotional issues and find ways to transform them.

Step 3: Surrender to a Higher Power

We can never heal by ourselves. Surrendering to a Higher Power is necessary to transcend our problems. Surrendering includes letting go of our own ideas about what is helpful and allowing ourselves to be flexible and open to situations and people who might have answers for us. Be willing to try something new. When we pray for help, we are always answered, sometimes in ways that we don't expect. Let go of expectations.

Step 4: Prepare a Safety Net for Yourself

Do what is necessary to provide for yourself all the physical help or support you need along the way. This support may be financial, relational, and/or medical. After you have taken care of the physical or practical matters, you may need to address your emotional and spiritual needs.

Step 5: Houseclean on All Levels

Eliminate the physical, emotional, and mental baggage that stops you from healing. Physical baggage can include problems with your body, your relationships, and your surroundings. Fear, anger, and guilt may need to be acknowledged and released. Journaling can be a powerful tool to aid with emotional release.

Step 6: Forgive Everyone, Including Yourself

Forgiveness is the greatest healer of all. It releases us from our painful past and creates a world where we do not withhold our love from anyone, including ourselves.

Step 7: Learn to Love Yourself

Find ways to treat yourself gently and with love and celebration. There is only one of you. Be able to look into a mirror and say, "I love you!" Laugh often.

Step 8: Form a Life Code

Set a concrete and doable standard for yourself for who you want to be and how you want to behave. When you digress from your standards or code, you will be able to self-correct.

Step 9: Learn to Know Yourself

Spend time alone or with a person you trust reflecting on your life. Be willing to accept the parts of you that are your shadow. Learn the art of mindfulness. When you learn to watch or witness yourself, and become aware of how you are thinking and behaving, you move from being a victim or a reactionary person to being in charge of your life. Therapy, storytelling, and spiritual development are three of many tools in learning to know yourself.

Step 10: Become Your Own Parent: Set Boundaries and Communicate

Do not let others hurt you. Practice the art of compassionate communication. Know your limits.

Step11: Spend Time Each Day in Contemplation/Meditation/Prayer

Talk to your Higher Power, listen to your Higher Power, practice forgiveness when it is needed, and take time to feel gratitude and appreciation for everything in your life. Visualize your life as a success.

Step 12: Serve Others

We all have something to give. When we give, we receive. It is as simple as that.

Step 13: Take Time for Beauty

There is beauty all around us if we notice it. We can notice beauty in words, environment, in aesthetics, in relationships, in movement. Ultimately we can see beauty (God's perfection) in everything. Our spirits are lifted.

Step 14: Take Time for Inspiration

We each have difficult days. Sometimes they seem to follow each other until we get mired down in our own problems. To help keep your life in perspective, read about those who also had difficult lives and found a way to transcend them. Find a hero to inspire you to be more than you thought you could be.

Step 15: Live in Gratitude

Be grateful for everything and everyone who shows up in your life. There are no accidents. Even what you think is bad, has a gift for you. Recognize that you have been given the gift of life and that every moment, even though it may seem like a tragedy or a problem, has a gift in it. Learn to find the gifts waiting for you.

In the next three chapters I tell the story of healing and reconciliation as it relates to each of my parents and myself. Each of us experienced healing in different ways and different amounts, depending on our generational and geographical opportunities, our culture and education, on our spiritual beliefs, and on our willingness to heal and acceptance of the healing process.

I don't apply the steps as described above to my parent's healing process because I don't know what went on their minds. I could only observe their actions. In my own process, the steps became apparent after I started writing about them. They were not conscious steps I took in order to heal. Rather, one thing led to another in an organic fashion after, from the depths of my heart and soul, I asked to be healed.

EIGHTEEN

Charley's Healing Process

Charley suffered from PTSD symptoms for all of his adult life after the war. Until he started writing about his experiences in the 1980s, his suffering was chronic and debilitating. After Dad retired from the telephone company in 1980, he had less financial and relationship pressures in his life, and more time to reflect. We noticed that he became more mellow and that he exerted an effort to be kinder, and to include himself in family and social activities. Since he was not receiving any therapeutic help regarding his relationships, this change must have been an effort of will. Although he never said so, I believe that Dad experienced remorse about his treatment of Mom and me over the years, and resolved to do his best to repair the damage.

He also visited a veteran's hospital in Minneapolis for three months in the early 1980s in order to find a way to cure his depression and headaches. His doctor prescribed a change in medication that helped him to move through headaches without having to go to the hospital and receive a hypodermic injection every month. His doctor also told him to start talking or writing about his war experiences. He spent around two years writing his memoir, included here, and making copies of it to give to people. After he did so, we noticed that there were some further changes. There is no doubt that the acclaim he received from telling his story locally began to help him, but he couldn't erase the wound of his soul gained by bayoneting some Germans. He could never make that right.

He tried to make it right. Charley, after he retired in 1980, began to atone for his role in WWII by doing all he could to help others. I am not certain that this atonement process was conscious because he never talked about it. However, we noticed that he was more constructive than destructive in his attitude and behavior. His days were spent primarily in his garage making and repairing items for his family, friends, and neighbors, or outside snow-blowing his driveway and the sidewalks in the neighborhood, or mowing his lawn and doing other yard work. He often was called upon to refinish or repair some furniture, to help someone with a telephone problem, or to fix an appliance. He became known as a handyman, and others were grateful for his service. Charley never advertised or charged a fee for his work. Others "paid" him by offering gratitude and possibly doing a favor for him.

Mom and Dad volunteered their time to many community activities such as Meals-on-Wheels and spent time weekly helping the elderly or disabled. As part of a Telephone Pioneer's project, Mom and Dad fashioned dozens of teddy bears made out of scraps of fleece to give to traumatized children who had been in an accident. I always thought it ironic that this project was done to help other traumatized children, but no help, understanding, or empathy had ever been given to Dad's own traumatized child. I have no idea if Dad ever thought about this particular project as being atonement for my childhood. I did, however, receive a few of the bears as a gift even though I was an adult at the time. No words accompanied the gift.

In some ways making the bears seemed like an atonement project Dad had with Mom. Theirs was a joint effort: Mom did the sewing, Dad did the cutting and gathering of materials, and both of them did the delivering to the local police force who distributed them.

Prior to Dad's retirement, Mom and Dad had never joined together to create or do things for others: their lives were lived quite separately under one roof. They both were proud of the bears and their efforts to help children.

Dad also began to go to church again regularly. I don't know to what extent this was a comfort to him, but he seemed to gain pleasure from being an usher and involved in church activities. He also joined several civic organizations and felt himself to be a valued member of the community. After he wrote his war story and started distributing it, he was asked to be a speaker at various local events where he was publicly honored for his service. After this recognition, he seemed more socially adept than in the past and was not always so much in a hurry that he would leave a social event prematurely. Perhaps he gained pleasure from serving others, and this helped him to feel better about himself. I am certain that being honored by others in spite of his self-conflict regarding his war experience was very healing for him. Both Mom and I were happy to see him become more active in the community and in the church.

Other kinds of evidence that healing was happening included more social activities. He enjoyed being outdoors and started a walking regime that took him past the homes of people who often called out a friendly hello. He always thought of the surrounding area as beautiful and gained pleasure from being outside and seeing that everything was as it should be. He and Mom took long drives in the rolling hills of the countryside, which seemed to nourish him. He would remark, "Isn't that beautiful?" when seeing a fully grown corn crop. After the drive, they would stop at a local fast-food restaurant and enjoy a Coke with other seniors who hung out there in the afternoons.

At least once or twice a week, Mom and Dad would get together with friends and play cards then go out to dinner in a neighboring community. The laughter shared with friends was healing for both Mom and Dad. These same friends accompanied Mom and Dad on several trips out of state, which gave them some new experiences to relish. At other times Mom and Dad visited me in Oregon and Arizona, and we all traveled to Hawaii after Dad retired. Dad did his best to be open to new experiences and to treat me and my ex-husband kindly when we were together.

At home, Mom and Dad's open-door policy was an inspiration. Because our family was always small, other people outside our family were always welcome at family holidays. If a single person or couple did not have family nearby to celebrate with, they were welcome at our house. In the summertime, the open door became the open porch! Neighbors and walkers-by were always welcome to stop and chat awhile. Sometimes Dad could be seen dragging out the living room chairs to the porch so everyone would have a place to sit. Because they both knew so many people in town, and because they were always welcoming, friends and neighbors would often spontaneously stop by throughout the year to visit or, in the summertime, to bring some fresh produce.

As the years progressed, Dad had a chance to take some trips to see some old war buddies which seemed especially healing for him. He lit up when talking about them. He had bonded with his army buddies for life, and seeing them enabled him to talk about memories with others who were there and knew the story. There is nothing like the comfort of an old friendship where the bonding between you is deep.

What was most helpful for Dad's recovery, however, was storytelling. Storytelling is a divine gift. When we tell our stories, or when we listen to the stories of another, we get in touch with the sacred. We learn about ourselves and others in ways we would have missed without the telling of our stories. We see how we are each a part of the universe and that everyone is a necessary and valuable part of the whole.

The first time I experienced a person's story as sacred was when I was in a group therapy session. There were several of us sitting in a circle one night when one person in our group came in late. She said, "I have something to tell you tonight." The tone of her voice suggested that her something was momentous, and we became silent and focused on her as she stated that she had learned about her past that day. In previous therapy sessions she always had difficulty remembering any events or emotions from her childhood.

At the time of this event, she was near thirty years old, and we sensed that we were about to hear an amazing story. She told us that in a private one-on-one therapeutic session earlier that week she had remembered being spiritually abused by her parents. She then related the details of how her family had been part of a Satanic cult and how they had used her body as part of a demonic ritual.

As she described the ritual, a strange feeling came over me. In the profound stillness of the room, I knew with absolute certainty that I was listening to the sacred . . . to the story of someone who had experienced such extreme torture and horror that the only way to cope with it was to block it out. I remember clearly having a sense of awe at the power of the human spirit: first to protect a person and later to transform the memory into something greater.

My friend had been involved in therapy for many years and had built up a support system that allowed her to feel safe and accepted. That sense of safety and unconditional acceptance allowed her spirit to remember her past; in other words, her past was re-membered or brought into wholeness. Her spirit soared that night, and we all felt it.

I learned that listening to the story of another can be a profoundly healing and a transformative experience for both the storyteller and the story-listener. My friend had taken the experience of being tortured from the horror of extreme abuse to a place where she had compassion and forgiveness for her abusers. She later used her compassion to work with others who had been similarly abused. Those of us who were there that night were inspired to do the same.

After reading my dad's story, I had the same sense of the sacred, of bearing witness to the demands of the soul. I believe that our soul is always seeking what is in our highest interest, and when we are safe enough to tell our story, we reach a place where we can transform wounds to memories that have no emotional attachment. Then when we tell our story, we can help others experience and transcend their inner story.

Story is an essential structure of mind that integrates the elements of event and imagination. When we hear a story, meaning emerges in a flow of light and understanding for both the storyteller and the story listener. Both may be moved to a greater place of compassion and healing.

Dr. Tick, in *War and the Soul,* writes, "One person's story extends into others to reveal the larger story of what happened to us all and what meaning we might discover in it. A personal war story is always about everyone who participated in war, as well as their family members, their friends, and their communities. War stories are about the earth and the damage done to it. They are about the nations who wage war and the histories and politics, beliefs and values that lead up to them. And they are about the wounds and deaths that result and how they shape the future of everyone and everyplace involved." (1)

It was important for Dad to tell his story. Fortunately, he also experienced his story as being heard. Many people, including veterans, are afraid to tell their story, not only because of the pain evoked in the telling, but also they fear that their story will not be properly received. In our culture of denial, we often offer religious platitudes and sympathy, which leaves the storyteller with a sense of not being fully heard. We also often follow what we hear from another with our own similar story. (A practice known as stage-hogging). This discourages the storyteller from feeling safe enough to tell their story. The story becomes locked up in the heart and mind of the storyteller. Sometimes it is never expressed. When it isn't expressed, the storyteller will never participate in the healing and transformative experience of knowing that one is accepted unconditionally.

Jonathan Shay in his book *Achilles in Vietnam* writes, "Narrative heals personality changes only if a survivor finds or creates a trustworthy community of listeners for it. Several traits are required for the audience to be trustworthy." The traits that he names include having the strength to listen without personal harm, and the ability to cope with inevitable triggers to their own memories. Listeners must also be strong enough to hear the story without having to deny the reality of the experience or to blame the victim. And finally, a listener must be ready to experience some of the terror, grief, and rage that the victim did. "Without emotion in the listener, there is no communalization of the trauma" (2).

Besides strength, Shay continues to write that respect is important in the listening experience. Respect means readiness to be changed by the storyteller and to refrain from judgment, which is very difficult to achieve, especially when the victim of a severe trauma is also a perpetrator. The storyteller wants to be heard, not judged, or considered to be a problem that must be solved.

If someone in our family or community has gone to war in our name, we have a profound responsibility to listen and be a supportive audience to him or her. As Paul Tillich states, "The first duty of love is to listen." And the listening needs to happen in a live face-to-face situation, and not through media. Dad received his most important healing moments when he could tell his story and see and feel the supportive response of his listeners. While it helped him to write his story, he could not tell what the response was until he interacted in person with others. Feeling their acceptance helped him to accept himself.

Tick suggests that in order for a combat war survivor to heal, the story must be delved into deeply. "Otherwise, a survivor might endlessly repeat the details of an event but not experience the release of related emotions, the accurate recording of history, or the making of meaning—all of which are essential in the recovery of PTSD" (3).

My uncle Orv was very repetitive. At almost every holiday gathering, he would start to tell us something about his war experiences, "When we were in the Pacific . . ." Unfortunately, he did not have a receptive audience. Instead of encouraging him to talk about his experience, his story was brushed aside, and he was never given the opportunity to heal his war wounds.

I am saddened to think about how many veterans experience not being able to tell their story. We, as a society, need to learn how to listen.

I wish that I had learned how to listen deeply and compassionately by the 1980s when my dad was telling his story. As I said, he wrote it over a two year time period and then distributed it widely among his friends and fellow veterans in his community. His work was printed in several local newspaper articles, and my mother sent me a copy. That was the first time I knew his story. Since I lived so far away and he was so reticent about talking, and I was still afraid of him, I never asked him any questions or acknowledged his experience other than through a "Thanks for letting me read this," and a few platitudes. And then I put his story in a scrapbook and the back of my mind without letting it impact me.

Now, upon reflection, I realize that there were a few other times in our lives when we could have talked deeply about my dad's war experience, but Dad chose to not talk about his experience, and I didn't know the questions to ask or how to listen. The first time was when I took German classes in high school and later in college. Another time was when I was in a college play, *The Diary of Anne Frank*. Dad chose to not say anything about the liberation of Nordhausen or even that he had been in Germany. Another time was when I married a man whose birth parents were taken to a concentration camp. Again, Dad never said anything about the memories this must have evoked. These missed opportunities of storytelling could have invoked more compassion and understanding in me and possibly some earlier steps toward reconciliation and healing for both of us. But we didn't know how to do that.

After some experiences of telling his story to a receptive audience, it was clear that the social isolation of early years had ended, and Dad was mellowing. However, some of the other symptoms of PTSD were still running his life: he still had headaches, he still had pain, he still belittled Mom, he still had control issues, and he still had nightmares and flashbacks. Even so, life was much better for Mom and Dad.

Although my dad had started his healing process, I am convinced that he never achieved full healing or reconciliation because he never could let go of the fact that he had killed, and he believed that was wrong. He began to feel that he did what was necessary, and he began to be able to accept other people's expression of gratitude for his role in the war, but self-forgiveness was elusive.

For the last six years of his life, Dad had Alzheimer's disease. As memory problems increased, his dread of what was to come also increased. Earlier in life, Dad watched his sister, Amy, die from complications associated with diabetes and dementia and often said, "Kill me first before putting me in a home." Once he started having problems with his memory, he put all of his affairs in order so that my mother would have no financial worries. She was his biggest concern because she had always been dependent on him to make the important decisions about their lives. He then went into the veteran's home in Luverne, Minnesota, for the remainder of his life.

He received excellent care there, although at first, he continually wanted to go home. After approximately a year in the home, I noticed a change. He became more accepting of being there, and he always seemed to be happy when Mom and I would visit. His face lit up when he saw me . . . my first experience of seeing my dad happy to be around me!

If I had not been available to visit my dad on a regular basis, we never would have experienced the final peace that we achieved between us, and I always would have regretted that.

Even though I had forgiven him many years before this and felt complete in my part of the healing process, I knew that Dad had not completely forgiven or accepted me. This changed when he realized that I had returned to be a caretaker for my mother. I could sense that he was able to move into an inner space of inner serenity and acceptance and that he felt free to transcend his earthly experience.

Many people talk about how Alzheimer's is a dreaded disease and that losing one's memory is horrific. In our experience, Dad's failing memory was a blessing since he no longer had nightmares about his war experience, and he acted like he was more peaceful. He lived comfortably in the home for three and one-half years and was free to explore it at will. Many of the nurses there told Mom and me stories about Dad picking up after others, of attempting to look out after others, and getting mad if he thought something was being done wrong. Even though his memory was almost gone, his deeply ingrained character traits evidently survived memory loss, as did his recognition of us!

My mother was always uncomfortable when visiting my dad in the home. She could not easily just hang out with him. I was able to do this and also notice his needs and take care of them. Perhaps, even though he was not fully functioning cognitively, he understood at a deeper level that I was there to take over the role of caretaker for my mother and that I loved him unconditionally. He could let go. I felt a bond forge between us that had not existed before.

Alzheimer's became the catalyst for a deeper form of healing and reconciliation than we would otherwise have experienced.

One day, toward the end of his life, he was sitting on the deck at the veteran's home when a beautiful monarch butterfly came to rest on his hand. He studied it for some time before it flew off. I was so struck with how butterflies are a symbol of metamorphosis and how my dad had in these last weeks of his life seemed to find his own transformation into peace. I was deeply grateful.

I was able to be with Dad on the night he died. During that time, I felt as though there was a peaceful resolution between us. I intuitively knew that he knew that all I felt for him was love and acceptance and had long ago put all of my earlier emotions of hate, anger, guilt, embarrassment, and shame behind me. Through my complete forgiveness of him and of myself, I believed I paved the way for him to forgive himself. Through my return to my Minnesota home, I showed him that all was forgiven, and he could transcend peacefully.

My spiritual belief is that we never really die—that our spirits or souls live forever and transcend the human experience when our bodies die. We are not our bodies or just physical beings. Our body is our vehicle for our spiritual evolvement. We are spirit having a human experience.

In the last hours of my father's earthly life, I was blessed to witness and sense his transformation. The spirits of various relatives and people he had known and loved throughout his life were present to help usher him to his soul's next experience. Their presence was a great comfort to me as well. Some I knew by name. Others had passed on before I was old enough to know or remember them. I told him that it was time to go, that he was loved greatly, and that God loved him deeply. I also told him that I would take over as my mother's caretaker and he could leave free to pursue his own spiritual development. A sense of calmness and peace filled the room, and he left his body. I was filled with deep gratitude and love for my dad and his role in my life. Our healing and reconciliation was complete. At last my dad was free of his pain and self-imposed demons, and his soul could move freely toward his Creator. I believe that all is well with him now and that he is at peace.

I was also able to fully appreciate his legacy: Dad always modeled to others his ideal. Throughout his life, he demonstrated to others that he was a man of courage, dignity, self-sacrifice, honesty, responsibility, compassion, creativity, loyalty, honor, integrity, and service.

By observing him demonstrate these characteristics, I learned to appreciate and love him and attempt to follow in his footsteps. I am grateful that this thought of him is what fills my heart now as I remember him rather than my earlier feelings. A great man had passed on. All of his lesser attributes had died with his body, and he could be remembered for what he truly was, a humble hero.

At his funeral service in 2006, I gave the eulogy to a small collection of family and friends. Many told me afterward that was the first time they had heard the story of my dad. I find it remarkable to think that one can live in a small town for over eighty years and be an acquaintance of many and known by few.

The following pictures were all taken at the Veterans's Home between 2003 and 2006

At home away from home

A hero's medals

Charley, Jean, and Janelle at the Veteran's Home

Janelle, Charley, and Jean

January 25, 2006

A butterfly visitation

NINETEEN

Jean's Healing Process

At the time of this writing, I am not certain that my mother has completely healed from the trauma of living with Dad's PTSD. She doesn't talk much about days gone by.

By the standards of today, her entire life with my dad was spent as a second-class citizen. Dad's needs and desires always took precedence over hers. He would ask for or demand something, and she would immediately comply. "Jean, bring me the newspaper." "Jean, when are we going to eat?" (The latter was said with the expectation that the time to eat better be now!) She never spoke up for herself or said no or insisted that they both get help. In fact, there was no help in small-town Minnesota in the 1950s or 1960s, or even later. Nor did she confide in anyone besides me. I was the only witness to her struggle. And sometimes she tried to hide her struggle from me. Others knew parts of it, but no one knew the extent of the abuse she endured. She put up with the way things were and tried to make the best of it. She, like Dad, suffered in relative silence with no relief.

One of her coping strategies was to find an outlet in being creative with her hands, and throughout the years she spent untold amounts of time knitting, painting ceramics, doing Hardanger embroidery, and other crafts until arthritis made doing handwork impossible. Creating something of beauty in a life full of turmoil is a testament to her character. Her handwork was masterful, but never offered up for public recognition and retail. She, like Dad, gave away anything she made or kept it in drawers hidden from view. She, like Dad, did not want to be the center of anyone's attention or praise.

I believe crafting was therapeutic for her but didn't provide all the therapy that was needed for a complete healing. She never experienced therapeutic or spiritual support that was specifically addressed to her needs. She never learned any kind of communication strategy that would help her cope or speak up for her needs. She was a prisoner of her generation's traditions and belief systems.

Because my mother did not grow up in a religious household and never seemed to acquire any particular religious beliefs that she discussed with me or anyone else, I don't know if she has ever appealed to God for help in healing her trauma. I also don't know if she has ever forgiven Dad or herself, or even has a belief in the power of forgiveness or in God. Perhaps she thinks that there is nothing to forgive. She always seemed to find someplace inside herself where she could accept the way things were and persevere in continuing to live her life as peacefully as possible. Throughout her life, regardless of what she was experiencing at the time, she always remained kind to others and selfless in her actions.

When I have attempted to talk about these kinds of subjects, she doesn't have answers to my questions. Recently, she did say, though, that she rarely thinks about Dad and "those days." Her memories of him do not have an emotional component to them, so perhaps she has forgiven him. Or perhaps her memory has deteriorated enough as the years have gone by, so that the past no longer matters.

Instead, her life seemed to be more about perseverance throughout difficulties, and about lying in the bed you made, than it did about valuing self. When asked, she often told me that she was proud of how she didn't let the life she had "bother her." "I always remained strong inside," she told me.

My mother's attitudes about her life sometimes conflict with my attitudes about her life. We grew up in different times and traditions. Because of this, my mother is largely a mystery to me, and I marvel at her ability to accept what is, and to keep plodding on, steadily and quietly, regardless of outer circumstances.

There are many women of my mother's generation who are like her: quiet, nonassuming, nonassertive, living for others, and forgetful of self. I wonder how many of them, like my mother, adopted this persona as a way to cope with living with PTSD.

Before being married, my mother had shown her own independence by moving to Ohio and working for TWA. Most independent actions disappeared after marriage. My dad became the decision maker, and her life revolved around his and my needs. I can recollect one major exception to this statement. In 1990 she visited me in Oregon. Her visit followed a time of deep wounding from Dad, and she needed to get away. She took it upon herself to travel independently of him and seemed to relish the freedom from his domination and criticism for the two weeks we spent together.

After that trip, there were no further trips or acts of independence. In the early 1990s her mother was admitted to a nursing home, and my mother became a caretaker of her mother. Every day for over ten years she spent time with her mother and saw to it that her needs were met.

Sometimes she talked about feeling guilty if she considered not going to the nursing home. She always did what she felt she had to do even though it may not have been what she wanted to do. She always gave of herself in order to serve others, often to her own detriment. Like my dad, my mother sacrificed herself for others: for my grandmother, for my dad, and primarily for me.

Certainly the hardships of the Great Depression contributed to her outlook on life—to persevere in spite of your situation. But what had once been a healthy part of her personality, to be independent and to stand up for herself, was lost after her marriage. She gave that up so that she could provide a nurturing household for me. Along with her independence, she lost her self-respect.

I think that the writing of this book has been somewhat therapeutic for my mother. For the first time as we talk about some of the events described here, she realizes that my dad's problems were connected to PTSD and not her fault. She is reaching a place where she is understanding more about what happened in our family and as a result is feeling more compassion.

She is also beginning to release some suppressed anger. Recently, we were playing a card game of Skip-Bo and reflecting on life with dad when out of the blue, she said, "Charley was a real shit!" My mother never uses this kind of language, so it was a shock to hear her say that with some amount of passion. In the past, she referred to things he had done that had hurt her but never seemed to separate herself from the action. Now, it was clear that she was looking objectively at my dad's actions and labeling them with some amount of anger. Implicit in that event was my understanding that she no longer was blaming herself or feeling like his victim. It was a relief to hear the anger since that is all about releasing suppressed emotions.

Elizabeth Kubler-Ross in her book *Death and Dying* talks about the stages of grief over the loss of a loved one. These stages include denial, anger, bargaining, depression, and acceptance.

Following her example, Barbara Ann Brennan talks about the seven stages of healing in her book *Light Emerging: The Journey of Personal Healing*. Brennan adds two more stages to Kubler-Ross's list: rebirth and a creation of a new life. Brennan states, "All dis-ease requires change within a patient to facilitate healing, and all change requires the giving up, surrender, or death of a part of the patient—whether it be a habit, job, life-style, belief system, or physical organ" (1).

After one has surrendered the old, one can embrace the new. My mom, all her married life, lived in denial that anything was wrong or out of the ordinary, even though part of her knew that was untrue. When she first started to exhibit some anger over her past, she was moving from the denial stage to anger. Brennan states, "Anyone going through the healing process will hit some anger" (2). Noticing my mom have some real anger was a wonderful sign of her progress on her own healing journey. I believe that her anger was a healthy kind of anger that is an acknowledgement about what has taken place and a refusal to allow that kind of behavior to happen again. I believe that today, if she were subjected to the same kind of behavior from Dad that was once part of her daily life, she would at least consider taking appropriate steps to take care of herself, if not actually take the steps. This is indication of movement toward self-esteem, or loving oneself, that is part of a healing process.

Another indication of her healing is that she now more readily will speak up on her own behalf. Sometimes she will request a latte, or that I run an errand for her, which is a new behavior pattern. She seems to be learning that it is okay for her to express her preferences and needs.

She has not reached a place yet where her self-esteem is completely healthy though. She was demeaned so much by Dad that it is hard for her to completely believe that she is a good and worthy person. She also has a lot of self-blame for not doing something about the abuse to me and to herself. She has a hard time to recognize and accept that she did the best she could given her life circumstances, beliefs, and culture. If she could realize this and forgive herself, I think her healing would be complete. Perhaps this will happen yet. After all, healing is a process, not a destination. And there is hope that she will realize this. She stated recently, "When your dad was alive, we were all doing the best we could." She is getting closer to a complete healing!

However, as time wears on, she, like my dad, is falling prey to mild dementia. And again like my dad, dementia is serving her in that she seems to be at peace. She doesn't dwell on the past and lives more in the present. She seldom brings up the subject of Dad and the years they spent together. She also seems to accept all aspects of her life. This is truly remarkable when as many seniors say, "Being old isn't for sissies!"

After Dad's death, Mom became more dependent on me as she began to experience declining eyesight, hearing, memory, agility, responsiveness to situations, and loss of balance. Even though her world became narrower, sometimes it seemed by the month, she remained at peace about it. After doing Hardanger embroidery for decades, there came a time when her fingers were no longer agile enough to ply the needle. She moved on to Sudoku. After falling, and injuring her back, she was at peace even when not having anything to do or any outside stimulation. She accepted her circumstances without complaint. In my eyes, she became a model, like my dad, for how to age gracefully and with acceptance. She, like my dad, and his sister, Amy, all seemed to understand and embrace the Goethe saying, "It is not doing the things we like to do but liking the things we have to do that makes life blessed."

During the past few years, Mom has developed a new appreciation for nature and its beauty. She thrives on going for country rides and taking in the changing seasons and wildlife. We go bird-watching every few days, and she never fails to be appreciative of seeing the eagles, pheasants, Canadian geese, American coots, egrets, swans, pelicans, ducks, wild turkeys, red-winged and yellow-headed black birds, robins, and many, many more birds that make Minnesota their home. "Isn't that good!" she will say when she notices a Canadian goose couple by the roadside. Often on our jaunts, we will also spot deer, which are a special treat. I stop the car, and we spend some time staring at them while they stare at us.

At a time in her life when much is leaving (friends, family members, physical abilities, memory), her interest in country life by the roadside has increased and developed into a passion and gratitude for life that was never there before. She has come into an acceptance of all that is in her life and is grateful for it. She often tells me how grateful she is for the small things: a Hardee's hamburger and fries, a McDonald's caramel latte, something that I have done for her, the rides we take and what she sees in the country. Profound healing has taken place within her.

I am grateful for her presence in my life and for her support of my writing this book. She, like me, is hopeful that the contents of this book will help someone else experience relief from PTSD. Some friends have asked me if my mother, a deeply private person, minds that so much about our family is revealed here. When I asked her this, she said, "No. By the time this is published, most of my friends will be gone. We have no more immediate family who are discussed in this book who are still alive. It is time to tell the story and hope that it will be helpful for others. I especially hope that other spouses will receive some help. What a difference it would have made in my life if therapeutic help had been available for me, you, and Dad." This is also a part of her healing process—to take what was once part of a hurtful past and transform it into a story that may help others.

TWENTY

Janelle's Healing Process

Ronald Reagan's presidency lasted from 1981-1989. During this time there was a massive military buildup in an arms race with the USSR (Russia). In March 1983, Reagan introduced the Strategic Defense Initiative (SDI), a defense project that used ground and space-based systems to protect the United States from attack by strategic nuclear ballistic missiles. Reagan believed that this defense shield could make nuclear war impossible, but disbelief that the technology could ever work led opponents to call SDI "Star Wars" and argue that the technological objective was unattainable.

Critics throughout the world noted that the increase in nuclear armaments made the world less safe rather than more safe. How many nuclear bombs are needed to destroy the world, they asked. The answer was one. How many nuclear bombs did the United States have? Between 1945 and 1990, more than seventy thousand total warheads were developed—much more than was needed.

At what point is being armed with weapons that mass kill others, even destroy the planet, obscene or crazy? Schoolchildren were depicted in the media as being so scared of nuclear war that they would have nightmares about it.

Organizations like Beyond War, a grassroots campaign in several states in the mid-1980s, formed to educate people about how important it was to create a spirit and ideology of cooperation among people rather than using force, which included nuclear arms. People around the world understood the destruction of nuclear arms and did not understand the need to have many more weapons than were needed to annihilate an enemy. They also knew that problems are not solved by duplicating the cause of the problem. More and more and more arms were not the solution for being safe.

This was a time of fear for many in America. We were afraid of being attacked and annihilated and afraid of being provoked into attacking and feeling the effects of annihilating others on all levels. Nuclear destruction would not only destroy the planet but make it uninhabitable for untold years to come. What would happen to the soul of a nation that destroyed on this level? It was clear that nuclear warfare was a lose-lose situation for everyone on the planet. And the likelihood of experiencing complete annihilation was great.

I was one of those who was afraid. This fear was not a casual fear but a pervasive, underlying fear that many people experienced. We knew that in an instant our world could be destroyed. And we knew that a mistake by one person pushing the button for the wrong reason could bring about the destruction of our planet. Any moment in time could be our last.

In November of 1983, the television movie *The Day After* was aired. The film portrayed a fictional nuclear war between NATO forces and the Warsaw Pact that rapidly escalated into a full-scale exchange between the United States and the Soviet Union, focusing on the residents of Lawrence, Kansas and Kansas City, Missouri, as well as several family farms situated next to nearby nuclear missile silos.

I remember sitting on a yellow bean-bag chair in the comfort of our family room while watching this movie. I cried with deep, wrenching sobs as I realized how our collective humanity's thinking and actions could bring us to the point of total earth destruction. Again in my life, like when I first saw the pictures of the victims at the

Nordhausen Concentration Camp, I could not understand the horror that one person or a nation could inflict on another.

I intuitively knew that we could stop an event such as nuclear destruction but that we, as a nation, would have to change our collective thinking to do so. The answer was not in creating more arms but in each person taking responsibility for their beliefs that led to the arms proliferation. We could no longer glorify war or think of war as the only valid response to some other country's actions. Force only begets force. We could no longer think of our nation as superior to other nations and try to get other nations to remodel themselves with the United States as their image to emulate. Countries, like people, cannot be forced into a way of thinking and acting without retribution, especially if they are not similar in culture, values, education, and history. Change like this would be very difficult to accomplish. But if we did not do these things, the cost would be enormous: we could possibly destroy our planet.

We had to learn as a nation how to have mutual respect for other nations, just as individuals in any relationship need to learn to trust and respect each other in order to live peacefully with each other. Intuitively, I knew that we as a nation could not continue to try to solve our problems with the same tactics that created them. I knew that we must rise above the problem in order to solve it. Retaliation solves nothing. Love solves everything. I cried out to God from deep inside myself, *God, I want to be part of the solution and not part of the problem.* I recognized that being part of the solution involved finding my own internal peace. I couldn't wait for peace to be declared. I had to do my part. I had to be the change I wanted to see.

In 1985, I joined the Beyond War movement that was growing on the West Coast and for the next two years spent much of my free time working with others in my area to educate people about the dangers of nuclear arms and promoting peace. The Beyond War community of activists grew to be similar to an extended family. We enjoyed each other's company, supported each other's efforts, and found ways to grow together.

After about two years of devoted involvement, I began to realize that I was talking a lot about the importance of peace, but I didn't have peace in my own inner life. I realized that in order to talk about peace authentically, I needed to *be* peace. I quit taking part in the Beyond War movement and began to spend my free time in an inner quest dedicated to becoming a peaceful and loving human being, the solution to the problem. (A goal I am still pursuing, decades later!)

I believe that inner decision was a pivotal point in my life and triggered my healing journey. Around this same time, I had experienced my own personal wake-up call discussed earlier, which clearly showed me that I needed to heal. I could no longer deny that changes had to be made. In retrospect, it seems as if everything changed in my life from that point on in order to help me come into harmony with this desire. Everything! The changes made were not always easy. The rest of the 1980s were a time of fundamental transformation. However, I didn't stop when the new year of 1990 rolled around. My transformation has become a lifelong journey with major overhauls every few years along the way.

Step 1: Decide to Change

> Every process has a beginning point. Begin by being willing to change and then making a decision to change. Ask for change sincerely, and then be willing to accept it. Often willingness to change is a result of "reaching bottom".

A decision to change is not made easily. Often people have to reach bottom as people who participate in Alcoholics Anonymous and any twelve-step program confirm. For many people, life circumstances have to be so bad that change to something better is critical for survival or well-being. I had definitely reached bottom. I no longer wanted to repeat my old patterns, and I wanted peace for myself and the planet. I could see that the personal is political. How I thought and acted was the microcosm of the macrocosm. If I continued to be a victim and blame others for my unhappiness, and believe in force as a way to get what I wanted, then I would continue to live out a lifestyle that would lead me to more unhappiness. If I was surrounded by a lot of people with the same belief system, then we collectively would live out the same circumstances with individualized stories. Our collective thinking would become nationalized and predictable. Destruction of any relationship, personal or national, was inevitable. Nobody likes to be forced.

Accompanying my decision to change—to be part of a solution rather than part of the problem—was a deep desire to change. This longing for change seemed to come from my soul, or the deepest part of my being. I knew I wanted to change, "no matter what!" Change was necessary for survival, and I was ready and willing to do whatever it took to make my life better.

When fear of change engulfed me, I said to myself, "It is only change!" The word *only* brought me huge comfort because it diminished the magnitude of the change and made change feel more familiar. I told myself that change was inevitable and my choice, and it was necessary if I wanted something better in life.

The first step for healing then is a decision to change accompanied by a deep desire for healing. This decision will take you on a journey (God answers our prayers!), and you must be willing to heal no matter what happens. Courage and faith that you will survive the changes are necessary companions for the journey. You must believe that if you ask God for healing, that healing will occur. If you were in charge of the healing, you might not accomplish the task in the same way God does. Therefore, you need to have faith that whatever happens is in your best interest and a part of the healing process, and you must have courage to persevere, even though the journey may become scary. Often as we let go of things and people that are not in our best interests, we become scared and want to hang on. Believe that all that is happening is in your highest interests.

Then look for the next steps in your journey as they show up in your life. A person, a book, an event, anything that is perfect for you can be the catalyst for the next step.

Step 2: Take Responsibility

> Instead of blaming others or waiting for others to change, take responsibility for making your own changes. Notice where you have some emotional issues and find ways to transform them.

One significant part of my journey in the early 1980s was when I recognized that I had married my father and that it was up to me to heal myself and stop playing the victim role. The victim role, as it is used here, means that we operate from the viewpoint that others cause us to think, feel, and act in ways that we ordinarily would not, if it wasn't for the input of the other person. Common phrases that depict the use of the victim role are "You make me so mad!" or "You made me do it!" When we play the victim role, we blame others for what happens to us.

Much of our society operates from this kind of thinking. Note the popularity of court cases and insurance claims whose entire purpose is about creating an industry around victimization. Politics is all about blaming one party or president or another. What a major change we would have in our society if institutions along with individuals were self-responsible!

For several years into my marriage, I blamed my ex-husband for my unhappiness. I thought, *If only he* _____, *my life would change for the better*. I filled in the blank with "worked less", "paid more attention to the house", "did more things at home", "loved me", and various other phrases. I played the role of victim beautifully and made sure my friends and family knew how much of a victim I truly was. Of course I did this with a certain amount of "Minnesota nice" so that I would not be seen as a complaining nag. I was part of the great tribe of female victims (martyrs) who were misunderstood and unloved by their husbands, or so I thought. I generalized my personal experiences to all females and thought of women as weak and ineffectual. After all, as a daughter, I had learned about being a victim (Dad was the cause of all my problems!) very thoroughly and convincingly. In both of my primary relationships with men I felt powerless to make any changes.

At this time in my life, I was attending graduate school at the University of Oregon and was working to obtain a certificate in women's studies along with a rhetoric and communication degree.

Women's studies fascinated me since I had never before thought of women separately from men. I had not known that until women insisted on the right to vote, they were considered the property of men and had no rights. A few women were fortunate to be educated, or to have money, but the majority had no income, no property, no prospect of higher education, and lived out their lives as subservient to men. I learned how they had been traditionally victimized until individual women stood up to say, "No more. I deserve to vote. I deserve to work outside the home or have my own business. I deserve to make decisions in my family! I deserve to serve my country and play sports and run for any political office. I deserve to make my own health decisions." My view of women historically began to change, and I understood my female ancestors better. I also, for the first time in my life, became motivated by an image of a strong woman and decided to be one.

My studies in communication skills helped me. In the 1970s and early 1980s when I was attending graduate school, a new kind of study emerged in the field of communications—interpersonal communication. This was a course of study that was made for me, I thought. I longed to learn the skill-set that would make my personal problems in my relationships disappear. I thought that if I spoke perfectly, and used the right phrasing, that my troubles would be over. I didn't realize that no matter how skilled one person is, if the other person in a dialogue is not skilled, doesn't care, or has a motive to be an obstructionist, the dialogue is doomed to poor results, and the relationship doesn't move forward.

The more classes I took, the stronger I became. As I built my observational abilities about relationships in general, gained knowledge about different kind of relationships, and learned some skills in interacting in them so that my needs had a chance of being met, I discovered that my existing relationship with my husband was not satisfying to me. We did not have an equal marriage. I was as subordinate to him as my mother had been to my father. I decided that I wanted a marital relationship where both parties valued each other equally and negotiated the outcomes in their lives with the end goal being happiness for both. I started thinking about divorce but was afraid to proceed.

I, like many women of my generation, was getting ready to take the monumental leap of leaving behind our parents' kind of relationship, which was primarily complementary where each person in the relationship had a gender specific or complimentary role, but the male was more dominant, and both people were considered one-half of a whole unit. We were beginning to believe that another kind of relationship, a relationship grounded in the belief that each partner was equal to the other, was preferable. In an equal relationship, both parties were already considered whole people because their roles were not gender specific. Both parties could experience their emotions, both parties could work inside and outside the home, both party's views and needs were equally important and taken into consideration when negotiating the outcomes in their lives.

Then on the memorable night discussed earlier, I remember experiencing horror and anguish at the realization that I had married my father. I felt betrayed by myself. I thought I had been so careful to marry someone who was not like my father. *How can I ever trust myself again to make choices that are right for me?* I cried silently to myself. How could I have been so blind as to be with someone who seemed to not care about me, who didn't want to spend time with me, and who's conversation with me happened during appointments set two weeks in advance? I screamed out "I hate you!" to my husband, but he wasn't there to hear my outpouring of anger.

Finally, as I lay sobbing on the bed, I realized that my anger and hate were primarily directed at my dad and myself, and it was time to do some personal housecleaning. At last, I took the second step toward healing: self-realization and self-responsibility. I moved away from the victim role of blaming others for my circumstances and started to take charge of myself. My dad and my husband were not responsible for my anger and unhappiness in life. I was. I was also responsible for how I dealt with all my emotions. I had to deal with the anger and the consequences of that anger inside of me, and not rely on someone else's transformation to heal my pain.

My next step was to ask for God's help. People turn to God when they experience a horrible human dilemma. I knew that I was going to need help in healing my wounds. They were too deep for me to heal by myself, and I had no idea about where to begin. I realized that transformation doesn't happen without the help of a Higher Power.

Step 3: Surrender to a Higher Power

> We can never heal by ourselves. Surrendering to a Higher Power is necessary to transcend our problems. Surrendering includes letting go or our own ideas about what is helpful and allowing ourselves to be flexible and open to situations and people who might have answers for us. Be willing to try something new. When we pray for help, we are always answered, sometimes in ways that we don't expect. Let go of expectations.

When I was a child, my aunt and uncle took me to the Methodist church where I attended Sunday school and sang alto in the choir while standing next to my aunt. She made sure I attended choir practice, confirmation classes, and the Methodist Youth Fellowship. All of my exposure left me with many questions like, Why does God only love Methodists and not everyone equally? I couldn't warm up to the God depicted in the Old Testament as one who punished people with horrible natural disasters. And the concept of sin and evil totally mystified me. Why did some people consider some things a sin and others did not? Did God really care if someone ate fish on Friday night or cut their hair, or danced, or shopped on Sunday? Who was really right? What happened to the millions of people who didn't embrace the same beliefs? And there seemed to be some confusion around the notion of just who Jesus was. Jesus and God were often used interchangeably. I could not understand how Jesus was the Creator of all things. How could He have created anything prior to his birth around two thousand years ago? I had the same problem with Mary who sometimes was called the Mother of the World. How could she have mothered everyone who was born before she was born? What did evil really mean? Were some people born without a soul? How could that happen? If they had a soul, how could they be evil? Why do the followers of so many religions believe that their religion is the right one and they need to make other people believe the way they do? Why do people or groups pray to God to favor them in any conflict or war and then believe that God will favor them and not the other side? Why is the idea so common that I'm better (holier) than you because I am a (fill in the religious denomination) when we have been told to love each other? Why can't Christians of all denominations get along with each other? Indeed, why can't people of all religious faiths get along?

I was suspicious of dogma, especially of dogma that stated that they (a specific religion or religious group) were the way and the truth. I reasoned that it was impossible for there to be only one way when there were so many different beliefs, traditions, and religions in the world. I couldn't believe that a loving God would say that only one group of people knew the truth and would ascend into heaven. Was knowing the peace of God, then, an accident of place of birth and luck?

I also was greatly disturbed by how many religions went to war with other religions claiming that they each were the way and truth of whatever they called God. Equally disturbing was learning about how Christians were responsible for genocide regarding the Native American population and other atrocities in the United States and abroad. This made no sense to me.

Where was "Love thy neighbor" in war? The Golden Rule in the Christian religions is a spiritual truth repeated in all of earth's major religions. How can warring with one's neighbor be possible if we love them? Why are there so many wars and so many religions? Why is there so much missionary zeal to make non-Christians Christians? Why can't we learn to appreciate, respect, and love each other rather than hold ourselves separate and better than others?

Throughout those early years, I didn't give voice to my questions because I feared that my aunt and other church members, including the minister, would disapprove of me. At that time in my life, it was very important to me, as it was to my mother, to not make waves. When I grew old enough to attend college, I chose a Methodist-affiliated college in Iowa where I thought my questions might be answered. They were not. I did, however, add more questions to my list.

Throughout this time, my relationship with God was not personal—just a puzzling concept in my mind. After moving to Oregon I decided to seek out other religious beliefs, so I attended a progressive church for a while before marriage. This church was satisfying to some degree because the congregants were intellectuals with a social conscience. Asking questions was allowed, and anyone who attended the church was welcome. There was no attempt made to transform other people's ideas about God into a replica of the church's ideas. I appreciated those values, but I didn't feel closer to God.

After I got married, my ex-husband was not interested in religion, so even though we were married in a church, neither one of us went to church for the duration of our marriage.

Since I had grown up with the belief that one's religious life was important, I always felt that there was a hole in our marriage and in my life, but I didn't actively seek to fill that hole.

One afternoon shortly after my waking-up experience, I felt sleepy so went to lie down on my bed. I fell into a light trancelike state unlike any previous experience. An incredible calm fell over me, and then I experienced a life-changing vision. From far away, a picture frame of blazing light came toward me. I couldn't read the words inside the frame until the lighted frame was close. Then I read part of the Twenty-third Psalm:

> Yea, though I walk through the valley of the shadow of death,
> I will fear no evil;
> For Thou art with me; Thy rod and Thy staff they comfort me.

The vision faded away, and I felt a sense of peace wash over and through me. Upon opening my eyes, I knew with certainty that I had been walking in the valley of the shadow of death for my entire life. The choices I had made to blame others, to feel anger, pain, hate, embarrassment, and shame were all choices leading me to choose death literally and metaphorically. I knew that if I continued on that path, I would eventually shut down and die because the emotional and spiritual pain of that path would lead me to addictions, illnesses, and numbing. I understood with complete clarity that I was harming myself with my beliefs and emotions.

I also knew that I now needed to choose life. I cried out to God from every part of my being, "I choose life!" and slowly got up from bed feeling completely refreshed and at peace. I knew deep inside myself that I was going to be okay and that I would have help on my healing journey. I was not alone.

I also knew with certainty that the process of choosing life included divorcing my husband and being open to whatever was next in my healing journey. Divorcing him meant that I was releasing both of us from a marriage that wasn't working in a positive way for either of us. We could each move on to our highest potential without the interference of destructive emotions.

Not everyone will have the same kind of transformative experience as I did when I surrendered to a Higher Power. It does not matter what your religious or spiritual belief system is. What seems necessary, however, is to surrender to a power higher than yourself for help. Any plea for help will be answered.

Many religious traditions as well as various organizations like Alcoholics Anonymous believe that surrendering to God is a fundamental step in our spiritual growth, and release from our addictions and other troubles in our lives. When we surrender to God, we surrender to something bigger than ourselves, to an intelligent universe. Events fall into a natural order when we stop trying to control them. We trust that the power that holds the universe together can handle the circumstances of our lives. God is an impersonal love of all life and a provider for all life. Since we are life, we are loved, and our prayers will be answered.

Surrender means, by definition, giving up attachments to results. Instead of trying to make something happen, we allow God's will to happen. God's will is always loving and in our highest interests. (I believe this is true for everyone!) We cannot know the most loving or perfect solution to our individual problems, but God does. A sincere prayer such as the following prayer will bring transformative change: "Dear God, my desire is to heal and to bring healing to others so that I and others may know inner peace. I don't know how this will happen. But I trust that You do. May Your will be done in and through me. Thank you, God. Amen" Then we begin noticing how our prayers are answered.

I was finally experiencing a personal relationship with God.

Step 4: Prepare a Safety Net for Yourself

> Do what is necessary to provide for yourself all the physical help or support you need along the way. This support may need to be legal, financial, relational, and/or medical. Besides taking care of the physical or practical matters, you may need to address your emotional and spiritual needs.

The next few years were remarkable transformative years. In order to make the changes that I knew were necessary, I began to prepare for the changes by taking care of some physical or practical matters as well as emotional and spiritual matters. Providing support for yourself on all three levels, I believe, is necessary for transformation.

Practical matters for me consisted of seeing a lawyer and financial advisor to get the information I needed to make changes. Until I did this, I realized that I scared myself by fearing the unknown. I had several misconceptions about what was involved in a divorce procedure. Fear immobilized me and prevented me from taking positive action. Once I started asking questions, I had less fear about proceeding forward.

Others may not need to see a lawyer, but there may be some other practical changes that need to be made. For instance, one may need to set aside some money, or enroll in a class, or move, or learn how to use a computer, or . . . Taking steps toward doing what needs to be done in order to move forward gives one a sense of accomplishment and encouragement to proceed.

Eventually, I gained the courage to start divorce proceedings. Until this time I thought, like previous generations in my family, that I should stay married until "death do you part." I did not have any personal money, and I was afraid of starting out on my own without a guarantee that a way to support myself would be forthcoming. I had a graduate degree from the University of Oregon and was teaching at a university in Oregon, but I had no tenured job and no self-confidence. I realized that if I was sincere in my choice of life over death, I had to take a leap of faith, and know that I was going to survive and thrive on my own. I took the leap.

Helping me to take the leap in good faith was some research I did while working on my master's degree. I wanted to know about the rhetoric of divorce so spent much time researching how humanity's perception and discussion of divorce has changed over the centuries. Much to my amazement, I learned that how we think of divorce is largely due to the culture of the times, and a patriarchal and political need for control. It has nothing to do with a spiritual truth that must be obeyed, although there are many who want us to believe that.

I also learned that marriage throughout the ages had largely been considered a financial or property arrangement. Women were considered to be property and had no rights of their own until the twentieth century. Love had nothing to do with most marital arrangements over the ages. When I looked back in history and realized that people hundreds of years ago typically had a much shorter life span than people do today, I could understand how it might be easier to stay with one person.

Today there are so many ways to grow apart over a period of many years that divorce seems like a healthy solution for some people. Of course men and women can stay together throughout the years if they desire it. But if they grow apart, they are better served to go it alone. Divorcing can be a powerful impetus to grow emotionally and spiritually.

After realizing all of this, I finally felt at peace about choosing divorce over a dysfunctional marriage. I didn't believe that I had failed because I had learned what I needed to learn from our relationship. I knew deep within my soul that it was time to move on and that in order to spiritually grow and thrive and to transform my pain into peace and love, I needed to divorce. I needed to let go of the marital dysfunction we had and the manipulative messages I was giving to my husband about his not being good enough as he was. He also needed to be able to freely move into what was his best and highest good.

Later I realized that because I thought I was not loveable, I had entered into a codependent relationship that was modeled on the marriage of my parents and others of their generation. Their marriage was based on a need for each partner to take care of the other so so that they wouldn't have to take care of themselves. A partner in life was seen as a completion; a person became whole when they found their other half. I wanted my ex-husband to supply all the needs I had as a result of feeling unloved by my dad. I wanted him to complete me and fill my hole. (No one can supply all of our needs or fill the holes inside us, but I didn't realize this at the time. That is our task as an individual.)

When I understood that I had entered into a marriage with false beliefs and expectations about marriage in general, our marriage could no longer function as it had been doing without both of us changing.

Since my ex-husband did not want to change at that time, divorce became the only option that I could see. Divorce became part of a transformative process in my thinking rather than a failure. It became a gift rather than a wound. All of the pain that I felt for years was transformed into compassion and understanding when I began taking the steps to divorce. I knew that I loved my husband the most when I divorced him because I was no longer trying to make him into a replica of my expectations. I loved him without conditions. He was free to be himself. I was free to transform myself. (Once again!)

As the years rolled by, I realized that one of the gifts of divorce for me was that I grew much stronger as an individual. I became a person who could take care of herself in all ways. No longer would I enter a relationship out of neediness or an attempt to complete myself. I already was complete!

Emotional and spiritual support took more time to evolve. During divorce proceedings, which lasted two years, a lot of what had been familiar fell away. Several friendships changed or disappeared. I lost my ex-husband's family whom I deeply cared about, and I sold my home and moved away from my community. I also started the process of moving away from the academic world and toward becoming a mind-body therapist.

One day I had the startling realization that the academic world was filled with many practices that were unhealthy for the individual. (Extreme competition and grading practices using a bell curve were at the top of my list!) Since my newfound mission in life was to heal and be part of the solution, I could no longer ethically remain a teacher in a system that I thought was so unhealthy. Movement toward becoming a therapist seemed natural and necessary.

On the surface, there was substantial loss. However, I found that when some doors closed, new ones opened. And behind the new doors

I found something more fulfilling than the old. Moreover, the new doors that opened did so without any plan or effort on my part. All of my needs were perfectly met, sometimes in surprising ways.

During this time, I found some resources that were right for me: inspirational and motivational books to read, body-mind work that helped me to understand myself and my needs and offered healing support, and changes made in nutrition. I decided to go to church again and found many new friends and resources in the progressive church I joined. I also began to learn about and practice new skills—especially communication skills.

None of this was done quickly or in a linear, goal-oriented fashion. Instead, over the course of about ten years, my life consistently changed. Sometimes the changes were noticeable only to me like changes in diet or color preferences. Sometimes the changes were noticeable to everyone who knew me like when I moved to a different city five times in ten years. I used to joke to myself that the one thing I could count on in my life was that change would be happening soon if not immediately. "Be flexible" became my mantra since it seemed that every time I made a decision to do something, an event would occur that would make my decision moot.

I learned to trust my intuition instead of the dictates of social conventions. I also began to learn that when I made a decision to do or not do a particular thing that somehow it best served the other person involved as well as myself. That seemed miraculous to me. The more I listened to my intuition and followed it, the more I learned to trust God. God always works in ways that provides for the best for everyone concerned.

Finding the human support you need to feel safe in making changes is advisable. It is particularly important to have a group of people in your life who are good listeners and supportive of your growth. These people may or may not be your family members.

In my case, my family members were not my best support. However, I was fortunate to have one friend who had traveled a similar road a few years earlier. Her encouragement and support of me was so helpful. She listened patiently to my woes and provided me tools to take my next step. In fact, one of the best gifts I have ever received came from her. For a Christmas gift one year, she gave me a beautiful place setting for one. At first this struck me as odd. Then I realized that this gift had a hidden message to treat myself well. I was enough. I didn't need another person in order to be whole and worthwhile. Most importantly, she believed that I had the inner strength and wisdom to make the right changes for me. Her belief in me helped me to believe in myself.

Besides having a good friend, therapeutic help can be valuable, as can joining a group of people who are working on similar issues. At a later time in my process, I was part of three different therapeutic groups that provided the safety net for me to delve into my inner shame and emerge feeling loved. Being able to tell your story to someone who will truly listen in a compassionate and nonjudgmental way is to experience unconditional love. The first time in my life where I received this kind of love and acceptance was outside of my family, my marriage, my job, my church, and my old friendships. I began to heal.

Step 5: Houseclean on All Levels

> Eliminate the physical, emotional, and mental baggage that stops you from healing. Physical baggage can include problems with your body, your relationships, and your surroundings. Fear, anger, and guilt may need to be acknowledged and released. Journaling can be a powerful tool to aid with emotional release.

My first experience of internal housecleaning came shortly after my ex-husband and I decided to separate. I had adopted a white cat that had been abandoned and quickly bonded with Frosty. Having a new animal to love seemed to partially fill my hole.

One foggy day, I came home from the university where I was teaching to find Frosty wanting to go outside. She usually spent an hour or two outside before meowing to come in. After two hours passed and Frosty hadn't returned, I called for her to come in. She didn't. I went outside to look around but saw no Frosty. For the rest of the night I went outside to search for her every two hours or so. After daylight, I found that she had been hit by a car. Evidently, she was chasing a mouse because the mouse's remains were nearby.

Frosty's death became the catalyst for an enormous outpouring of grief and anger. I took a couple days off from work and cried. And cried. And beat the shower walls in my grief. I remember feeling so surprised that I could let myself go in this way, but it felt cleansing. I just let all the emotion out until I could cry no more. Peacefulness settled in me, and I felt renewed when I returned to work.

Being able to let the emotions out that need to come out is very important in the healing process. Some people may be able to do it as I did, alone and in a safe environment. Others may need the support of a therapist or some other catalyst to help them release their toxic emotions.

There is no time limit for doing this. It takes as long as it takes.

Of course two days of crying did not take care of all the housecleaning that I needed to do. It just paved the way. There is an old saying that until you let go of the old, there is no place for the new. Housecleaning, or the letting go of toxic emotions, unnecessary items, practices, beliefs, and relationships may not happen all at once or in consecutive order in a transformational process.

During the next few years, housecleaning happened for me when it was appropriate throughout the process. Sometimes I scheduled housecleaning around moves, the season of the year, or the day of the week. Sometimes housecleaning was spontaneous. I continually embraced a willingness to change and to go with the flow rather than to resist change and hold on to what I had. Everything from garage sales and recycling to confronting the beliefs that I had and needed to change were tools for my transformation.

One of my most powerful tools was journaling. In 1992, Julia Cameron's book *The Artist's Way* was published. I was intrigued with its subtitle, *A Spiritual Path to Higher Creativity,* because I felt blocked in expressing my creativity, and I was attracted to anything spiritual at that time. As a child, I had been very creative and artistic and felt I had lost that part of myself. As I read, I discovered that Cameron had a much broader vision of the artist than most people. All of us are artists, or creators of our own life. With her guidance, I opened up to expanding my understanding of what artistry is all about.

I had journaled before I read *The Artist's Way*. My journal entries read like a diary with notations about the events of a day or how I was feeling about my life at a particular moment. But my journaling never gave me the insights into myself that occurred after I started following Cameron's guidelines.

Cameron uses journaling as a primary tool to help people become unblocked. She has very specific rules that are non-negotiable for the journaling process. First thing in the morning, her students are instructed to write three pages of stream-of-consciousness meanderings. There is no wrong way to do it. They are also instructed to not go back and reread or to write from the perspective of writing for someone else. No one else will ever read what is written.

When I started my first page of writing, I finished a half page before I realized I had nothing else to say. I wrote, "I have nothing to say, I have nothing to say." Before long, I realized that I had nothing to say because I was judging what I already had written. I also was writing as though someone else might read it. I was trying to be impressive. In half a page I had learned a lot about me! I wrote all that down and thus began a daily exercise that taught me a lot about myself and offered me an opportunity to let go of thoughts and emotions as I became aware of them. Writing morning pages also helped me to get beyond my internal censor, the place inside me that sat in judgment about everything I did, thought, said, and felt.

At one point well into my journaling routine, I began to elaborate on my practice and started to write once in a while with a specific goal in mind. One of my most memorable and useful goals was to look at and release all of the anger I directed toward my parents. I started writing down all the reasons I was angry at both of my parents. I made a list of "I am angry at you, Dad, because _____." And I filled in the blank. Then I did the same thing regarding my mother.

Several pages later I ended with "Mom, I don't even like the clothes you wear!" I read that again and burst into healing laughter.

The laughter lasted a long time. That last sentence was so ridiculous. It was like I had been relieved of all the weight of my grievances, some petty, some more legitimate. I realized that all of my judgmental and critical thoughts directed at my family were released, and I could forgive and let go of those thoughts. If more came up later, I knew how to release those too. No longer was I the victim of my own negative thoughts. The power of journaling was becoming very clear to me.

From somewhere I heard that after writing like this, it is a good idea to conduct a releasing ritual of lighting a fire and burning the list. Metaphorically, the anger or other negative thoughts turn into smoke and waft away. I tried this, and it worked. I no longer felt those same angry emotions directed at either of my parents. What a relief! I also had taken ownership of my thoughts and proactively was changing them to something positive. After I released the negative, I could look for what I admired about my parents because I no longer was consumed by my grievances. I journaled that too and much to my amazement found a lot to admire in both my parents. I started seeing them from a different perspective. I began to see how they had both contributed great gifts to me and that I had some similar characteristics to both of them. This was a shock to realize since I had spent a considerable part of my life working on being different from them.

After a time, journaling became a tool where I could access my subconscious thoughts and beliefs and write from the perspective of my inner child, and find answers to my problems by accessing my higher self. I heard from another source that if one would pose a question with their nondominant hand, this would access their inner child and/or subconscious beliefs. Answering the question with their dominant hand would access their inner parent or higher self.

I tried this, and it became a profound process for me. My wounded inner child found much relief, support, and unconditional love from my higher self.

Susie Michelle Cortright in her online article "*Journaling—A Tool For Your Spirit*" states that "the fountain of personal wisdom may be as close as your nearest pen. That's because the single most essential instrument for nurturing your spirit is a personal journal." She further elaborates on the power of journaling by summing up its benefits:

- It can ease worry and obsession.
- It can identify hopes and fears.
- It can increase your level of energy and confidence.
- It can tap into your subconscious mind and zap your nervous, passive energy that leads to guilt and worry.
- It can help you discover the wisdom you already possess that will empower you.
- It can help you feel a unity within yourself and dispel feelings of loneliness and confusion (1).

Journaling has proven to be a very powerful tool for me. It is free and can be done at any time. Best of all, its benefits are enormous in eliminating the fear and negativity inside.

Another useful housekeeping tool I used was nutrition. I decided to eat a primarily vegetarian and organic diet and noticed a huge benefit in clarity of mind and lightness of body. Over the years I have not always stuck to this diet and notice that when I digress, I feel heavier and am clouded in my thinking. Finding the best diet for you can be important to your health and well-being.

The most comprehensive tool for me, however, was getting rid of stuff. During my twenties and thirties, I was a consumer of goods. I would go shopping for therapy. I would go shopping to manage the image I wanted to create of myself. I would go shopping when I was bored. I enjoyed shopping; the colors, textures, smells were all inviting and stimulating to me.

When it came time to divorce, I was faced with having to make a decision to let some things go. I sold my home and moved to another town into an apartment that was not big enough to contain all of my previous belongings. I let go of things I didn't like much, had never used, or could see no future use for. This was relatively easy. I also took the time to go through my file cabinets, which had been the repository for all academic and personal memorabilia for fifteen years and discovered parts of myself and my life that I had completely forgotten about. Gail Sheehy in her book *Passages* states that every seven years we go through a passage where we leave the old behind and move into something new. When I was housecleaning my files, I found clear evidence of this. I celebrated what I had written or done but was no longer in my present or foreseeable future and let it go.

During the next ten years, I repeated this process every two years. I moved further and further away from where I had set down roots in Oregon, each time not only leaving stuff behind but also jobs, friends, and lifestyle. After each move, I felt lighter and more ready to take on life's challenges unencumbered with stuff.

An illuminating moment happened for me when I moved to Tucson, Arizona. I arrived a week before the moving van and lived for that week with only a few necessities that I had carried in my van. I realized that all I really needed in life was a foam cushion to sleep on and a sleeping bag, a lawn chair to sit or lay on, a plate and utensils, a pan to cook in, a few clothes and hygienic items. If I had more than I could pack in my van, I had luxuries, not necessities. This was liberating to realize. The less I had, the freer I felt. Simplicity became my lifestyle.

Since that time I have gained a few more possessions but attempt to live lightly with low impact on the environment. My motto is to get rid of everything that is not useful, beautiful, inspirational, or fun. Sometimes I miss something that I once had but generally feel freer and less weighed down by stuff than I once did. Because I feel unencumbered by stuff and all the decisions that one makes about what to do with their stuff, I listen to my intuition more and respond to what life offers me without guilt or wondering "What will happen to my stuff if I do a particular thing?"

Most of us have too much stuff. We are told by politicians and advertisers that we should consume stuff for the good of the economy, and to make us better human beings. (More beautiful, more healthy, more appealing to our friends and relatives, more likely to get the job or partner of our dreams.) Consuming things we don't need is a way of life. Once we realize that our identity and well-being are not tied up in possessions, it is easy to let them go and to be freer and happier as a result.

During the time that I was housecleaning and finding support for myself while getting a divorce, I discovered what became for me one of the three most important tools for my life transformation. It helped me with releasing old thought patterns and adopting the kind of beliefs that were healing and life affirming. This tool was a book, *A Course in Miracles,* which became for me, a miracle!

Step 6: Forgive Everyone, Including Yourself

> Forgiveness is the greatest healer of all. It releases us from our painful past and creates a world where we do not withhold our love from anyone, including ourselves.

In 1984, a few days after my ex-husband moved out of our home, I went to my therapist in tears because of the loss of my husband, dog, and cat all around the same time. I had hit bottom and didn't know how to deal with any of it. My therapist couldn't see me right away, so I sat down in his waiting room to wait. On the table by my chair, I saw a book, *Love is Letting Go of Fear* by Gerald Jampolsky, MD. There were no other books in the room. I picked it up and started reading. As I turned over the first few pages, I was struck with the thought *This is just what I need*. I immersed myself in the book and didn't look up until I had completed reading it.

Somehow, my therapist (and the universe) was cooperative and didn't come for me until after I had completed the book.

In the book there were many references to the *Course in Miracles*. I had heard about the course before this and thought I wanted to start it but was afraid of making the commitment in time and energy. After reading this book, I knew for certain that I wanted to start the course.

And that was the beginning of "better days ahead" for me.

The course, or CIM, is a self-study metaphysical thought system that teaches forgiveness as the road to inner peace and the remembrance of the unconditional love of God.

In the preface to the *Course in Miracles* it states, "The forgiven world becomes the gate of Heaven, because by its mercy we can at last forgive ourselves. Holding no one prisoner to guilt, we become free. Acknowledging Christ in all our brothers, we recognize His Presence in ourselves. Forgetting all our misperceptions, and with nothing from the past to hold us back, we can remember God. Beyond this learning cannot go. When we are ready, God Himself will take the final step in our return to Him."

The purpose of the course is to provide a way in which some people will be able to find their own internal teacher. It is not affiliated with a religion or religious group, and because of that, it appealed to me greatly. It claims no monopoly on God. Instead, it contains universal spiritual themes and is one path of many to knowing God. The course uses Christian terminology but in nontraditional, nonreligious ways.

Religiosity always has disturbed me because in my experience it did not lead me into a connection with God. I learned in confirmation classes and in Old and New Testament college classes *about* God and the Christian religion, but I did not learn to *experience* God. What I didn't know at the time was that God was within me. I had always believed that God was in heaven somewhere, but where exactly that was, I didn't know. I just knew that heaven was outside of myself somewhere in some vague place.

What attracted me to the *Course in Miracles* and made it such a life-changing book is that by following the workbook section of the course, I began to think of God as a Creative Force that is a part of us all rather than as a kindly or judgmental spirit in the sky somewhere who had distinct preferences in people and behavior.

Most importantly, I learned how to connect with my inner truth, or God within. I was not told what my truth was or should be as is done in so many religions. There were no guidelines to follow such as don't cut your hair, don't eat meat on Fridays, don't dance, don't wear colorful clothes, etc. I found that by following the workbook's suggestions, I was freed from many of my negative emotions and belief systems.

The *CIM*, a self-study program of spiritual psychotherapy, is divided into three parts: the text, the workbook for students, and the manual for teachers. The workbook is divided into daily practices that help the student to undo their misconceptions and opens them to their inner teacher. In my experience, it is the most powerful part of the course because through participation it fosters transformation.

Three ideas offered in the workbook were especially thought provoking for me: "We are not our bodies," "Would you rather be right than happy?" and "There are two emotions: love and fear. Fear is nothing more than a cry for love."

For the first time in my life, I realized that I was a spiritual being having a human experience and that there was much more to me (and to everyone else) than the physical body. This understanding began to lead me on a quest to find out more about who I was on all levels.

The idea of choosing happiness over being right changed all of my relationships. I started to notice when I had some investment in being right and realized that position was an alienating one in my friendships. When I let go of my need to be right, I listened more deeply and found some commonality between myself and the other person. Empathy prevailed instead of judgment, criticism, and alienation.

And when I reduced emotions to two, I began to see how anger, jealousy, resentment, and other so-called negative emotions were really a cry for love. This understanding helped me to view and respond to others with compassion rather than with condemnation.

For a year, I met with a small group of people weekly to process our experience with the course, and I went through the lessons daily, as suggested. As the weeks progressed, I began to notice changes in me and my friends. We all seemed to become more loving, more forgiving, and happier. I remember feeling like I was getting in touch with my internal integrity and was so grateful for that. I had a new guidepost in my life. My anger, resentment, shame, fear, and hate melted away, and my outlook on life became positive and forward looking.

As a result, I was able to get through my divorce and the succeeding years of change with more compassion and peace. At one time during my divorce proceedings, I realized that I had more self-esteem because of the way I was handling my divorce than I had experienced in the preceding many years of marriage. I noticed that I no longer was motivated by pain and blame and that I no longer had angry words said to or about my ex-husband. The two best years of my life as a legal partner were the two years of separation at the end of the marriage. I was no one's victim: I was in charge of my life and emotions.

At one point in the course forgiveness for oneself and all others is the lesson. This was pivotal for me. I found that when I forgave my father, I discovered his positive characteristics.

Until the time of forgiveness, all I had seen were his negative characteristics. I began to write down his positive characteristics and feel gratitude for the gifts he had given me such as the gift of reading, of knowing how to fix things, and of following through with my formal education. I made it a point to tell him in person and in letters what I valued about him as well.

I also realized that because life was so difficult in our household, I had gained a certain strength and independence that I otherwise might not have attained. I began to see the adversarial positions that my dad and I had as a great gift and understood that only can someone who loves us very deeply take that kind of adversarial position with us in order to help us grow. I began to believe that on a spiritual level my dad loved me deeply, as I did him. Only those who show up in our lives as our adversary can teach us to be stronger. By experiencing difficulties and trauma we are forced to grow in order to overcome. Trauma is a gift, not a curse.

Many spiritual paths suggest it is important to love your enemy. While Dad wasn't exactly my enemy, he was the person I feared the most in life. As I progressed through the course, I began to understand that my dad reflected back to me everything I disliked about myself. He was impatient, I was impatient, he was intolerant, I was intolerant, he was controlling, I was controlling. He showed me exactly where my fears and insecurities were. Only one who opposes you can be such an effective teacher. Once I realized this, I turned my hate and fear into love and gratitude and understood why it is important to love our enemies. They mirror the hidden, shadowy part of ourselves. Part of the healing process includes looking at all of the dark places in your mind and bringing love to those places.

Our enemies or adversaries bring us the gift of seeing ourselves. When we see how we are alike and learn to see ourselves through the enemy's eyes, we develop compassion and move beyond conflict. For example, there are many stories of combat war veterans who experience shooting someone at close range, and then they realize that they both have a lot in common, for each warrior is a person who is doing the best they can do for their country, and each believes passionately that the other is wrong or evil. After realizing this, the warrior often will wonder how they can kill someone like themselves. They are moved emotionally and spiritually into a place of being unable to kill again.

When I let go of the many negative beliefs I had about my dad, I also discovered that we had some commonalities such as leadership qualities, honesty, and service to others, and began to focus on them rather than our differences. Because I changed my perception, I learned more about myself and him that was positive. I was impressed with the fact that both of us had chosen as part of our life's work something to do with communication: Dad with making connections for conversations through telephones and my making connections through nonviolent talking skills. My inner world turned around from dark to light, and I realized that in forgiving Dad and myself that we had both received a great gift. My dad's presence in my life changed from a curse to a gift, and I was grateful. My self-esteem grew, as well as my respect for my dad.

Not only did I benefit from my change in attitude, our family benefited. When I spent time with my parents during a vacation, our relationships changed because I had changed my perception. I was no longer reluctant to be in the same room as Dad. I know he felt the difference too and seemed to want to spend more time in the company of Mom and me. Card playing became a nightly activity when I visited them, which was a major change from Dad spending time isolated in his room.

Because of my change in thinking about Dad, I began to practice forgiveness for everyone who I believed had wronged me at one time or another. I made a list of those people and everything I could remember that I had a grievance about. Then in a meditative state, I imagined myself talking to that person and telling them my grievance and then saying to each one, "I forgive you!" Then I imagined what they would say back to me. In all cases, it was something like, "I'm so sorry that happened, and you felt that way. I am glad you told me." And some kind of understanding or solution would emerge. After each session with each person, I felt immense relief and knew that I was complete with that person. Compassion took the place of resentment for each person, and afterward I began to notice a change in how I felt about my parents, ex-husband, and other people in my life who I had previously judged and found lacking.

As I started to view the people in my life with more compassion, I noticed that my relationships with these people began to change too.

There were a few people I knew I had to approach in person and apologize to. When I did so, even if a long period of time had elapsed between the event and the apology, I felt immensely relieved. Sometimes the relationship improved; sometimes it did not. But I was certain that I had done my part in healing the relationship between us. That was all I could do. I was not in charge of anyone else's response.

I was particularly grateful for the attitude shift I had about my ex-husband. I began to realize that like my father and I, my ex-husband and I had an adversarial relationship that helped me to grow stronger and more compassionate. I began to see the gift that our relationship had given me, rather than the emotional turmoil of self-doubt and lack of self-love that I had experienced while I was married.

I found it hardest to forgive myself. Throughout my life, I held myself to high standards. I expected myself to be nearly perfect. After all, I had been told that I had to be perfect so that my Dad would not be disturbed. I felt deep remorse when I started realizing the negative impact that I had on some of the people in my life, especially my dad and my ex-husband. I finally understood how when we think we are victims, we victimize others in response. For instance, when I was "escaping" from my circumstances, I was hurting my parents. It was hard to forgive myself. The course taught me how to do that too. It was a great relief to realize that, like everyone else, I was always doing the best I could do at that moment given what I knew at the time.

I really began to understand what a therapist had told me long ago, "You must change yourself, if you want to change your circumstances. You can't change anyone else." The changes that I experienced did not happen because others had changed themselves but because I had changed myself. I was no longer a victim. I no longer harbored resentment and blame.

Because I was no longer a victim, I did not demonize the other people in my life any more. My inner war was over.

In succeeding years, I have found that forgiveness is a continuous process, not something that is done once and then forgotten about. As we live our daily lives and find ourselves in judgment or criticism of ourselves or others, forgiveness eliminates our emotional pain and brings harmony to our relationships and inner selves. It erases our painful past. As Catherine Ponder reminds us, "When you hold resentment toward another, you are bound to that person or condition by an emotional link that is stronger than steel. Forgiveness is the only way to dissolve that link and get free." Forgiveness brings us peace of mind and peace of heart. It deepens our connection to all that is and to what we call God. We begin to see humanity's oneness and connection to God.

Forgiveness may also improve our physical well-being. A few of the physical problems that may be eased by the practice of forgiveness include the following: depression, headaches, backaches, lack of energy, anxiety, irritability, insomnia, and stomachaches and ulcers. Studies have shown that our immune system becomes stronger when we forgive.

When I remember my dad and all the years he spent with PTSD, I recognize that he endured all of the symptoms above. He never forgave himself for his role in killing others. He never understood the power of forgiveness. He didn't know that God loves all of creation, and that included him. If God can forgive anything and everyone, then we can too, including ourselves.

Forgiveness doesn't mean agreeing with the act or condoning an outrageous behavior. It doesn't mean that you deny the other person's responsibility for hurting you, and it doesn't minimize or justify the wrong. You can forgive the person without excusing the act. When forgiving my past, I did not change my beliefs to include hitting me or giving me the silent treatment were acceptable and loving behaviors. I did not make myself a bad person because I believed that hitting me and the silent treatment were really acceptable, and I just didn't know it at the time. Those acts were not loving or acceptable behaviors or how I wanted to be treated.

However, I realized that my father truly was doing the best he could, given what he knew at the time, and he had his problems too. I had to let go of the past and those old wounds and stop revisiting them. I learned to love my father anyway, in spite of the past. I learned to see the light within my dad and, consequently, the light in myself.

Forgiveness extends to everyone. If we can forgive the person to whom we hold our deepest resentments, we can forgive everyone, including ourselves. Forgiveness opens the door to feeling joined in spirit to everyone and with everyone to God. It opens the door to reconciliation with others.

Until I started to practice forgiveness, I paid the price of harboring resentment and anger by bringing it into all my relationships, especially with men. This led to depression and being at odds with my spiritual self. I lost a valuable connection with others.

When I forgave my dad, I opened my heart's door to empathy and understanding. I realized the gift that had always been there for me—love enough to inspire me to grow and become the best person I could be.

A prayer for forgiveness that I find very powerful is the following: "If there is anyone or anything that has hurt me in the past, knowingly or unknowingly, I forgive and release it. If I have hurt anyone or anything in the past, knowingly or unknowingly, I forgive and release it. I ask for the highest good for everyone and for myself. And I forgive myself." (This prayer did not originate with me, but with Marci Shimoff, a celebrated transformational leader, author, and trainer of numerous Fortune 500 companies. I took a tele-class from her once, and she offered it as a wonderful tool for forgiveness. I agree.) Of course this needs to be said with deep sincerity and accompanied with time for reflection. I have found that when I use this prayer, a number of people or situations crop up in my mind as though they were waiting in line for my specific attention. I then go back and address each one until I feel like I have completely forgiven that person. When it is complete, a feeling of peace washes over me, and I end with gratitude, "Thank you, God."

Step 7: Learn to Love Yourself

> Find ways to treat yourself gently and with love and celebration. There is only one of you. Be able to look into a mirror and say, "I love you!" Laugh often.

Shortly after I started the course, I took a workshop in Portland, Oregon, presented by Louise Hay that moved me to work on loving myself more. It came at a time when I had just learned that I didn't love myself at all. I had attended yet another workshop (for a period of time, I called myself a workshop junkie) where in a guided meditation the participants were asked to imagine themselves getting ready to go to a party and then being present at the party. The first time we did this, we imagined ourselves as our fattest selves, and the second time, we imagined ourselves as our thinnest selves. Then we were asked, "What was the difference in how you acted at the two parties?"

I found out that for me there was no difference. I hated myself at both! This realization really shook me because I had anticipated that I would not love myself as my fat self but would love myself as my thin self. After all, that was what advertisers had been telling us for years. I realized that I had some serious work to do around the issue of self-love.

Then the work of Louise Hay entered my life. Louise Hay is a motivational author and the founder of Hay House, a publishing company. She has authored several books and is best known for her

1984 book *You Can Heal Your Life*. The workshop I attended she said would be one of her last workshops.

When I saw her for the first time, I was so struck with the love that emanated from her. I vowed to myself that "I want to be like Louise Hay!"

During the workshop, some of her messages were about forgiveness and self-forgiveness, and she gave the workshop attendees some important tools to help them in their healing process. I left the workshop feeling like some significant shifts had happened, and I was lighter after letting go of some more of my baggage.

I really admired the work of Louise Hay, and when an opportunity came up soon after the workshop experience to attend a weeklong training in California where people could learn how to facilitate the "Love Yourself, Heal Your Life" workshops, I jumped at the chance to attend. Offered in 1987, this was Louise Hay's first training of this kind and was so helpful and inspirational to me. I focused on many ways to love and heal myself, including forgiveness, the use of positive affirmations, which I quickly put all around my house so that would have a constant reminder of who I was becoming, on body work and purification exercises, and organic vegetarian nutrition, to name a few. I returned home with a variety of tools to help me transform into a more loving and compassionate person, and with the will to apply those tools.

At the workshop, she made available to all of us some simple ideas that would help us to take charge of our mind and our attitudes. These ideas were the kind of tangible things we could do to learn to love ourselves. I came home with the list and promptly hung it up in my home where I could read it and forever keep it in mind. That list is:

- **Stop all criticism.** Criticism never changes a thing for the better. It breaks down the inner spirit. Refuse to criticize yourself. Refuse to criticize others. Accept yourself exactly as you are. Don't expect others to change. When you approve of yourself, your changes are positive.

- **Don't terrorize yourself.** Stop terrorizing yourself with your thoughts. Find a mental image that gives you pleasure and immediately switch a scary thought with a pleasant or positive thought.
- **Be gentle, kind, and patient.** Treat yourself as you would someone you really loved. Imagine yourself relating to a child you dearly love and treat yourself with the same patience, kindness, and gentleness.
- **Be kind to your mind.** Self-hatred is only hating your own thoughts. All hatred is a call for love. Gently change your thoughts.
- **Praise and celebrate yourself.** Praise builds the inner spirit. Praise yourself as much as you can. Tell yourself how well you are doing with every little thing. Each day, take time to savor your gratitude, your appreciation, and yourself acknowledgment. Celebrate your accomplishments and special days.
- **Support yourself.** Find ways to support yourself. Reach out to friends and family and allow them to help you. You are strong when you can ask for help when you need it. You also give others the pleasure of giving. Surround yourself with others who support you becoming the best you can be.
- **Be loving to your negatives.** Until now your negatives have fulfilled a need. Now, find new, positive ways to fulfill that need. Lovingly release old, negative patterns.
- **Take care of your body.** Learn about nutrition. What kind of fuel does your body need to have optimum energy and vitality?

Learn about exercise. What kind of exercise can you enjoy? Cherish the temple you live in.
- **Mirror work.** Look into your eyes often. Express the growing sense of love you have for yourself. Say at least once a day, "I love you, I really love you!"
- **Love yourself.** Do it now. Do the best you can.

The mirror work can be especially important. I had a client once who claimed to hate herself. I asked her if there wasn't some part of herself that she didn't hate. After prolonged serious reflection, she said, "Well, maybe my big toe is OK." I was shocked that her big toe was the only thing that she didn't have a negative judgment about. I decided to suggest mirror work for her.

She agreed to spend some time every day looking into the mirror and telling herself that she loved herself. At first, she could not look into a full-length mirror. (I later found out that there are many people who do not have full-length mirrors in their home for this very reason. Some do not even have a small hand mirror.) Eventually, she graduated to being able to look into a full-length mirror completely clothed, and finally, she could see her unclothed body and say to herself with sincerity that she loved herself.

She did some additional work besides mirror work to help herself overcome her self-hatred, but there is no doubt that the mirror work was profoundly helpful. There is something about looking deeply into the eyes of someone else, or into your own eyes, and saying "I love you" that moves us and convinces us of the truth of our statements. Even looking into the mirror and smiling at ourselves is helpful.

If we look into the mirror and produce giggles or negative thoughts about ourselves like "I'm too fat, or have too many wrinkles, or, or, or," we are finding those judgments about ourselves that keep us from self-love. If we can notice those thoughts (be mindful), we can change them to something more positive like "My wrinkles remind me of all the times I have laughed" and "I love my wrinkles too."

Part of my client's other work besides mirror work was to notice the "buts" and "except fors" that were part of her thinking while she was doing her mirror work. She wrote them down then found something else to say to herself that was positive. She pasted her new thoughts on her mirror and repeated them when she looked at herself. In this way, she trained herself to regard herself with acceptance, compassion, and self-love.

Over the years, I have used this list frequently to keep myself reminded of the places where I need to love myself more.

Another tool that I learned from Louise Hay is the use of affirmations. Her work offers wonderful examples of the use of and useful affirmations.

Self-affirmations are positive statements that can condition the subconscious mind so that a more positive perception of yourself can be developed. Affirmations can also help undo the damage caused by negative scripts, those things that we repeatedly tell ourselves (or which others repeatedly tell us) that contribute to a negative self-perception.

For years, walking into my home was like walking into rooms filled with words. Where others hung pictures, I hung affirmations. The really important ones, I framed. Others found their way to my mirrors, wallet, car visor, and other places where I often looked. My intent was to fill my mind with ideas about who or what I wanted to be. After realizing how unlovable and undeserving I thought I was, I knew I had to make an all-out effort to change my thinking about myself. I had to constantly bombard my mind with a more positive outlook on myself and my life.

Instead of believing that I was bad or unlovable, my affirmations read, "I am loveable." Instead of believing that I only had male relationships that were destructive and emotionally unrewarding, my affirmations read, "The men in my life love me and treat me kindly" and "The men in my life are emotionally available to me and others." Hundreds of other words reminded me of who and what I wanted to be.

I also learned around this same period that it was important to add emotion to the words in order to make change. Every feeling we have makes an impression on our subconscious mind. Most of what we do in daily life is programmed by our subconscious. Feeling love, or other positive emotions, is critical in our transformation. Whatever feeling is dominant becomes destiny. Adding an appropriate positive emotion to an affirmation increases the likelihood of the manifestation of the affirmation in one's life.

These practices, along with forgiving myself and others, have been responsible for changing my self-image and relationships for the better. They are no longer concepts on a mirror or wall but deeply held core beliefs.

Not on Hay's list, but very important, is laughter. We all experience laughter as good medicine. During the time of my life when I was so intent on bringing my shadow to light, I had to take time to laugh. I found that somehow laughter put everything into perspective, and I no longer took myself so seriously. There was also a relief that came with laughter. I was no longer taking the world so seriously either.

Norman Cousins was one of the first people to discuss openly the healing effects of laughter in his book *Anatomy of an Illness*. After he started promoting the idea that "laughter is the best medicine," research began to reveal that this was true. For instance, we now know that laughter reduces stress, pain, and blood sugar levels, increases job performance, connects people emotionally, and improves the flow of oxygen to the heart and brain.

Many people, in their healing process, use laughter to offset the seriousness of their illness. I have found, like so many others, that if I watch something funny on TV and laugh out loud, I instantly feel better. It is always a good idea to leaven our healing with laughter. Taking time to play with children or a pet, watching or reading something that gives us a good belly laugh, or joining together with friends and family for a lighthearted time that includes much laughter is good for the soul and for PTSD.

Marmelade and Apricot, two cats who were litter sisters, came into my life right after my ex-husband and I separated. For the next sixteen years, they were a source of laughter, service, companionship, and joy in my home. For the first time in my life, I truly looked forward to spending time at home because my cats were there. Every day they brightened my life with their antics and their love. My home became my refuge rather than just a place to go to change clothes and sleep.

Pets not only offer companionship to humans but health benefits to many as well. The medical establishment and people in general are beginning to recognize and accept the healing impact pets have on the human being. Studies have shown that the simple stroking of a pet, such as a dog or cat, can lower the heart rate, respiratory rate, and blood pressure. Even watching fish in an aquarium creates similar effects. It is both soothing and meditative. Many groups of people including invalids, the elderly, veterans, and the lonely notice how having a pet changes their lives and their health for the better.

One of the practices from the list above that I took especially to heart was "Take care of your body!" Because my inner war was over, some healing and rebuilding had to take place like they do after any war. Partway into the study of the *Course in Miracles*, I discovered a flyer on a community bulletin board advertising Reiki, a form of energy healing using chi (Chinese) or ki (Japanese), or universal life energy, the energy that enlivens and animates matter. The ad used the word *light*, and I was immediately attracted to learning more. I went to the class and two years later became a Reiki-Seichim teacher.

Learning and practicing Reiki, like studying the course, was life changing for me in many ways. Not only did it help me to heal emotionally and physically, it also offered me a way to experience my connection to God. It even helped me to support myself after I had stopped teaching at an Oregon university and decided to start a therapeutic practice involving mind-body work.

Because Reiki is boundless, transformational, and knows no denomination, it is a nonthreatening and simple way to treat one's self and others. The practice of Reiki focuses universal life energy and directs it through the hands of the practitioner. The concentrated flow of this energy accelerates the healing and balancing of body, mind, and spirit. It is a gentle, noninvasive transfer of energy that helps the body to heal physical and emotional disorders.

When receiving Reiki, I began to understand the emotional and mental causes of my physical problems, thus enabling me to take responsibility for my own wellness. When practicing Reiki on others, I noticed that pain and acute problems were often relieved quite rapidly while chronic illnesses usually took a number of treatments.

One wonderful benefit of learning Reiki was that I was able to help both my parents. When my dad had heart bypass surgery, I had just become a Reiki teacher. When I found out when he was going into the hospital for the surgery, I started sending him long-distance Reiki. My mother later told me that the doctors were amazed at how quickly he healed. He was out of the hospital in about half the time that patients usually took to recover from heart bypass surgery.

A couple months later during that same year while on vacation to Minnesota, I offered to do some Reiki on him, and much to my surprise, he accepted. We spent around two hours together with no words, just gentle touch and a transfer of energy. He told me afterward that experience was the most relaxing one that he could remember. Ever. I could tell that was true and was grateful that he had that opportunity to deeply relax and receive. I also benefited by being with my dad in a profoundly intimate way. All I did was send love. No words were involved. He never accepted any more treatments from me although they were offered. I wondered if this was because he couldn't accept love. Was he so convinced that killing condemned him to hell that he couldn't let himself experience peacefulness?

My mother was more open to receiving treatments. She has both osteoporosis and arthritis, and sometimes feels a lot of neck, back, and finger pain. Reiki has been a wonderful tool for easing her pain and for helping her to heal quickly from a few falls she has taken. Later in life, she learned how to work with energy herself so she could send it to herself when needed.

Working with energy has increased the bond between us.

To say I fell in love with Reiki is an understatement. I noticed that when I practiced Reiki, a calm peacefulness washed through me, and I could more easily become a witness to what I was experiencing. By becoming the observer, I was no longer attached to outcomes or emotions and could report on the experience and let it be. For the first time, I understood the practice of "Let go and let God!" I began to easily see that the thoughts I had were just thoughts—some worked in my best interests and some did not. If they did not, I could change them and utilize thoughts that were in my best interests. I also began to notice the connection between the thoughts I had and what I was experiencing in my body through the messenger of pain. If I had pain, discomfort, or disease in any part of my body, I could find the thought or sometimes the story that was attached to that area.

Pain no longer was an enemy that needed to demonized and eradicated but a friend who helped me understand myself. Often, after I understood the message that pain was giving me, the pain disappeared completely as though to say its job was done.

Reiki became the tool that helped me move from conceptualizing spirituality to experiencing spirituality at a deeper level. Through the practice of "allowing," I became the vehicle (or straw, as I like to call it) through which healing energy coursed on its way to the recipient. I had no agenda about the results; I just played the part of detached observer who was greatly privileged to be the straw. By being willing to show up as the straw, I also received healing energy at the same time as the person, plant, or animal I was working with. My trust and faith in God increased, as did my willingness to be of service of others.

I loved working with Reiki so much that I decided I wanted to teach it to others. I also wanted to learn more about energy healing and other forms of nontraditional healing. For several years, I took a variety of classes devoted to the healing arts and energy work and immersed myself in practicing what I was learning with my friends. I also decided to become a certified massage therapist so that I could practice energy work legally in Oregon.

When I was taking massage classes, I learned about Hakomi, a method in psychotherapy developed by Ron Kurtz. In 1988 I moved to a different location in Oregon so that I could take Hakomi training, which became another life-changing experience and the third major part of my spiritual, physical, and mental transformation.

The Guiding Principles of Hakomi

Hakomi is paradoxically powerful: it is gentle and nonviolent, yet yields dramatic results rapidly. In many ways, its subtle power flows from the congruence of its methods and techniques with the underlying principles and assumptions that guide it:

MINDFULNESS is a powerful tool for helping persons study the organization of their experience. It is an exploratory, relaxed and alert, meditative (though non-hypnotic), state of consciousness, which allows us to move beyond our normal, habitual thoughts and actions to the often richly non-verbal intuitions of our deeper states. The process also supports the mobilization of our essential or core selves, which have a presence, centeredness, compassion, and wisdom that transcends the limitations of our historical experience.

NON-VIOLENCE is a principle that promotes safe, non-forceful, cooperative exploration through honoring the signs and signals of our organic processes, especially those that manifest as "resistance." In contrast to confronting or overpowering such "defenses," the Hakomi methodology respects and literally supports such occurrences, which then allows them to be befriended for the wisdom they contain, and willingly yielded when appropriate.

The principle of **MIND-BODY INTEGRATION** affirms that mind and body jointly manifest and reflect the beliefs we hold about ourselves and the world, which in turn organize how we creatively experience and express ourselves in life. Hakomi has many ways of exploring the mind-body connection to help bring to awareness this somatic material, and the core beliefs and experiences that generate it.

The **UNITY** principle assumes that, as people, we are living, organic systems that are integral wholes, composed of parts, which also participate in larger systems. The interdependency of all levels of the system, including the physical/metabolic, intrapsychic, interpersonal, family, cultural, and spiritual are taken seriously in Hakomi.

ORGANICITY assumes that when all the parts are communicating within the whole, the system is self-directing and self-correcting, and has an inner wisdom of its own. In Hakomi, we support our clients' organic unfolding toward wholeness, and trust that this is the direction that their system will naturally seek. Rather than imposing their own agenda, the therapist works cooperatively with the client's system.

www.hakomi.org

Step 8: Form a Life Code

> Set a concrete and doable standard for yourself for who you want to be and how you want to behave. When you digress from your standards or code, you will be able to self-correct.

I started Hakomi training in 1988 and committed to the principles outlined above as an individual and as a budding therapist. When I first heard these principles, I knew deeply inside myself that living by those principles was how I wanted to live my life. The next few years became years of deep introspection and release of old core beliefs that no longer worked for me, and dedication to serving others through the combination of mind and body work.

My dad became my teacher by example of how the body and mind interface. I could see in my dad and other family members, including myself, how what was happening in the body was an extension of our core beliefs. I knew that our beliefs control our lives, and I was inspired to look at my beliefs and weed out the ones that didn't serve me.

One of the many great gifts of Hakomi therapy sessions for me was that I began to experience other people's unconditional acceptance of me. For the first time in my life, I began to see myself as loveable. Until this time, I had seen myself as lacking. (I was not as good as a boy, and I wasn't someone my ex-husband wanted to spend time with.) These wounds were deep within, and I tried to cover them up with a holier-than-thou attitude and other identity-management techniques. I ended up by not being authentic, honest about what I was thinking or feeling, or truly present with others.

One night during Hakomi training, another trainee said to the group, "I realized during the last month that I need people to be honest with me." Those words charged into my being, and I erupted into tears, much to my own amazement and the amazement of the others in the group. I knew deeply inside myself that I hadn't been honest with others or myself about who I was. I was so engaged in being Minnesota nice and a "spiritual" person that I had lost touch with what all my feelings were. I only accepted and gave voice to positive feelings. I had not yet got in touch with the deeper, hidden, and secretive emotions connected to my past. Becoming honest and authentic became another part of my code. I deeply desired to know myself and accept myself fully. That included all of my emotions and all the parts of me that I thought of as negative.

What I discovered through the process of owning up to the parts of myself that had been hidden in shadow was that I was loveable in spite of them. I began to experience for the first time in my life other people's unconditional acceptance of me. I was loveable. Love was not based on how well behaved I was, or what my achievements were, but instead was based on who I was, flaws and all. In fact, the flaws made me more vulnerable, more approachable, and more like my fellow humans. As a result, I began to experience true emotional intimacy for the first time in my life. The shell around my heart cracked, and I became more open and compassionate toward others as I heard their life stories and flaws too. What a gift honesty can bring.

As I began to seek my truth inside myself and treat myself compassionately, I vowed to treat others with compassion as well. The Hakomi code included nonviolence, which deeply inspired me to explore the meaning of that. How was I violent toward myself and toward others? I had seen the effects of violence firsthand and abhorred even the thought or threat of physical or verbal violence. Upon deep reflection though, I found many other ways that one can be violent, even ways that I had been violent toward others and myself. I had been guilty of lying, of saying hurtful things, of making threats, of practicing conditional regard, of being judgmental, and of trying to manipulate or force others to do the things that I wanted them to do. I also had been guilty of not recognizing my own needs and vulnerabilities and instead pushed myself aside in an attempt to do something for someone else so they would like me or approve of me.

As I realized this, I also understood that at the time that I had done these things, I hadn't known any better. I was just acting out my past programming. I had compassion for the me who felt she had to do those things in order to make her life better, and forgave myself. Then I set about learning other ways to get my needs met.

Another piece of my code came into being when I realized that I had always acted in the best way I knew, and that others are just like me. No one does anything that they feel is the very worst they can do. We are all doing our best given our education, upbringing, culture, and life circumstances. Recognizing this allows me to treat others accordingly. I don't assume they are evil, or bad, or doing their worst out of choice. I don't demonize. Rather, I assume that they are doing their best. When they have other information to draw on, they may make a different choice.

One of my experiences that illustrated this idea actually happened a few years earlier than Hakomi training. At the time of the experience, I didn't put it into the context of a life code. It was just an impactful event. I was still teaching and offering workshops called *PowerTalk,* (another name for assertion) to various groups in the area. A few days after giving this workshop in Salem, OR, I received a call from an inmate at the state penitentiary. He told me that he was given the privilege of making one phone call a month, and he had read the article about me in the paper. He wondered if I would come to the penitentiary and give my presentation to a small group of inmates there. He said, "All of us are in here because we don't know how to get our needs met in healthy ways! And we all want to change that." After some discussion, I agreed to do it.

I will never forget my arrival. So much steel clanging down all around me as I walked through a variety of gates, and so many guards and searches; I felt extremely intimidated as I walked with two guards to the room where I would give my presentation. It occurred to me, as I got closer, that it really was presumptuous of me to think that I had anything to offer to these men. After all, we had nothing in common; I was a young female, college educated, and a teacher, and they had all been convicted of murder. How could I begin to offer anything of value to them? One of the first requirements of a good speaker is to find what you have in common with your audience and to build from there. I couldn't see anything that we had in common at all.

Finally, I reached the room where I would be offering my class. On one side of the room the entire wall was made of heavy glass and guards were on the other side watching every move that we, the occupants of the room, made. I asked the eight or so participants to move their chairs into a circle, (a symbol of equality) which they did with a little grumbling. Perhaps this was the first circle they had ever experienced. I then asked each participant to tell a bit of his story. My thought was that I would like to get to know each of them a little, so I could tailor what I would say to their specific needs.

The first person looked me in the eyes, and then proceeded to tell me why he was incarcerated. When he mentioned how he had murdered someone, I could tell that this was a test. Would I act horrified? Would I leave the room? What would I do? What happened was a miracle. I felt a calmness settle over me as I listened to each one in turn tell their murder story. I did not feel intimidated. Instead I felt compassion. I realized as I listened that I too had done some violent things. While I had not consciously murdered someone, I could identify with committing violence. Our difference was in degree. I could find some part of myself in them.

When it got to be my turn to tell something about me, I said that they had taught me about myself, and I too had experienced anger that resulted in violence. They seemed to accept that, and we went on to have a productive workshop.

I realized afterward that what made this workshop successful was that I did not see evil or pass judgment on these men. Instead, I saw our commonalities and recognized that everyone had done what they had done given what they knew at the time. They were now learning other ways to respond to the situations in their lives and could make other choices. I have nothing to fear when I see myself in others. This understanding, learned earlier in my life, was instrumental in attracting me to Hakomi training and to embracing wholeheartedly the idea that "everybody is doing the best they can" and adding that to my code.

This realization enabled me to let go of my tendency to demonize people, and to think of violent behavior as a cry for help or love. As I embraced this new perspective on other people, I realized that I no longer had any need to engage in hateful conflict with others. Could it be that ending war might be this simple—a change of perspective from some people are evil to all people are doing the best they can? Self defense is the result of the first perspective; compassion is the result of the second.

I was learning that having a personal code was important to my transformative experience. I needed to have something concrete that I could expect from myself in order to become the best version of myself that I could create. I had learned that we can never change another, but we can try to live up to our personal standards or ethics in our interactions with others. In fact, it doesn't matter what others do as long as we hold ourselves accountable for our own actions. We are not responsible for other's behavior, nor are they responsible for ours.

I believe most people who run their lives from their victimhood do not bother with codes. They don't accept responsibility, they just blame others for their lives. Having a code demonstrates that you take responsibility for yourself. Only you know if you are living up to your code or not. If you do not, you can take appropriate action like making an apology or asking for and giving forgiveness to another. You are in charge of your life, and you feel better about yourself after you have done so.

If a person takes responsibility for their own behaviors, violence and war become unnecessary. Behaviors like blaming others, demeaning and demoralizing others, and forcing others, becomes obsolete. Feeling humiliation, resentment, shame, fear, and anger are no longer emotional by-products of these behaviors. Better health and happiness are the result, instead.

Your code is not about your goals in life. Nor is it about how you want to be treated. (Examples of what not to include: I want to learn how to play the piano. I want to become a firefighter. I want others to like me or accept me.)

Instead, it is about how you expect yourself to treat others when you are interacting with them. Examples taken from my code:

- I choose to treat others with compassion and nonviolence.
- I choose to believe that others are always acting in the best way that they know and I treat them accordingly.
- I choose to tell the truth to others.
- I choose to be self responsible in my interactions and not play the blame game.

- I strive to do no harm to any person, or other living beings, to places, or things, or to the earth.

After much reflection, I put my code in written form in various places around my home and office. It was always available to remind me of who I was and what was important to me.

Eventually, I no longer needed to read my code because it was so deeply engrained within me.

Having your own personal code is an act of empowerment, accountability, and self responsibility. When you have a standard that you want to live up to, you have an opportunity to become the highest version of yourself that you can imagine. You also have a tool that will allow you to self-correct. If you are not honest when speaking to a friend, for instance, you can self-correct by apologizing and telling the truth. You are no longer any one's victim when you take responsibility for yourself.

While I was involved in the Hakomi learning process, the next two steps began to happen in my life simultaneously because they were part of what I was learning and practicing.

Step 9: Learn to Know Yourself.

> Spend time alone or with a person you trust reflecting on your life. Be willing to accept the parts of you that are your shadow. Learn the art of mindfulness. When you learn to watch or witness yourself, and become aware of how you are thinking and behaving, you move from being a victim or a reactionary person to being in charge of your life. Therapy, storytelling, and spiritual development are three of many tools in learning to know yourself.

Learning to love yourself implies learning to know yourself. Both involve a deep understanding and acceptance of who you are. The relationship we have with ourselves is the most important relationship we have. After all, we are the only person who will never leave us.

To listen to ourselves, to understand ourselves, to love ourselves unconditionally may be the most important tasks in our lives.

Many people think that the words "love yourself" means being egoistic, to put yourself first and have no regard of anyone else. Often egoists will brag about themselves and their accomplishments and be self absorbed.

In my view, egoism and loving yourself are not related. In fact they may even be opposites. Loving yourself unconditionally means that we accept ourselves (and others) with all of our flaws and weaknesses. When we accept those parts of us that we perceive as a flaw, we bring it out of the shadows and learn to deal with that flaw. When we accept our flaws and weaknesses, and don't denigrate or punish ourselves or others, we empower ourselves to change and improve ourselves. We can become the best person we can be.

Loving ourselves is a prerequisite for transformation. Our willingness to love ourselves unconditionally acts as a catalyst for allowing ourselves to fully know and accept ourselves. Knowing ourselves and loving ourselves are two sides of the same coin.

There are many tools to use to learn to know yourself. The few I share here were useful for me. You may find others. The important thing for each of us is to take time to know ourselves.

What are your core beliefs? How do they operate in your life? What are your feelings at any given time? Do you have access to the full range of emotions or are you cut off from some of them? Are you only a sum composite of your family and career, or is there more to who you are?

If you define yourself this way, what happens to yourself if you no longer have a family or a career? What is your body in relation to your Self? Are you more than a body? Are you only a role in life: a mother, a father, a son, a daughter? What do you hold dear? What (or who) would you die for?

You might begin the quest for knowing and loving yourself by answering the question, "Who are you?" on paper or word doc. If words don't come readily to mind, you might try answering some of the questions above. You may find this exercise revealing, and if done periodically throughout your transformation process, ever changing.

In the quest to know myself, I was fortunate to find the most useful tool for me, talking with another, during Hakomi training where I was confronted with my shadow on a daily basis.

Fortunately, I had fellow trainees who became very close friends to talk and evolve with. Because of them and their growing skills, I felt safe enough to reveal the parts of my life that had been hidden, and I found that they had hidden parts too. We all bonded as we shared our life stories and core beliefs, and found commonalities. Our hearts expanded as we each became more compassionate and wise in the ways of listening to each other. At first I found it difficult to share the hidden parts of myself, but when I discovered that I was accepted anyway, and even loved for who I was, I felt encouraged to delve deeper and trust more in the process. I discovered the truth of the old saying that "an unexamined life is not worth living" (Socrates).

Learning to be mindful was a key part of Hakomi training. Not only did we become mindful about our own process, we learned how to follow another so that they could become mindful as well. This led to deep sharing and transformative growth. Fortunately, becoming mindful is not exclusive to Hakomi. Mindfulness is a common practice taught by many.

According to Ron Kurtz in *Body Centered Psychotherapy: the Hakomi Method*, "Mindfulness is a special state. It is self-observing. It is noticing one's present experience. It is also a special kind of availability, an openness of the mind, a willingness to be affected" (2). Being in a mindful state allows the observer to notice what is happening in the moment without having judgment or commentary about it. This provides the safety to go further into the story or experience of what one is discovering about the self. One can study one's own experience and decide if the core beliefs that are at the heart of the memory really are in one's best interests. If not, a decision to change can be made. In this way, one becomes empowered to create one's own experience or story, rather than have one's life be a reaction to something outside of self. Transformation becomes real.

To become mindful, we need to be able to move into the place of observer, rather than reactor. Spending some quiet time alone can help. Ask yourself, "What am I thinking now? How am I feeling now? Where am I feeling that? What is associated with that thought or feeling? A color, a memory, a picture? And continue on with questions that are asked from the perspective of tracking what is being experienced in the moment. The process is somewhat like what a tracker in a forest might do: follow the signs. A mindful person, or self observer, tracks, or follows the thoughts as they occur. Only what is happening in the moment is noticed.

By paying attention to what is happening in the moment, the tracker can find out about how they organize their thoughts and what their core beliefs are. When this is discovered, a point of empowerment has been reached. The tracker can then decide if the core belief they just uncovered is really their truth. The unconscious becomes conscious. Freedom of choice has been realized. In fact, this may be the most important freedom there is.

Most conversations that people have do not allow for this kind of healing introspection because they lack depth and a safe space to explore the self. Most people consider themselves to be excellent listeners, but are in fact, very poor listeners. They think that hearing the beginning of another person's story is an invitation to tell their own story, or an opportunity to offer their opinion about the story, or to give some practical advice. These tactics shut down the storyteller, and stop the flow of self observation. Conversation becomes more like a competitive tennis match than an opportunity for connection, growth, and transformation.

Several years ago I taught a class called *Couples' Communication*. Each of the couples had a complaint that their partner did not listen to them. They were so desperate for understanding that they were on the verge of divorce. In fact, often couples of both genders will say that the number one thing that is causing them to leave their marriage is their partner's lack of listening.

Over the years I have been amazed at the number of people I have met who feel like no one has deeply listened to them for their entire lives. Finding someone to listen becomes a mission, because somehow we all understand that satisfaction in life comes from knowing and accepting another and ourselves.

In the communication revolution that is going on now with so many people texting and e-mailing instead of talking face-to-face, the problem is deepening. In the age of multi-tasking, people don't often slow down enough to really be attentive to another. There is no chance of healing through listening if we don't connect with another. Nor is there an opportunity to find ourselves. For it is in the other that we find ourselves. So many times when I am talking with a another person, I find out more about my own feelings and thoughts than I knew before the conversation started. Through conversation, we explore ourselves, and we find our commonalities. We build our trust and respect for each other, and open our hearts. When we listen compassionately and without judgment, and accept others for who they are, they will usually do the same for us. When we listen and accept others and their shadow self, we experience unconditional love. This allows us to forgive and love ourselves and helps us transcend our problems.

Deep listening happens when the listener is fully present and then reflects back what the other person has said. That is all. No comments, no problem-solving, no assurances of "There, there," or "It will be OK." are added. Usually the speaker understands that the listener is listening without judgment and without interjecting themselves in the conversation, and then they feel safe to continue with their story at a deeper level.

Storytelling took on a new meaning for me when I witnessed how a story is deepened if there is a mindful listener following every word and body expression. We all desire to connect deeply with another. Reflective listening is love in action. It is the simplest way I know to demonstrate unconditional acceptance and love.

Everyone has a life story. The more tragic a story is, the greater the opportunity for growth and transformation. Often we stop ourselves from deeply listening to another because we think we have to solve the problem or in some way take care of the other person. We view the other person as damaged or "lesser" than ourselves. Somehow, they understand this hidden message that we are sending and feel themselves become disempowered. ("I need fixing!")

When we listen non-judgmentally and just offer ourselves, not solutions or similar stories, the other person feels loved and accepted and can heal. It is really very simple. Everyone is capable of solving their own problems. Talking about them in the company of a good listener can help each person to find their own solutions. When we find our own solutions, we become empowered. When we know we can find our own solutions, we are more willing to tackle bigger or deeper problems. Our growth and transformation becomes boundless.

One experience I had which deeply embedded this idea into my psyche happened in the midst of Hakomi training. One day while we were role playing therapist and client, I happened to be playing the part of the therapist working with a client on the table before me. One of the trainers was nearby watching our interaction. Her intent was to help the therapist become a better therapist and to find the blocks that were occurring in the mind and practice of the therapist.

At first, the session seemed to move along very well. The client was opening up and revealing a lot of rich material to explore in a mindful way. At one point I became aware that her dialogue stopped. I started to panic, and my head became filled with thoughts like "What do I do now?" and "What is happening here?" The silence became awkward. The trainer looked at me, and asked, "Janelle, what is happening now?" Immediately, I realized that I was engaged more in me and wondering what I could do to lead the situation and solve a problem, than I was in listening. My inner-enabler was in control of the situation.

The trainer then gently reminded me to move into my heart and listen, rather than be engaged in my thoughts. I did so, and a miracle occurred. I stopped trying to be a problem solver and therapist in charge of an outcome, and just listened. The client took a long breath, relaxed, and resumed her story. She eventually found her own solution too. I learned that all we really have to do is show up in the lives of others and deeply listen.

Learning some effective listening habits can benefit not only our relationships, but also our health. Our sense of connectedness with others increases our happiness. There are many studies available that show how people who are in happy relationships are longer lived and have less heart problems and other serious illnesses. It seems to make sense to learn to listen to ourselves and others.

Besides talking with another, interacting with a group can offer a tool for knowing ourselves.

While I was involved with Hakomi training, I attended several self-help workshops including one offered by John Bradshaw based on his work with family dynamics and healing dysfunctional patterns. This workshop was attended by approximately six hundred people and was very well received. The concept of self-help was popular in Oregon at the time, and all the participants were on a similar journey of healing past trauma.

John Bradshaw is an American educator, counselor, motivational speaker and author best known for his PBS television programs on topics such as addiction, recovery, codependency and spirituality. When I attended his workshop, I heard for the first time about such ideas as the "wounded inner child" and the "dysfunctional family," and as a result began to understand myself better. At last I had some language that began to explain my life situation. I found that when one has a diagnosis, one can find a way to heal.

After attending his workshop, two female friends and three male friends and I met consistently over a period of a year and worked on our dysfunctional family issues and learned new coping strategies such as boundary work, and making the inner child safe. For the first time in my life, I developed a friendship with three men and two women where it was totally safe to reveal myself, where sexuality was not an issue, and where honesty and authenticity were the values practiced. I felt a deeper emotional connection to these people than I had yet experienced with anyone, including my family and ex-husband, because we shared our wounds as well as our strengths. We also were helpful to each other in turning our pain into triumphs.

A third tool I have used to learn to know myself better is writing my life story. I find that as I write, insights occur continually. A few years ago, I became interested in exploring genealogy and began to add to my life story by including the stories of my ancestors. I was struck not only by how much I was learning about myself and family connections, but also about the personalities and life story of my ancestors. Then I began to see commonalities in various people in my family tree and understood them even more clearly. We all realize how some illnesses may be genetic and passed to various members of a family. I believe that themes run in families too. For example, the theme of being nonviolent was part of my Quaker heritage as explained earlier. Another theme I have detected is learning acceptance of the way things are instead of how we want them to be. I never would have understood any of this if I had not started writing about my family. This understanding has raised some questions for me about soul families and what we are here to learn and experience together. Understanding this has also led to a deeper connection with my roots and with myself.

History for me is now personal. I always have been interested in history, but purely from an objective viewpoint. Now, I realize that

I had an ancestor on the Mayflower, Quaker ancestors who were involved in the western migration, ancestors in the Civil War, etc. Their journeys and personal trials and triumphs are the experiences out of which I was eventually conceived. I find that very humbling and fascinating at the same time.

What has really amazed me is to find that I, along with a few other descendants from some of the same ancestors, have similar characteristics and interests. For example, three second and third cousins and I have followed a communication related path in our choice of work. We each have similar personalities and interests as well. It is almost like a twin experience spread out among the descendants.

Similarly, I have realized that some of the things that have happened in the past have also happened in my present lifetime. For instance, some of my ancestors lived in Witham, England. For a few years, I lived on Witham Hill in a community in Oregon with no knowledge at the time of my ancestors. A great, great grandmother left a brief memoir that explained some of her life story so that her children would have a sense of their history. In her memoir she talked about her life of hardship and how she healed through her belief in God. Our experiences are similar in pattern if not in kind. As mentioned previously, I have from childhood on had an interest in Quakerism although at the time there was no talk or understanding of how some of my ancestors were Quakers who helped in the founding of this country. Realizing the similarities between people and places has resulted in asking myself more questions about who we are.

Knowing your family ancestors can lead you to greater knowledge of yourself. You understand yourself in the context of history and past generations, rather than as an isolated event in the life of two adults, your parents. You understand yourself to be part of a collective, not just an individual.

In this discussion about knowing self, I neglected to mention KNOWING THE SELF. It is one thing to learn to know and express your story. It is another to KNOW WHO YOU ARE.

One task I used to ask my students to do in my classes on Interpersonal Communication, was to tell the class who they were. Many said things like "I am my family." Others referred to their chronology, their careers, their interests or hobbies, etc. and said they were that. In all of the years that I asked students to complete this exercise, no student ever said anything about their relationship to God. No one ever said that they were a child of God, or spirit in a human body, or anything similar to that. That really surprised me. I always expected that to be the first thing that someone would say when describing who they were, because that is the most fundamental thing about ourselves. We are all children of God. We are all a part of Divine Creation. We are all loved by God unconditionally no matter what we have done. Completely understanding that will change our lives and our relationships.

Step 10: Become Your Own Parent:
Set Boundaries and Communicate

> Do not let others hurt you. Practice the art of compassionate communication. Know your limits.

At the time in my life when I was learning to know myself and my core issues, I also began to learn about boundaries and assertion. Boundaries mark our personal territory including our land (house, car, possessions, office space), our physical self, emotions, ideas, our spiritual selves, and our rights and freedoms (personally and nationally). All that we call "ME" is established by our boundaries.

Assertion helps us communicate our boundaries in a non-blaming, healthy way. Instead of being silent and hoping that the other person will intuit our needs, instead of using manipulative behavior to get our needs met, instead of using aggression or demands to make our needs known, we simply and clearly, perhaps even politely make a request. The request is often more powerful if accompanied with a statement about why the request is important to you. Referring to yourself rather than the other makes the request free from blame placement and the other person becomes more likely to grant the request. "I feel unloved and unappreciated when I am left alone night after night. I would like to have you come home by seven at night at least two nights a week." A statement made like this is non-threatening and may be easily granted if the other person is in the same mind frame as you are. If the other person has a different agenda, then an opportunity for negotiation may arise. The goal is for both parties to feel satisfied about the end decision.

My divorce was the first time I drew my line in the sand and established a boundary. I essentially stated that I did not want to continue living the way we were living. When I stated my frustration and made my needs known, my ex-husband did not want to meet my needs or negotiate any compromise. The only option I had, I believed, was to leave my marriage. I no longer could continue to live as though I didn't matter in the relationship. If my ex-husband wanted to continue living as though work was the primary focus of his life, that was alright with me. I would no longer advocate for something different. He was okay the way he was. I was the one who was wanting change. I needed to make my life okay too.

In the next few years, several opportunities arose where I needed to assert my boundaries. They provided practice for the big challenge of my life: confronting my dad, the person who I feared most.

Around the time I was forty years old I visited my parents for two weeks and after the visit fell victim to my typical depressed, child-like state. Then began a remarkable time period, even for my dad and me. For the next two years, Dad did not talk with me on the phone, nor did he write a letter. (I later realized that this time period was when he was starting to reflect deeply about his combat experience and was beginning his journaling process.)

I heard about his activities through conversations with my Mother. At first, this was alright with me. I told myself I didn't want to talk with him anyway. Then I began to wonder why he wouldn't talk with me. I didn't know about anything that could have led to his silent treatment of me this time. The longest period of time that he had previously been silent was three months.

Something was definitely wrong. I stewed about what to do, but could make no decisions. I thought that I could forgive him and let it go. I thought that I should confront him, but that thought terrified me. I knew deep inside though, that I would have to confront him at some point.

The inner tension I felt about my dad continued to build. Finally, one day close to his birthday, I realized that I could not send him a birthday gift as usual and remain true to myself. If I did, I would be essentially saying that it was okay to not speak with me. And it was becoming resoundingly clear to me that this was not okay.

One night three days before his birthday I had a dream where I wrote a letter to my dad.

> Dear Dad,
>
> For the past two years when I have called or written a letter, you have not responded. Your not responding or talking to me has reminded me a lot of when I was a child and you would be silent for days or weeks at a time. I was terrified of you then, and I am afraid of you now. I need you to talk with me about why you are silent. Why haven't you talked with me in two years? Please write to me about this. Janelle

After I wrote the letter in my dream, I woke up and realized I had to write that letter on real paper and send it to him. I did so. When I put my letter in the mailbox, I noticed an important change take place in me. As a very real energetic weight lifted from my shoulders, I realized I was no longer afraid of him, and his response no longer mattered to me. He could answer me or not. Whatever he chose had nothing to do with me. I knew I was going to be able to take care of myself regardless of how he conducted himself. What matters to ourselves is what we do, not what the other person does. For the first time in my life, I truly stood up for my inner child. A wave of relief washed over me and I, for the first time in years, felt very good about myself and strong in my ability to take care of myself. I was doing what I needed to do for me. I was not responsible for my dad's response. I was finally an adult.

A few days later a letter came from Dad. He said he was sorry he had not spoken to me for such a long time, and he would try to do better. He also included a story of why he was so silent much of the time:

> *Dear Janelle,*
>
> *Here is a little something that I wrote to give as a Trip down Memory Lane to the Golden Kiwanis. It might serve partly to explain things between us.*

At the peak of the American endeavor in Europe during WWII, there were some three million men and women on the continent. Of these, about 750,000 were in the shooting war. In a typical infantry division only 11% were riflemen actually in the front lines, the ones who had to carry the battle.

Ernie Pyle, our beloved newspaper man who visited us several times, once wrote, "The front line soldier I knew lived for months like an animal. He was filthy dirty, ate seldom, and then not much. He slept on bare ground without cover, his clothes were greasy, and he lived in a constant haze, with a 2000 yard stare, pestered by flies, heat and cold. He had to move constantly, deprived of all things. He had to harden his insides as well as his outside, or he would crack under the strain."

I saw guys that I knew personally crack: guys who had been wounded several times and who were always sent back to rejoin the fighting. Sometimes they would lay on the ground, shaking, unable to move, and slowly pass away from the shock. The medics were too busy taking care of the wounded to pay any attention to them.

Whether wounded or sick in the hospitals, men would hear their outfit was moving out, and if they could possibly do so, would go AWOL (absent without leave) from the hospitals, just to get back with their friends. We who were overseas together formed friendships that can never be broken, especially those who spent over three years together. Men cried when their friends got killed or seriously wounded.

There was always another hill to take, or a river or stream to cross, and you had to keep moving. After a few months in a line outfit you began to think that you were there for the duration, and the only way to find shelter, or a cot to sleep on, was a wound serious enough to get sent to the hospitals. New faces came on the scene nearly every day, and soon they would look as old and weary as the rest of us. The day-to-day living and the terrible grinding pace would soon grind them down. If we went into reserve for a day or two to rest and get cleaned up, it seemed as if we would be camped near a heavy artillery outfit, and they would have heavy firing missions all night long. It seemed as if we were always trying to get a little sleep, in the rain, in the mud, or sitting up in a foxhole.

During the winter when we got into a firefight, there was frostbite and trench foot to contend with. The rear echelon was provided with overshoes and gloves months before the fighting forces got them. It seemed as if we never really got dried out and warmed up.

There was always firing from the enemy, and once in a while, we would catch friendly fire, something that was hard to put up with. Probably the worst cases of friendly fire that we had was at Macnassy in Africa when we were blown off a mountain we were trying to take by our own artillery. And again in Normandy when our bombers killed over seven hundred and fifty men at the time of the St. Lo breakthrough. Another bad case was in Sicily when the paratrooper planes were shot down by the navy.

General Patton, "Old Blood and Guts" (our blood and his guts), said there wasn't such a thing as battle fatigue, and he slapped a couple of patients in a hospital who were being treated. He was made to apologize to all the troops he commanded personally. He certainly didn't know what the front line troops had to put up with in those days. It was tough to survive, and the only thing that brought you through were your friends. Our weapons were adequate, but some of the German weapons were better than ours. It was the attitude of the GI and the manpower that made it possible to defeat the enemy.

We, who were there the longest, over three years, paid a terrible price. I still have nightmares often and wake up only to spend hours reading before I can drift off again. I had ulcers for years and wanted to shoot myself and threatened to do so. I was sent to the VA hospital and spent three months there under treatment trying to find my way out of this mess.

One of my biggest problems was trying to reconcile myself to the fact that I had severely wounded and killed three Germans in hand-to-hand combat. Something that I had been brought up to believe was a terrible sin. Of course, I had fired my weapons many times at the enemy, and probably done plenty of damage. To me it was so much more personal to engage in hand-to-hand.

These are the things I still think about, and it has only been in the past few years that I can talk about them. It helps to talk about these things, but I suppose it is pretty boring for someone who has never had to experience the rough life that an Infantry GI had to put up with.

After reading this letter, my heart broke open for the man who had experienced all of this horror and who also thought that it would bore me. How could he think that? All my life I had longed for a real connection with him. His letter seemed heartfelt and like a genuine attempt to explain himself and reach out to me.

For the first time in my life, I noticed that my feelings about my dad included compassion and understanding. In two letters I had gone from fear and victimhood to strength and compassion. I never again reverted to my fear of him, thankfully, and our relationship changed significantly. We talked more, and when I visited my parents, he didn't avoid me as much as before, nor did I try to avoid him. He seemed eager to play card games with Mom and me and to go with us if we went shopping or out to eat. We even started to spend some time together without my mother being present to provide a buffer between us. I believe he wanted to heal our relationship as much as I did. Communicating my boundaries with my dad brought him closer.

This letter had an interesting by-product. My dad's birthday and my birthday were close together in November around the Thanksgiving holiday. I sent my letter to him a few days before his birthday and received his letter to me on my birthday, which was one day before Thanksgiving that year. It just so happened that for Thanksgiving I had invited five of my special friends to spend the weekend with me. We had been meeting for several months to work on our boundary and inner child issues and had developed a deep sense of trust and bonding with each other. The subject of war had come up in our group since I was intent on working on my issues with Dad. One of the men had revealed earlier that he had avoided being involved in the Vietnam war by going to Canada. He always felt some shame about this.

After my friends arrived for the weekend, and we settled down to catch up emotionally with each other, I read my letter to them after telling about my dream and process of writing. My friend started to tear up while listening to the letter. He said afterward, "I now know that going to Canada was a good decision for me. What happened to your Dad was horrific. I wouldn't have wanted that for me." Not only were my dad and I beginning to find peace, my friend, by listening to my dad's story, began to find peace in his heart too. No longer did he feel so guilty about having sought amnesty in Canada instead of becoming a warrior. He understood more deeply the horror of the effects of combat war and was grateful that he hadn't experienced that.

Knowing our boundaries and communicating them to others is one way of demonstrating our willingness to parent ourselves and to be a responsible adult. Unfortunately, too many of us don't do that effectively. Instead, we take our communication with others for granted. We do and say the same kind of things that our parents and others in our lives taught us without any thought regarding whether our strategies are helping us to get what we want out of life. Most of us would say we want love and connection with others as our first priority. Yet we use communication tactics that guarantee that we won't get what we want. My dad belittled my mom. Instead of bringing them closer together, his tactics wounded her and eventually isolated them from each other. My mother didn't speak up for herself, or establish any boundaries, so the wounding continued.

This book is not meant to be a communication class on personal relationships, but in my opinion, everyone needs to take such a course. We all need to be more aware of how we communicate toward each other, and whether or not we are getting our needs met. There is growing awareness of how the thoughts we think can bring us closer to healthy self-esteem and success in life. Hopefully, people will begin to recognize that they must pay attention to the words and actions they use if they want to achieve healthy and happy relationships.

I wish so much that I had the communication tools when I was a child and young adult that I do now. I would have avoided much personal misery and would not have inflicted as much misery on others.

A smile, a compliment, some time spent with another, can all send the message, "I love and appreciate you." In fact, Dr. Wayne Dyer, in his book, *The Power of Intention* states, "The positive effect of kindness on the immune system and on increased production of serotonin in the brain has been proven in research studies. Serotonin is a naturally occurring substance in the body that makes us feel more comfortable, peaceful, and even blissful. In fact, the goal of most anti-depressants is to stimulate the production of serotonin chemically, helping to ease depression. Research has shown that a simple act of kindness and or appreciation directed to another improves the functioning of the immune system and stimulates the production of serotonin in both the recipient of the kindness and the person extending the kindness. Even more amazing is that any persons observing the act of kindness have similar beneficial results. Kindness and appreciation extended, received, or observed impacts the physical health and feelings of everyone involved" (3)!

After some reflection, we all would probably agree that a genuine compliment is a day brightener.

One teacher of communication strategies who has significantly impacted me is Marshall Rosenberg, an internationally known mediator and peacemaker. His first book *Nonviolent Communication: A Language of Life* inspired me to practice the art of nonviolent communication, or, as it is sometimes known, compassionate communication.

Nonviolent communication (NVC) is a life-changing way of interacting that facilitates the flow of communication needed to exchange information and resolve differences peacefully. With its focus on human feelings and needs, the practice of NVC emphasizes emotional intelligence over intellectual analysis in expressing what's going on in people. With its reliance on objective observations rather than evaluations, NVC avoids making people defend themselves from value-laden judgments. And finally, by employing clear requests in place of demands, NVC raises the bar for communication skills by allowing everyone to get their needs met on their own terms, without coercion, fear of retribution, or loss of self-esteem.

I first learned about NVC several years ago when I was living in Oregon. Because the word n*onviolent* was such a magnet for me, I immediately picked up the book when I first saw it.

The skills taught are simple yet profound. I joined a group of people who were practicing NVC and found this to be a helpful way to hone my newly emerging skills.

You might find a book or a class or more to be helpful to you too as you seek to find ways of communicating with your loved ones that will bring you together rather than provide further wounding.

As a child and young adult, I just didn't have the words or communication strategies in my repertoire to be able to approach my dad. I didn't know how to effectively listen, or ask questions, or stand up for myself. My mother didn't have those skills either. As a result, we all interacted in dysfunctional ways that served neither our relationships or our self-esteem. As the years rolled by, even our physical bodies were affected. I knew that communication skills would help, but nothing was taught of this nature until the 1970s. How I could have benefited if only I had been exposed as a child to healthy communication strategies. Life for all of us might have been significantly different.

The next four steps have no particular order; they can be practiced at any time throughout our healing journey, or all of the time. They all help us move outside of ourselves and our self-involvement and concentrate on what works in life, and what is good and beautiful.

Step 11: Spend Time Each Day in Contemplation/Meditation/Prayer

> Talk to your Higher Power, listen to your Higher Power, practice forgiveness when it is needed, and take time to feel gratitude and appreciation for everything in your life. Visualize your life as a success.

There are many forms of contemplation, meditation, and prayer. Choose what works best for you. Spending some time each day talking and listening to your Higher Power helps you get through the day when change is happening all around you, and you are confronted with life's challenges. You may find that journaling helps you in this process. More importantly, aligning yourself with spiritual intention expands the meaning and significance of your life and draws on the creative power of the universe to help and guide you.

My intention here is not to teach how to commune with God but only to suggest that considering doing so will impact your healing enormously. There are numerous resources available that will teach you various methods and illustrate the benefits of doing so. The same techniques will not work for everyone.

The God I communicate with is not a religious God. He/She is the Creator of all, a Supreme Being who is omnipotent and who loves all of creation without judgment and exceptions. God has many different names in many different languages.

After searching for the right church for me for several years, I finally gave up dogma in favor of becoming a "seeker," someone who finds God's words in the messages of many spiritual teachers and belief systems. I don't believe that one system of thought has all the answers. Instead all systems of thought have a part of the answer. Each person needs to find what works for them. What works for one does not mean that the same thing will work for all.

I call myself a spiritual being but do not apply any other label to my belief system such as Christian, Buddhist, Muslim, Jewish, or any other religious belief.

Instead, I embrace some of what each has to offer and especially take to heart their common teachings, such as loving each other as ourselves. Traditional Native American philosophy which includes living in harmony with and having respect for all life forms seems especially meaningful to me as does the Buddhist teachings about compassion for self and others.

I call the Supreme Being or Creator God because it is a simple word and part of my heritage and language system. You, of course, will do what is right for you.

Contemplation

The *Merriam-Webster Dictionary* defines contemplation as (a) concentration on spiritual things as a form of private devotion, a state of mystical awareness of God's being, (b) an act of considering with attention, (c) the act of regarding steadily. I have found contemplation to be a state of mind where I can calmly reflect and be introspective while my eyes are open. Because of this, it can be practiced at any time during the day while I am doing other things. Because it doesn't require a time set apart to practice like meditation, it is easy for people to do within the perimeters of their day. For this reason, it may be the most popular avenue to communing with your Higher Power.

During contemplation, the practitioner is in a state of effortless unfolding, as opposed to being goal oriented. The practices of observing, allowing, and mindfulness, are all closely related to contemplation. The result is often heightened awareness, solutions to problems, a sense of peacefulness, and/or feelings of awe or wonderment at the glorious nature of the universe.

While I spend time every day in contemplation, I don't always have memorable insights. However, they can happen. For instance, when I was living in Tucson, Arizona, I decided to go camping with a friend in northern Arizona for the weekend. I started gathering my camping gear and took it out to my van, which was parked in an open air, covered parking area. As I approached the door of my van, I happened to look down and saw a line of fire ants marching down the white line defining my parking space. When I looked beyond the white line, I realized that the row of marching ants extended well beyond the line and covered the space of the parking lot and perhaps was in the grass on the other side. I couldn't see the end of the line! What I could see was that they were marching in a very determined way, one after the other, and that I had to confront them to get into my van. Unfortunately, I stepped on a few in order to reach my van and immediately felt the sting of being bitten. I managed to finish loading my gear and took off, all the while feeling the pain of fire on my feet and legs.

When I hit the open road beyond Tucson, I began contemplating what had just happened. I had never seen such a parade of ants before and brought it back to my mind's eye. As I moved into a state of quiet introspection, I began to sense the wonderment of what I had just experienced. The ants marched steadily and purposefully ahead on their journey, around, over, under, or through any obstacle. Even though they were small, they were formidable, and by working together they could accomplish things that an individual ant could not hope to accomplish.

Then I realized that the ants were reminding me of something that I needed to know for me. I needed to be like the ant and be willing to find a way around my obstacles and stick to my path forward in life. As I realized the teaching that the ants had for me, I began to see the ants in an entirely different way. They were not some insect to be crushed beneath my feet and disregarded, nor were they a pest that needed to be destroyed with bug spray. Instead, they were part of the creative universe with a purpose of their own, and needed to be respected.

Over the years, whenever I see an ant, I am reminded of this event and the meaning it had for me. God works in mysterious ways. Contemplating what shows up in life can give us insights into what lies ahead and how to approach it. It can also humble us as we realize the wonderment of the universe and the perfection of all of God's creations and events.

Meditation

Meditation is a time-honored means by which to access spiritual truth. Many specific techniques have evolved over the centuries in various cultures and religions. There have also been many scientific studies of altered brain physiology when meditation occurs. For instance, according to http://www.medicalnewstoday.com/articles/238093.php, "A new brain imaging study led by researchers at Yale University shows how people who regularly practice meditation are able to switch off areas of the brain linked to daydreaming, anxiety, schizophrenia and other psychiatric disorders. The brains of experienced meditators appear to show less activity in an area known as the 'default mode network,' which is linked to largely self-centered thinking. The researchers suggest through monitoring and suppressing or 'tuning out' the 'me' thoughts, meditators develop a new default mode, which is more present-centered. A report of their findings is published online in the *Proceedings of the National Academy of Sciences*." The same article continued, "Meditation can help deal with a variety of health problems, from quitting smoking, to coping with cancer, and even preventing psoriasis, one of the researchers said in a statement" (4). We don't yet know all the benefits of meditation. We do know there are many.

When I first started practicing meditation, I tried several different styles, some more or less complex than the others. I found that quieting my mind, closing my eyes, and concentrating on looking out straight ahead through closed lids worked best for me. Often what happened is that I began to see colors, usually purple or blue, and I felt myself going into a deep state of calm and observation. I watched my thoughts speed by, and as I started to slow my breath, my thoughts slowed down to a drift. The result of spending some time like this was a deeper state of peacefulness and readiness to meet life challenges from a higher perspective than reactivity. Often answers to my challenges occurred to me during the meditation or soon after.

Some people find it difficult to meditate for various reasons: they don't have time in the day to sit down and quiet their mind, their thoughts race by, there are too many distractions, etc.

I have found that if this is the case with me, I try to find ways to make it easy. I give myself a minute to meditate rather than fifteen. If I notice myself criticizing myself because my thoughts are racing, I allow my thoughts to race for a while. When I give myself permission to be me, my thoughts eventually slow down. I do what I can to be still and listen.

Prayer

While meditation is about listening to God, prayer is about talking to God. Because God is my best friend and knows everything about me, I don't limit my talking to God to requests like "Please send me money." (Or whatever.) If I limited my conversation with friends-in-the-flesh to requests, we would have a shallow relationship or a nonexistent relationship. In fact, I start each conversation with God with gratitude. I thank God for whatever comes to mind. Usually the list is long. Sometimes, my prayer doesn't include anything else.

Sometimes my prayer does include a request usually followed with "whatever is in the best interests of all concerned." I know that I can't see the whole picture and leave it up to God to supply me with exactly the right thing. My requests are not usually about stuff as in "Please give me a new car" but about attitudes or personal challenges such as "Please help me to find the courage to overcome my fear in moving forward in life." Sometimes my prayers are just a conversation with God that is similar to a conversation I might have with any of my good friends.

Group prayers are very powerful. We hear stories frequently about groups of people holding a prayer vigil for someone who is ill or experiencing adversity. Numerous studies about the power of prayer to affect change show that the biblical idea of two or more gathering together to pray does indeed affect the outcome in a positive way.

For years I practiced a form of prayer called Partners in Prayer with a group in Oregon. This prayer strongly affirmed what we were wanting to create in life. There were several steps to the prayer that we each stated alike. Then, one by one, each of us named our particular growing edge or struggle and our vision for what we wanted to create in our life. After we stated our individual vision, the others in the group affirmed for us that they saw us experiencing what we desired.

Then we all, as a group, focused on visualizing the manifestation of that prayer request.

For example, if I said that I would like to become more loving to others and myself, the others told me that they could see me accomplishing that. This form of prayer seemed particularly powerful because I heard firsthand and immediately that others believed in me when I didn't believe in myself. I realized that if others could believe in me, then maybe I could believe in myself. Those of us who practiced this form of prayer were continually amazed at the results and how quickly our prayers were answered. We also bonded as a group when we heard the struggles and desires of each other, and experienced each other as a powerful support system.

However I pray, I know that my prayers are answered, sometimes not immediately and not in the manner I would have expected. But they are answered in a way and timing that suits the best interests of all.

Visualization

Besides contemplation, meditation, and prayer, I have found the tool of visualization is another way to affect change that is more proactive. Instead of asking and receiving as we do in prayer, we imagine the wanted outcome in complete detail and happening now. We use our own power as creative individuals to institute change through our intention.

I personally believe that prayer is ultimately more powerful than visualization because we are putting the Supreme Creator of all things in charge of our lives, but I know that both processes work, and work well.

Visualization is the technique of using your imagination to create what you want in life. There is nothing at all new or strange about visualization. We all do it every day. Our self-talk, our beliefs and attitudes, the things we tell ourselves about our self (self-fulfilling prophecies), all contribute to how our life works. We can take charge of our life and success in life by becoming aware of how we tell ourselves negative things and change that to more positive ideas. Then we can visualize ourselves experiencing the positive. Because the body cannot distinguish between a vivid mental experience and an actual physical experience, the chances of succeeding are greatly enhanced.

When I used to teach public speaking classes at the college level in Oregon and Minnesota, I began every new class with a discussion about communication apprehension—more people fear public speaking than just about everything else. Most people fear it because of some past incident in grade school where they were teased about getting up in front of a group. I found that when I taught my students about visualization, they quickly overcame their fears. They imagined themselves having a successful experience rather than a horrific experience.

I personally use visualization techniques frequently to help me reach some wanted outcome in my life like bringing in more money, getting a job, buying a car, answering questions at an interview, confronting another person about a boundary issue, etc. I find it very helpful to focus on what I want in life and visualize having it complete with all the emotional satisfaction.

Group visualization works well too. Many years ago when I was living in Tucson, I belonged to a women's group called WOVA, or Women of Vision and Action. There was quite a large group of us one day focusing on what we would like to bring in the world. One woman stated that she would like to see a beginning of white people atoning for the atrocities that they inflicted on the Indian population in the past. She specifically stated that she would like to see white people asking for forgiveness in a public way and making amends.

After she said this to the group, we all visualized that happening for a few minutes then went on to the next person speaking about what she would like to see. I forgot about this incident until our next meeting.

When we gathered at the next meeting, one of our members brought with her a newspaper clipping saying that a minister of a church in Texas had begun the process of publicly asking for forgiveness of atrocities conducted against the Indian population in general—not just in Texas. We were all astounded by the synchronicity of this event and our visualization.

Of course, I can't prove that our visualization exercise produced this outcome. But I do believe that it had an effect. After hearing more about visualizations that resulted in specific outcomes, my respect for the power of visualization strengthened. A few examples: One of my students once told me that in his life as a pilot before going back to school, he used visualization at every takeoff and landing. He believed that helped him to maneuver his plane successfully. Numerous students who were athletes of one kind or another talked about using visualization before a game; they believed that helped them to play successfully. There also are many stories about people with various illnesses using visualization to overcome that illness. Dr. Bernie Siegel's book *Love, Medicine, and Miracles* offers a few of these stories and a good explanation of how visualization works.

Anything that we set out to accomplish can be made easier if we use visualization as a tool. Imagining ourselves being successful is far better than imagining ourselves being a failure! In our imagination we create our own self-fulfilling prophecy.

Every year for several years in a row, I used visualization in another way. Either alone or with a group of friends, I created a vision board, which sometimes is called a treasure map.

First, I gathered various pictures, words, or objects that were symbolic of what I was wanting to bring into my life during the next year. (I found that doing this as part of a birthday celebration, anniversary, or new year was especially meaningful.) Then, I glued these objects onto poster board in a way that was meaningful to me. Finally, I created a story to accompany my vision board and told it to my friends or spoke it aloud to myself. Then with my friends or alone, I visualized that happening during the next year. If I was doing this with friends, they would tell their story too, and we would all spend time affirming for each other that we could see each vision being manifested. After I had completed the creative process, I hung my vision board in my bedroom where I could see it several times a day. It helped me to keep my focus on what I was wanting to accomplish in a year.

Over the years that I have done this, I have been amazed at the results of the process. Most of what I have visualized has come to pass.

I hope that some of my experiences in using these tools will inspire you, my readers, to try out a variety of ways to commune with God and your higher self. There is no one right way; find out what works best for you.

Step 12: Serve Others

> We all have something to give. When we give, we receive. It is as simple as that.

Another tool for healing that can be practiced anytime is serving others. When we focus on someone else, we are not focusing on ourselves. What we give to another, we receive ourselves.

I have already mentioned how serving others was a major part of my dad's healing experience. After he retired, serving others through community programs like Meals-On-Wheels, or through individual help like repairing a broken piece of furniture, snow-blowing a sidewalk, or fixing a lock on a door became a daily occupation. He was always ready to help another and seemed to thrive on being asked. He never accepted payment and often did something for another without being asked or seen.

For years, I thought of his desire to serve as unhealthy and sometimes intrusive in the life of another. "Dad, you need to charge for your services!" "Dad, what if (name of neighbor) doesn't want you to shovel his sidewalk?" I didn't realize that he was already receiving much more than he was giving. What he was giving was an expenditure of time and talent. What he received was healthier self-esteem and a sense of being a valuable member of the community. He also was experiencing himself as a constructive person, rather than a destructive person.

"In about the same degree as you are helpful, you will be happy." This quote by Karl Reiland sums up what service to others is all about. Service can involve very simple things like picking up a piece of trash on the lawn or helping a neighbor or family member, or more complex things like starting a non-profit organization. Each time we give to someone else, we feel better about our lives and ourselves. It is that simple. Service is a wonderful cure for depression!

Each day we can start the day by asking ourselves, "How can I be of service today?" The opportunities will then show up. Perhaps someone needs a smile or some kind of acknowledgment or appreciation. Maybe, they just need someone to listen to them. Sometimes we serve by doing more than our share of something. For instance, I may shovel my neighbor's driveway as well as my own.

However we serve, whether we are doing simple things or something that requires more thought or even training, service is all about doing whatever we do from the heart. What we will receive as a result of the service is not the reason for doing the service. When we are selfless in our service, we are the most rewarded.

A woman I know has frequently complained about being friendless. One day she decided to try out the idea of "If you want a friend, be a friend." It worked. Her perception shifted from "Poor me" to "How can I serve?" It changed her life. She no longer complains about being friendless.

Volunteering can be a wonderful outlet for providing service. Many volunteer situations offer opportunities for practicing the skills you already have or train you to master new ones. When I lived in Tucson, I was a volunteer mediator for the Attorney General's Office. They trained a group of us, and then we mediated several different kinds of cases including small claims, victim and offender, and civil. When I moved back to Oregon, I mediated for two local agencies, (again as a volunteer) and helped to train other mediators. I loved doing that work and learned so much, especially about being a nonjudgmental listener. I will never forget some of the disputes I heard because they also involved a process of reconciliation that at times was heartrending and inspirational. By starting with some skills you already have and adding new ones, you can benefit not only in nonmonetary ways, but also you may be led to skills and jobs that have monetary rewards.

However we choose to serve, we are uplifted in the process.

Step 13: Take Time for Beauty

> There is beauty all around us if we notice it. We can notice beauty in words, environment, in aesthetics, in relationships, in movement. Ultimately we can see beauty (God's perfection) in everything. Our spirits are lifted.

Beauty is one path toward healing and inner peace. The recognition of beauty in words, in nature, in aesthetics, in relationships, in movement, in objects, in architecture, in people and animals, and within ourselves—in everything we see—creates a warm refuge for the soul in daily life. When we perceive beauty, our hearts and minds are lightened, our stress is forgotten, and we feel joy and reverence for what we behold. Beauty startles us out of our ordinary patterns, and both stimulates and soothes our soul. The by-product of what we experience as beautiful is more kindness and gratitude that we share with others.

The Navajo people have a ceremony called the Beauty Way, which means being in harmony with all things and all people, with all objects, all the animals, all the feelings, the plants, the weather, and all the events in your life. It means being at peace, serene in the knowledge that all around you is well and that you are well with everything in your life.

Even though I am not Navajo, nor have I ever experienced the Beauty Way ceremony, I resonate to this idea that peacefulness and healing are the result of seeing everything around you as beautiful.

When I was a small child, I saw beauty all around me: a snowy day, a butterfly on the lawn, a swan on the river. I remember that time seemed to stop as delight filled me. Sometimes I felt beauty surround me like a balmy, sunny day caressing my skin, or I heard beauty when a rooster crowed in the early morning hours saying, "All is right with the world."

As I grew older and became influenced by what others called beautiful, I became more selective about my ideas of beauty. I began to take my surroundings for granted and didn't see them with fresh and appreciative eyes. Ugly entered my world after I heard others apply that word to many of the things they experienced. Certain people, things, and vistas became ugly.

After I moved to western Oregon, my definition of what was beautiful became tall evergreen trees, rhododendron gardens, mountains, and the ocean. Since I saw what I defined as beautiful every day while living in Oregon, I experienced a loss of beauty when I moved to the desert—first in eastern Oregon, then in Tucson, Arizona. I remember asking a friend, "Where is the beauty?" because I recognized that something very important was missing.

She said, "Look around you!"

"But everything is brown."

Her very wise answer was, "Learn to see the subtle shades of color in the brown."

As I contemplated her answer, I realized the truth of that old saying, "Beauty is in the eye of the beholder." If I don't immediately see the beauty, I need to look closer. It is there, I just have to change my perspective and definition of beauty.

When I took her advice and started to look closer at the brown, I saw subtle shades of pink, deep rose and purple, green, blue, and yellow. Over a period of time I began to recognize the amazing beauty that the desert has to offer. It wasn't lush like the western Oregon terrain; instead it was an entirely different expression of life. Each individual plant stood out as an individual statement of God's handiwork, and I learned to appreciate an entirely different kind of beauty: the beauty of survival in a harsh climate. I also began to experience beauty in other forms like jaw dropping sunsets and the diverse faces of people mingling in the marketplaces.

When I moved back to Minnesota several years later, I once again saw no beauty. This time, however, I realized that the problem was within me and not with what I was viewing. Other people saw beauty in the town where I lived. I even remembered experiencing beauty there when I was younger and hearing my dad and others be appreciative of a Minnesota scene. Why wasn't I experiencing beauty in my hometown? I knew I had to change my perspective, or I would be continually unhappy.

Shortly after this insight, I happened to watch a PBS documentary called "Chased by the Light," which was about Jim Brandenburg's journey to take one picture a day for ninety days.

His photographs were taken in the Boundary Waters area of Minnesota and were spectacular. I finally saw beauty in my home state. More importantly, I began to open my mind to see beauty all around me.

Creation Spiritualist Matthew Fox reminds us that we all share beauty: "It strikes us indiscriminately . . . There is no end to beauty for the person who is aware . . . we walk on beauty every day, even when things seem ugly around us." Learning to see beauty around me has been a key to my inner happiness and sense of peace. I now see beauty all around me . . . in the deer watching me as I watch them, in the migratory birds talking to each other as they fly overhead, in the plant life poking up through the concrete in my driveway, in the colors around me whether they be brilliant or subtle, in the centipede on my bathroom wall. There is beauty all around me at all times if I but recognize it.

Over the years, and through various means, I worked to create beauty around me. Surrounding myself with uplifting music, artwork

I enjoy, pleasing room décor and coloring, all have contributed to my sense of well-being. My home became my refuge rather than a place to change clothes. Sometimes I created beauty by making something I enjoyed: a special meal, sewing my wedding dress, various craft projects, putting together scrapbooks, an endless list. There is always a sense of accomplishment and satisfaction that accompanies a project well done.

But seeing beauty is not just about seeing objects or vistas that we call beautiful. It is also about recognizing that the words we use can be beautiful too. When I have an uplifting emotional response to a poem, book, or conversation, I experience beauty. When I hear music that gives me goose bumps or sends shivers down my spine, I experience beauty. When I taste an extraordinary piece of chocolate, I experience beauty. Beauty surrounds us if we choose to see it or create it.

When we fill our lives with beauty, we create a beautiful response to life, and we can give beauty to others. A smile, a few words of recognition and appreciation, a gift, some time spent with another with no distractions, all enhance our lives. Beauty startles us out of our ordinary patterns, and both stimulates and soothes our soul.

In your search for healing, embrace the power beauty has in comforting your spirit and giving you the gift of awe and wonder. Comforted with gratitude find a way to give beauty back to the world. You and the world will be enriched and blessed.

Step 14: Take Time for Inspiration

> We each have difficult days; sometimes they seem to follow each other until we get mired down in our own problems. To help keep your life in perspective, read about those who also had difficult lives and found a way to transcend them. Find a hero to inspire you to be more than you thought you could be.

Not only can beauty inspire us and help us to transcend our lives, but other people can too. Just when I thought I was alone in my troubles, I would find a story of another who had worse problems than I did and who didn't succumb to misery, apathy, depression, violence, addiction, or suicide.

A few of the most inspirational people in my life I include here as a resource. Perhaps you will find them inspirational too. Of course there are many others, and you will find your own.

The first person who inspired me was Albert Schweitzer. I remember hearing about him in Sunday school when I was in my early teens. I don't remember the teacher or the context of the lesson. However, the example of the man who gave his life in service as a medical doctor in Africa in very difficult situations and who had reverence for all of life never left me. He believed that respect for the life of others, including those who are often overlooked or discarded, like lepers, is the highest principle and the defining purpose of humanity. Knowing about Schweitzer and his work deeply inspired me to find other examples of nonviolence and attempt to follow that ethical code.

When I was in a college philosophy class, I read *Man's Search for Meaning* by Viktor Emil Frankl MD, PhD written in 1946 chronicling his experiences as a concentration camp inmate and describing his psychotherapeutic method of finding a reason to live. Frankl concludes that the meaning of life is found in every moment of living; life never ceases to have meaning, even in suffering and death. A prisoner's psychological reactions are not solely the result of the conditions of his life but also from the freedom of choice he always has even in severe suffering. The inner hold a prisoner has on his spiritual self relies on having a faith in the future and that once a prisoner loses that faith, he is doomed.

This was the first book I ever read about real atrocities and hope, courage, and inspiration. For the first time in my life, I realized that in spite of extreme adversity, we can retain our faith and inner dignity.

Much later in life I learned about Nelson Mandela, president of South Africa from 1994 to 1999 who was the first South African president to be elected in a fully representative democratic election. Before his presidency, Mandela was an anti-apartheid activist, and the leader of the armed wing of the African National Congress (ANC). In 1962 he was arrested and convicted of sabotage and other charges, and sentenced to life in prison. Ultimately, he served twenty-seven years in prison.

Following his release from prison in 1990, Mandela led his party in the negotiations that led to multiracial democracy in 1994. As president, he frequently gave priority to reconciliation, while introducing policies aimed at combating poverty and inequality in South Africa. He won the Nobel Peace Prize in 1993.

There is something regal in Mandela's bearing. He too is distinguished by being able to forgive the people who were his captors. His inner spirit was never captured and held hostage.

He is an international figure who has become a spokesperson and role model for many, including me. Every time I see his picture or hear him speak, I am comforted by knowing that such a great man exists.

Another person who has an amazing personal story is Immaculee Ilibagiza who wrote *Left to Tell: Discovering God Amidst the Rwandan Holocaust.* This book I found impossible to put down. The author's account of genocide survival is not only astonishing, it is inspirational. If Immaculee could forgive the atrocities she witnessed, then I could forgive anything in my past.

Many of my students also found this book inspirational. One student who was some thirty odd years old told me at the beginning of a term one year that she had never read a book in her life.

I was amazed to hear this. Since reading had been such a big part of my life, I could not imagine anyone not reading. This particular student had a history of trauma in her life, and I gave her *Left to Tell* to try out. The next week she returned the book saying she could not put it down and was now a confirmed believer in reading. For the duration of the term, at least, she continued to read books that were relevant and inspirational to her.

Another person whose personal story deeply touched me was Christopher Reeve who was an American actor, film director, producer, screenwriter, author, and activist. He achieved stardom for his acting achievements, including his notable motion picture portrayal of Superman, a fictional hero who had the ability to save the world. In 1995, Reeve became a quadriplegic after being thrown from a horse in an equestrian competition in Virginia. He required a wheelchair and breathing apparatus for the rest of his life. He lobbied on behalf of people with spinal cord injuries and for human embryonic stem cell research afterward. He also founded the Christopher Reeve Foundation and cofounded the Reeve-Irvine Research Center.

When Reeve was injured, I was a fan of his Superman movies. He seemed so indestructible in them, and I found it hard to believe that he wouldn't walk again. During the next few years when stories were told on the news about his indomitable spirit and efforts at recovery, I was so moved. He made it clear that even though we may have a beautiful body, we are not our bodies but something much more. He managed to be an inspiration to humanity even though he was a quadriplegic.

Of course, there are many, many others who have been a source of inspiration for me: Anne Frank, Corrie Ten Boom, The Peace Pilgrim, Mahatma Gandhi, Dr. Martin Luther King Jr., Mother Theresa, and Oprah, all have led amazing lives. Their lives show the way to remain true to ourselves and to continue to have faith in our Creator regardless of what is happening in our life. They each transcended their experiences, rather than let their experiences embitter and disempower them. They each used their experiences to be of service to their fellow humans. When we have experienced some difficult passage of life, it is very empowering to use our voice to be a way-shower for others. When you find people who have experienced something close to what you are experiencing, they become an authentic teacher for how to transcend problems.

During my years as a teacher, I would often ask students at the beginning of a term to talk about someone whom they found inspirational, their particular hero. Very frequently, the person they chose was not a public figure but someone from their family or circle of friends who had overcome extreme hardships. A single parent, a survivor of an incurable illness, a homeless person, or drug addict who turned their life around—all were examples of stories told. There are many heroes among us. Discover them and emulate their example. We are never alone. There is always someone who has worse circumstances than we do, and who wasn't destroyed. There is always someone who has gone before us, and who will show us the way to move forward in life toward transcendence.

Step 15: Live in Gratitude

> Be grateful for everything and everyone who shows up in your life. There are no accidents. Even what you think is bad has a gift for you. Recognize that you have been given the gift of life and that every moment, even though it may seem like a tragedy or a problem, has a gift in it. By seeing painful experiences as lessons we do not become embittered by our circumstances. Instead, by seeing the lesson, we transform the problem into a gift. Learn to find the gifts waiting for you.

For many years gratitude in my life was not a way of life but a duty. Before I was able to write sentences, my mother taught me to send a "thank you" note for everything I received from another. When my grandparents sent me a gift, they in turn received from me a folded piece of paper that had a bunch of scribbled circles and *X*s which were intended to convey my gratitude.

When I got older, the teaching was, "Always thank everyone for anything that they do for you." I attempt to follow this practice to this day because it is valuable in letting the giver know that their thoughts and deeds are appreciated. It creates good will and helps bring completion to a situation. No one is left to wonder if their gift has been received. This kind of gratitude is a helpful formality, but does not offer transcendence.

Experiencing the attitude of gratitude is transcendent.

Until I turned forty, my experience of life was that there were good and bad times that happened to me outside of my control. After I turned forty and had embarked on my transcendent journey, I still had some bad times that were difficult to transform. Days would go by when I would feel mired down by my challenges. Often at the end of the day, I reflected back on the day's events and judged them. Then I woke the next morning in the same mood as I had been in the night before.

Early in the 1990s I heard about writing a gratitude journal and decided to try it. The directions were to spend some time at the end of the day writing down five things that you were grateful about that happened that day. The promise was that "If you do this, you will find your life change at the end of three weeks!" I scoffed at the idea but decided to try it anyway because I thought my life was so horrible and I was ready to try anything. I was experiencing some financial difficulties and other challenges and sometimes thought about committing suicide. I knew this was unhealthy but didn't know how to fix it.

I bought a notebook and sat down to write the first night and couldn't think of anything to say. Not one thing came to mind that I was grateful for had happened that day! That shocked me. I wrote down something like "I'm grateful that the day was sunny." Just after writing one sentence, my mood lifted a tiny bit, and I thought of something else. "I'm grateful that I can take care of myself physically." I continued on like this until I had completed my list of five things. For the next few nights, I still struggled to come up with ideas, but I persevered. Then I began to notice a shift. I started to experience being grateful for more substantive things, and sometimes during the daytime I would feel grateful and express it. The result of this practice was that over the course of three weeks I shifted from being a person down on her luck and largely negative to one who noticed a lot of wonderful things in her life and was primarily positive in outlook.

This experience was so powerful for me that I began using it in my Interpersonal Communication classes as part of a unit on developing healthy self-esteem. At the end of my courses, students were asked to talk about the practices that worked well for them during the term. One male student said, "Just before the term began, my best friend was killed in a car accident. I was also in the car and didn't know why I didn't die too. I wanted to. At the beginning of this class I was thinking about committing suicide. Then we had the practice of writing about our gratitude. I started doing this, and it completely shifted me around. I no longer think about suicide, and wake up each day thinking about what I can do that is positive. I still miss my friend. But it's manageable!" The entire class cheered at this revelation.

I became a firm believer in this practice and now have many notebooks filled with gratitude lists. If I experience a downer of a day, I look at my row of notebooks and realize that I have much to be grateful for. That is an instant day brightener and mood elevator.

What is gratitude? It certainly goes beyond the formality of thanking someone for a gift. Paul Ferrini in his book *Love Without Conditions* states, "Gratitude is the choice to see the Love of God in all things. No being can be miserable who chooses to do thus. For the choice to appreciate leads to happiness as surely as the choice to depreciate leads to unhappiness and despair."(5)

For myself, practicing the attitude of gratitude led to being able to see the gift in all things. I am now old enough to reflect back on my life and see many times of reinvention. Many times I have closed the door to one part of my life in order to open the door to another. For instance, closing the door to childhood when I gave away my toys, closing the door to living with my parents when I went to college, closing the door to living in the Midwest, closing the door to my marriage and academic career, closing the door to my therapy business, and closing the door to my life in Oregon and Arizona when I returned to Minnesota. Heartache always led to transformation. When I understood that, I began to see how there was always a gift for me in the process. The gift of my marriage and divorce was that I became a stronger and mentally healthier individual who had more compassion and understanding for others and a closer connection with God. The gift from returning to Minnesota has been a complete reconciliation with my father and mother, and participating in a loving family living situation that I hadn't fully experienced previously. By seeing the gift in each situation, my life has been transformed.

Of course, life itself is a gift. When we fully realize that, we see ourselves as a gift as well. We are life being expressed. All that we see and experience becomes an expression of God's love and abundance. To live a life with this deep understanding is to live in humility and grace because we *know* that a force greater than ourselves is always at work.

PART VI

Reconciliation
2003-Present Day

TWENTY-ONE

Reconciliation with the WWII Experience of my Father

As I reflect back on my life, I am thankful that part of my journey during this lifetime is complete. I have reconciled with both of my parents and have turned my experience into a story that I hope will be helpful to someone else. Of course, I have more work, including personal growth work, to accomplish. That never ends. We are always in the act of becoming. It is good, however, to say one thing is completed. I look upon both of my parents with gratitude and love and realize that we are all part of a much larger picture.

I also believe that my parents have reconciled with me, an act that would not have been accomplished if I had not chosen to return to my home town to be a caretaker for my mother. By moving back, I demonstrated that not only had I forgiven my past but that I also had not divorced my past. For fifty years I was reluctant to embrace my past and live in my hometown, a fact that both my parents knew and grieved. By moving back, I was able to show them in a very concrete way that they were important in my life. We were a family. The value that was a part of my ancestral heritage—taking care of family—was alive in me too. Finding ways to help my family ultimately also helped me.

Before I started to write this book in 2007, I believed I had already completely healed from my childhood trauma. I had forgiven my father and mother, and no longer was uncomfortable in their company.

I had worked hard to change my thinking and communication strategies, release my negative emotions and their toll on my body, and to take charge of my own life by moving beyond victimization. I had accomplished much and thought I was at the end of my healing journey with my parents. I viewed life from my own perspective and had no remorse about anything from my past.

Then I started to write. For the first time, as I copied my dad's memoir unto my computer, I began to experience his story more deeply than I had in the past. The horror of what he lived through permeated my being as I contemplated his words and experiences, and often I would have to stop writing and take some time to recover from the deep emotions of horror and anger at all nations who send their people to war to experience such atrocities before I could continue writing. Wells of sadness cascaded down my cheeks as I contemplated Dad's experiences and how all of our lives were affected. Copying his memoir also awakened within me a deep desire to know more about killing and war and how they could happen and why they seem to be so much of our human experience throughout history. This led me to research these subjects that also evoked more horror and anger. Why can we not seem to evolve beyond war?

The end result of this part of my journey, the writing of this book, has been reconciliation with my family. I more deeply understand each of my parents and even see our life as a family from each set of eyes, not just my own. As a result, I have more empathy and understanding now than I did before I started writing, and have concluded that the journey to reconciliation is not the same as the journey to healing. Both are valuable, and the journey to healing may sometimes be a prerequisite to reconciliation. Reconciliation means coming together as a unit or "oneness." I understand this more deeply now since I have found myself looking through the eyes of both my parents and realizing my shortcomings in our family interactions. I've learned to see the whole picture, not just the part about how I was affected by my dad's war experience.

Recognizing that I too talked and behaved in ways that were wounding for my family has been humbling and the cause of more forgiveness work. I believe that I've deepened in compassion and understanding in ways that I couldn't have predicted before writing this book. I have enormous gratitude for the life I've lived and all the people, animals, and circumstances that have populated it and helped to give my life meaning. I now believe myself to be a part of a family unit instead of a victim who had to escape.

I've also realized that because of the war experience of my father, both my father and mother lost key parts of themselves. Their souls were disconnected and confused. Numbness set in for both of them, and they lost the capacity to love themselves. When we don't love ourselves, it is impossible to fully love another. They couldn't possibly love each other or me unconditionally. As a young person, I felt myself to be a victim of lack of love and looked for it in many different individuals. Finally, I realized that I had to love/heal myself. I could not look for love/healing in other people—especially those who didn't have the ability to love unconditionally. My parents were instruments in teaching me life lessons. Their job was not to heal me or to fill my hole. Healing comes from within and is something that I had to do for myself with God's help. Healing/love is a decision I had to make and continue to make, not an expectation for how I want to be treated. I am in charge of my own healing and decision to love myself and others. My hole has been filled, and the truth has set me free.

As you can see, telling your story can be immensely powerful and transcendent.

If you, my readers, are embarking on your own journey and find any of mine helpful, I am grateful. Together, all of us who have experienced PTSD in our households as a result of family members being in combat war, have an important story to share: a story that deglorifies war by telling the truth about the experiences of veterans and their families, and makes it imperative to help entire families of veterans in multiple ways. We can broaden our understanding of the impact of war and possibly make decisions to stop warring. A world without war is a dream that can come true. It is our choice.

APPENDIX A

WWII Timeline and Wartime Statistics

This timeline of WWII provides a brief synopsis of some of the major events of WWII with concentration on American involvement.

Dec 7, 1941—Japanese bomb Pearl Harbor; Hitler issues the Night and Fog decree.

Dec 8, 1941—United States and Britain declare war on Japan.

Dec 11, 1941—Germany declares war on the United States.

Dec 16, 1941—Rommel begins a retreat to El Agheila in North Africa.

Dec 19, 1941—Hitler takes complete command of the German army.

Jan 13, 1942—Germans begin a U-boat offensive along the east coast of USA.

Jan 21, 1942—Rommel's counteroffensive from El Agheila begins.

Jan 26, 1942—First American forces arrive in Great Britain.

June 1942—Mass murder of Jews by gassing begins at Auschwitz.

July 9, 1942—Germans begin a drive toward Stalingrad in the USSR.

July 22, 1942—First deportations from the Warsaw Ghetto to concentration camps; Treblinka extermination camp opened.

Aug 7, 1942—British General Bernard Montgomery takes command of Eighth Army in North Africa.

Aug 17, 1942—First all-American air attack in Europe.

Sept 2, 1942—Rommel driven back by Montgomery in the Battle of Alam Halfa.

Oct 18, 1942—Hitler orders the execution of all captured British commandos.

Nov 8, 1942—Operation Torch begins (U.S. invasion of North Africa).

Dec 13, 1942—Rommel withdraws from El Agheila.

Dec 16, 1942—Soviets defeat Italian troops on the River Don in the USSR.

Dec 17, 1942—British Foreign Secretary Eden tells the British House of Commons of mass executions of Jews by Nazis; U.S. declares those crimes will be avenged.

Jan 2-3, 1943—Germans begin a withdrawal from the Caucasus.

Jan 10, 1943—Soviets begin an offensive against the Germans in Stalingrad.

Jan 14-24, 1943—Casablanca conference between Churchill and Roosevelt. During the conference, Roosevelt announces the war can end only with an unconditional German surrender.

Jan 23, 1943—Montgomery's Eighth Army takes Tripoli.

Jan 27, 1943—First bombing raid by Americans on Germany (at Wilhelmshaven).

Feb 2, 1943—Germans surrender at Stalingrad in the first big defeat of Hitler's armies.

Feb 14-25, 1943—Battle of Kasserine Pass between the U.S. First Armored Division and German panzers in North Africa.

March 2, 1943—Germans begin a withdrawal from Tunisia, Africa.

March 16-20, 1943—Battle of Atlantic climaxes with twenty-seven merchant ships sunk by German U-boats.

March 20-28, 1943—Montgomery's Eighth Army breaks through the Mareth Line in Tunisia.

April 6-7, 1943—Axis forces in Tunisia begin a withdrawal toward Enfidaville as American and British forces link.

April 19, 1943—Waffen SS attacks Jewish resistance in the Warsaw ghetto.

May 7, 1943—Allies take Tunisia.

May 13, 1943—German and Italian troops surrender in North Africa.

May 16, 1943—Jewish resistance in the Warsaw ghetto ends.

May 16-17, 1943—British air raid on the Ruhr.

June 11, 1943—Himmler orders the liquidation of all Jewish ghettos in Poland.

July 9-10, 1943—Allies land in Sicily.

July 19, 1943—Allies bomb Rome.

July 22, 1943—Americans capture Palermo, Sicily.

July 25-26, 1943—Mussolini arrested and the Italian Fascist government falls; Marshal Pietro Badoglio takes over and negotiates with Allies.

Aug 12-17, 1943—Germans evacuate Sicily.

Aug 17, 1943—American daylight air raids on Regensburg and Schweinfurt in Germany; Allies reach Messina, Sicily.

Aug 23, 1943—Soviet troops recapture Kharkov.

Sept 8, 1943—Italian surrender is announced.

Nov 18, 1943—Large British air raid on Berlin.

Nov 28, 1943—Roosevelt, Churchill, and Stalin meet at Tehran.

Dec 24-26, 1943—Soviets launch offensives on the Ukrainian front.

Jan 6, 1944—Soviet troops advance into Poland.

Jan 17, 1944—First attack toward Cassino, Italy.

March 18, 1944—British drop 3000 tons of bombs during an air raid on Hamburg, Germany.

April 8, 1944—Soviet troops begin an offensive to liberate Crimea.

May 9, 1944—Soviet troops recapture Sevastopol.

May 12, 1944—Germans surrender in the Crimea.

May 15, 1944—Germans withdraw to the Adolf Hitler Line.

May 25, 1944—Germans retreat from Anzio.

June 5, 1944—Allies enter Rome.

June 6, 1944—D-Day landings.

June 27, 1944—U.S. troops liberate Cherbourg.

July 3, 1944—Battle of the Hedgerows in Normandy; Soviets capture Minsk.

July 18, 1944—U.S. troops reach St. Lô.

July 20, 1944—German assassination attempt on Hitler fails.

July 24, 1944—Soviet troops liberate first concentration camp at Majdanek.

July 25-30, 1944—Operation Cobra (U.S. troops break out west of St. Lô).

Aug 25, 1944—Liberation of Paris.

Oct 14, 1944—Allies liberate Athens; Rommel commits suicide.

Oct 21, 1944—Massive German surrender at Aachen.

Oct 30, 1944—Last use of gas chambers at Auschwitz.

Dec 16-27, 1944—Battle of the Bulge in the Ardennes.

Dec 26, 1944—Patton relieves Bastogne.

Jan 1-17, 1944—Germans withdraw from the Ardennes.

Jan 16, 1945—U.S. First and Third Armies link up after a month long separation during the Battle of the Bulge.

Feb 4-11, 1945—Roosevelt, Churchill, and Stalin meet at Yalta.

March 6, 1945—Last German offensive of the war begins to defend oil fields in Hungary.

March 7, 1945—Allies take Cologne and establish a bridge across the Rhine at Remagen.

April 1945—Allies discover stolen Nazi art and wealth hidden in salt mines.

April 1, 1945—U.S. troops encircle Germans in the Ruhr; Allied offensive in North Italy.

April 12, 1945—Allies liberate Buchenwald and Belsen concentration camps; President Roosevelt dies. Truman becomes president.

April 16, 1945—Soviet troops begin their final attack on Berlin; Americans enter Nuremberg.

April 18, 1945—German forces in the Ruhr surrender.

April 28, 1945—Mussolini is captured and hanged by Italian partisans; Allies take Venice.

April 29, 1945—U.S. Seventh Army liberates Dachau.

April 30, 1945—Adolf Hitler commits suicide.

May 2, 1945—German troops in Italy surrender.

May 7, 1945—Unconditional surrender of all German forces to Allies.

May 8, 1945—V-E (Victory in Europe) Day.

June 5, 1945—Allies divide Germany and Berlin and take over the government.

June 26, 1945—United Nations Charter is signed in San Francisco.

July 1, 1945—U.S., British, and French troops move into Berlin.

July 16, 1945—First U.S. atomic bomb test; Potsdam Conference begins.

Aug 6, 1945—First atomic bomb dropped, on Hiroshima, Japan.

Aug 8, 1945—Soviets declares war on Japan and invade Manchuria.

Aug 9, 1945—Second atomic bomb dropped, on Nagasaki, Japan.

Aug 14, 1945—Japanese agree to unconditional surrender.

Sept 2, 1945—Japanese sign the surrender agreement; V-J (Victory over Japan) Day.

Wartime Statistics

WWII was the deadliest war in history. Over 60 million people worldwide were killed. That was 2.5% of the world's population at the time. The following statistics refer to the United States.

- **Over 16.1 million** U.S. armed forces personnel served in WWII between December 1, 1941, and December 31, 1946. This was more than 12% of the American population at the time.

- **10,000,000** were drafted.
- Fewer than **1,000,000** saw extended combat.
- **11,200,000** served in the army, **4,200,000** served in the navy, and **660,000** served in the marines.
- **292,000** soldiers, sailors, airmen, and marines were killed in battle.
- **114,000** other deaths sustained by U.S. forces.
- **671,000** were wounded.
- **4,946** died of wounds later.
- **12,780** were missing in action.
- **183,000** children were left fatherless.
- Over **1.3 million** service personnel received some kind of psychological wound.
- **25%** of the military did not leave the United States.
- **33 months** was the average length of duty by military personnel.
- **73%** was the proportion of military personnel who served abroad.
- **16 months** was the average time military personnel served overseas.

I could not find any information on how many suicides there were among service men and women during WWII. I did find, however, information suggesting that the number of veterans killing themselves decades after the war was double the amount of veterans from the wars of Iraq and Afghanistan. "In California, World War II-era veterans are killing themselves at a rate that's nearly four times higher than that of people the same age with no military service. The suicide rate among these veterans is also roughly double the rate of veterans under 35, those who are returning home from Iraq and Afghanistan." http://www.baycitizen.org/veterans/story/suicide-rates-soar-among-wwii-vets/ Suicide Rates Soar among WWII Vets, Records Show. Aaron Glantz on November 11, 2010.

APPENDIX B

Distinguished Service Cross Award

CONFIDENTIAL
HEADQUATERS SEVENTH ARMY

APO758 U S ARMY   25 August 1943

AG 200.6 Misc.
SUBJECT: Award of the Distinguished Service Cross.

TO : Staff Sergeant Charles S. Willsher, Headquarters Company, Third Battalion, 60th Infantry

1. Under the provisions of Army Regulation 600-45, as amended, a Distinguished Service Cross is awarded to Staff Sergeant Charles S. Willsher

2. Citation:
Charles S. Willsher, Staff Sergeant, Headquarters Company, 3rd Battalion, 60th Infantry, United States Army, for extraordinary heroism in action during the campaign at Maknassy, Tunisia. On the afternoon of 29, March, 1943, Staff Sergeant Willsher, upon learning the enemy had launched an attack on the position held by Company "L", requested that the Battalion Commander allow him to take forward a group of volunteers from Headquarters Company to assist in driving the enemy to the rear.

Permission was granted, and Staff Sergeant Willsher helped a group of fourteen men.

They arrived at the scene of the heaviest fighting at about 1530 hours where they were led by Sergeant Willsher to the crest of a hill over which the enemy was attempting to storm. Using hand grenades, bayonets, and rifles, the volunteer group succeeded in driving the enemy from this hill, inflicting severe casualties on them. Staff Sergeant Willsher was seen to follow the withdrawing Germans and either kill or severely wound three of them with his bayonet. Staff Sergeant Willsher received a piece of shrapnel in his left ear but refused to be evacuated. He remained on the scene of the battle, personally supervising and assisting in the evacuation of the wounded and dead.

Having satisfied himself that all his men were accounted for and his assistance no longer needed, he returned to the Battalion Command Post, to resume his duties.

By command of Lieutenant General Patton

J. Y. Rahe
Major, AGD
Asst Adj Gen

APPENDIX C

Facts and Figures about the 9th Infantry Division

"The Old Reliables"

According to Wikipedia at http://en.wikipedia.org/wiki/9th_Infantry_Division_(United_States)

Commanding General(s):
- Maj. Gen. Jacob L. Devers (Oct 40 - Jul 41)
- Maj. Gen. Rene E. DeR. Hoyle (Aug 41 - Jul 42)
- Maj. Gen. Manton S. Eddy (Aug 42 - Aug 44)
- Maj. Gen. Louis A. Craig (Aug 44 - May 45)
- Brig. Gen. Jesse A. Ladd (May 45 - Feb 46)

Campaign(s):
- Algeria-French Morocco (8 Nov 42 - 11 Nov 42)
- Tunisia (17 Nov 42 - 13 May 43)
- Sicily (9 Jul - 17 Aug 43)
- Normandy (6 Jun 44 - 24 Jul 44)
- Northern France (25 Jul 44 - 14 Sep 44)
- Rhineland (15 Sep 44 - 21 Mar 45)
- Ardennes-Alsace (16 Dec 44 - 25 Jan 45)
- Central Europe (22 Mar 45 - 11 May 45)

(Charley participated in all of these campaigns except for the Northern France campaign because he was wounded in Normandy and spent some time in a hospital before returning to his company.)

Combat Chronicle:

The 9th Infantry Division was among the first U.S. combat units to engage in offensive ground operations during World War II. (Alongside the 9th in North Africa, were the 3rd Infantry and the 2nd Armored Divisions.) The 9th saw its first combat on 8 November 1942, when its elements landed at Algiers, Safi, and Port Lyautey, with the taking of Safi by the 3rd Battalion of the 47th Infantry Regiment standing as the first liberation of a city from Axis control in World War II.

With the collapse of French resistance on 11 November 1942, the division patrolled the Spanish Moroccan border. The 9th returned to Tunisia in February and engaged in small defensive actions and patrol activity. On 28 March 1943 it launched an attack in southern Tunisia and fought its way north into Bizerte, 7 May. In August, the 9th landed at Palermo, Sicily, and took part in the capture of Randazzo and Messina. After returning to England for further training, the division landed on Utah Beach on 10 June 1944, cut off the Cotentin Peninsula, drove on to Cherbourg and penetrated the port's heavy defenses.

After a brief rest in July, the division took part in the St. Lo break-through and in August helped close the Falaise Gap. Turning east, the 9th crossed the Marne, 28 August, swept through Saarlautern, and in November and December held defensive positions from Monschau to Losheim. Moving north to Bergrath, Germany, it launched an attack toward the Roer, 10 December, taking Echtz and Schlich. From mid-December through January 1945, the division held defensive positions from Kalterherberg to Elsenborn. On 30 January the division jumped off from Monschau in a drive across the Roer and to the Rhine, crossing at Remagen, 7 March.

After breaking out of the Remagen bridgehead, the 9th assisted in the sealing and clearing of the Ruhr Pocket, then moved 150 miles (240 km) east to Nordhausen and attacked in the Harz Mountains, 14-20 April. On 21 April the Division relieved the 3d Armored Division along the Mulde River, near Dessau, and held that line until VE-day.

Casualties: (Tentative)
    Killed 4,581
    Wounded 16,961
    Missing 750
    Captured 868
    Battle Casualties 22,292
    Non-Battle Casualties 15,233

In addition to these totals, countless survivors of the war went home with amebic dysentery, dengue fever, and malaria.

Individual Awards: According to http://www.mrfa2.org/9thWWII.htm

Medal of Honor: 4
    Distinguished Service Cross: 86
    Legion of Merit: 6
    Silver Star: 1,789
    Soldier's Medal: 55
    Bronze Star: 5,518
    Distinguished Flying Cross: 1

Prisoners of War Taken:
    Total: 130,000
    Total Casualties in WWII: 293,121
    Total Wounded in Action in WWII: 671,000

(These last two numbers are from hostile action and do not include all the other deaths.)

NONMILITARY NOTES AND REFERENCES

Chapter 10

1. National Center for Post-Traumatic-Stress-Disorder http://www.stanford.edu/group/usvh/stanford/misc/PTSD%20-%20Older%20Veterans.pdf
   USVH Disease of the Week #1: Posttraumatic Stress Disorder (PTSD) PTSD and Older Veterans: A National Center for PTSD Fact Sheet
2. "Post-traumatic stress disorder hitting World War II vets" by Brian Albrecht http://blog.cleveland.com/metro/2009/07/posttraumatic_stress_disorder.html. Published: Wednesday, July 15, 2009, 10:07 PM Updated: Thursday, July 16, 2009, 7:49 AM
3. Carol Schultz Vento, *The Hidden Legacy of WWII: A Daughter's Journey of Discovery.* Sunbury Press, Camp Hill, PA, 2011. P. 110
4. Carol Schultz Vento, *The Hidden Legacy of WWII: A Daughter's Journey of Discovery.* Sunbury Press, Camp Hill, PA, 2011. P. 112
5. Carol Schultz Vento, *The Hidden Legacy of WWII: A Daughter's Journey of Discovery.* Sunbury Press, Camp Hill, PA, 2011. P. 114
6. Carol Schultz Vento, *The Hidden Legacy of WWII: A Daughter's Journey of Discovery.* Sunbury Press, Camp Hill, PA, 2011. P. 114

Chapter 11

1. *Women and the Home Front during WWII.* At www.mnhs.org http://www.mnhs.org/library/tips/history_topics/131women_homefront.htm

Chapter 13

1. *Diagnostic and Statistical Manual* (DSM IV-TR) of the American Psychiatric Association Posttraumatic Stress Disorder DSM-IV™ Diagnosis & Criteria 309.81 Posttraumatic Stress Disorder http://www.mental-health-today.com/ptsd/dsm.htm
2. Medscape Education Psychiatry & Mental Health, "Improving Medical Care for Military Personnel and Their Families" PTSD: Principles of Diagnosis and Treatment CME/CE
3. Stellman, J.M., and S. Stellman. 1988. Post traumatic stress disorders among American Legionaires in relation to combat experience: associated and contributing factors. *Environmental Research* 47 (2), 175-210. Quote found in Grossmans ON Killing p 43
4. Jonathan Shay, MD, PhD, *Achilles in Vietnam: Combat Trauma and the Undoing of Character* Scribner, New York, 1994 pp165-181.
5. Tick, Edward, PhD, *War and the Soul,* Quest Books / The Theosophical Publishing House, 2005 p. 99
6. Tick, Edward, PhD, *War and the Soul,* Quest Books / The Theosophical Publishing House, 2005 p. 5
7. Gabriel, Richard. *Military Psychiatry: A Comparative Perspective,* Greenport Press, New York, 1986
   Quote found in Grossmans ON Killing p 43
8. Grossman, Dave, Lt. Col. *On Killing: The Psychological Cost of Learning to Kill in War and Society,* Back Bay Books / Little, Brown and Company, 1995 p. 43
9. Swank. R. L., and W. E. Marchland. 1946. Combat Neuroses: Development of Combat Exhaustion. Archives of Neurology and Psychology 55, 236-47 Found in On Killing pp 43-44

10. Grossman, Dave, Lt. Col. *On Killing: The Psychological Cost of Learning to Kill in War and Society,* Back Bay Books / Little, Brown and Company, 1995 p. 54
11. Levinson, Leila. *Gated Grief: The Daughter of a GI Concentration Camp Liberator Discovers a Legacy of Trauma,* Cable Publishing, Brule, WI, 2011 p. 24
12. Tick, Edward, PhD, *War and the Soul,* Quest Books / The Theosophical Publishing House, 2005 p. 20
13. Tick, Edward, PhD, *War and the Soul,* Quest Books / The Theosophical Publishing House, 2005 p. 5
14. Ingerman, Sandra. *Soul Retrieval: Mending the Fragmented Self,* Harper San Francisco, A Division of HarperCollins Publishers, 1991 pp. 11-16
15. Levine, Peter A. and Frederick, Ann. *Waking the Tiger: Healing Trauma,* North Atlantic Books, Berkeley, CA 1997 pp. 57-59
16. Tick, Edward, PhD, *War and the Soul,* Quest Books / The Theosophical Publishing House, 2005 p. 16
17. Tick, Edward, PhD, *War and the Soul,* Quest Books / The Theosophical Publishing House, 2005 pp. 97-118.
18. Tick, Edward, PhD, *War and the Soul,* Quest Books / The Theosophical Publishing House, 2005 p. 140

Chapter 14

1. www.FamilyofaVet.com
2. "When a Child's Parent has PTSD" by Jennifer L. Price, PhD, http://www.va.gov

Chapter 17

1. Tick, Edward, PhD, *War and the Soul,* Quest Books / The Theosophical Publishing House, 2005 p. 7
2. Levine, Peter A. and Frederick, Ann. *Waking the Tiger: Healing Trauma,* North Atlantic Books, Berkeley, CA 1997 p. 21
3. Lipton, Bruce, PhD, *The Biology of Belief,* Mountain of Love/Elite Books, Santa Rosa, CA 2005 p. 125-127
4. Lipton, Bruce, PhD, *The Biology of Belief,* Mountain of Love/Elite Books, Santa Rosa, CA 2005 p. 134
5. Myss, Carolyn. *Defy Gravity: Healing Beyond the Bounds of Reason,* Hay House, Inc. 2009 p. 206

Chapter 18

1. Tick, Edward, PhD, *War and the Soul,* Quest Books / The Theosophical Publishing House, 2005 pp. 218-219
2. Shay, Jonathan, MD, PhD *Achilles in Vietnam: Combat Trauma and the Undoing of Character,* Scribner, New York, 2003. pp. 188-189
3. Tick, Edward, PhD, *War and the Soul,* Quest Books / The Theosophical Publishing House, 2005 p. 223 Find where the exact quote is!!!!!

Chapter 19

1. Brennan, Barbara Ann. *Light Emerging: The Journey of Personal Healing,* Bantam Books, New York, 1993. pp. 83-84
2. Brennan, Barbara Ann. *Light Emerging: The Journey of Personal Healing,* Bantam Books, New York, 1993. p. 86

Chapter 20

1. Susie Michelle Cortright in her online article "*Journaling—A Tool For Your Spirit*"
   http://www.amberskyline.com/treasuremaps/journaling.html
2. Kurtz, Ron. *Body Centered Psychotherapy: the Hakomi Method*, LifeRhythm, Mendocino, CA, 1990 P. 68
3. Dyer, Wayne W. PhD, *The Power of Intention*, Hay House, Inc., 2004 p. 25
4. to http://www.medicalnewstoday.com/articles/238093.php,
5. Ruiz, Don Miguel. *Love Without Conditions: Reflections of the Christ Mind,* Paul Ferrini, 1994. P. 95.

GLOSSARY OF MILITARY TERMINOLOGY AND OTHER REFERENCES FROM WWII

𝔉or those readers who may not understand all of the military terminology discussed in Charley's memoir, I have provided a brief explanation here according to Wikipedia, the free encyclopedia:

- **Division** is a large military unit or formation usually consisting of between ten to thirty thousand soldiers. In most armies, a division is composed of several **regiments** or **brigades**, and in turn several divisions make up a **corps.** In most modern militaries, a division tends to be the smallest combined arms unit capable of independent operations; due to its self-sustaining role as a unit with a range of combat troops and suitable combat support forces.
- **Batallion** is a unit of 800-900 soldiers, divided into a headquarters company and three rifle companies; two to five battalions form the combat elements of a tactical brigade.
- **Infantry** are soldiers who are specifically trained for the role of fighting on foot to engage the enemy face to face and have historically borne the brunt of the casualties of combat in wars. As the oldest branch of the Combat Arms, they are the backbone of armies. Infantry units have more physically demanding training than other branches of armies, and place a greater emphasis on discipline, fitness, physical strength and aggression. Infantry can access and maneuver terrain

inaccessible to cavalry vehicles or armored tanks, and employ infantry support weapons that can provide heavier firepower in the absence of artillery.

- **Soldier** refers to a land component of national armed forces. In most societies of the world, "soldier" is also a general term for any member of the land forces including commissioned or non-commissioned officers
- **Company** is a military unit, typically consisting of 75-200 soldiers. Most companies are formed of three to five platoons although the exact number may vary by country, unit type, and structure. Several companies are grouped to form a battalion or regiment, the latter of which is sometimes formed by several battalions.
- **Battery** is roughly equivalent to a company in the infantry, and are combined into larger military organizations for administrative and operational purpose.
- **Platoon** is a military unit typically composed of two to four sections or squads and containing about thirty to fifty soldiers. Platoons are organized into a company, which typically consists of three, four or five platoons. A platoon is typically the smallest military unit led by a commissioned officer—the platoon leader or platoon commander, usually a lieutenant.
- **Headquarters company** is a company sized military unit, found at the battalion level and higher. In identifying a specific headquarters unit, it is usually referred to by its abbreviation as an **HHC**. While a regular line company is formed of three or four platoons, an HHC is made up of the headquarters staff and headquarters support personnel of a battalion, brigade, division, or higher level unit. As these personnel do not fall inside one of the regular line companies of the battalion,

brigade, or division, the HHC is the unit to which they are administratively assigned. The typical personnel strength of an average HHC is eighty to one hundred and ten personnel.

There are many other references made in Charley's memoir that people reading today may not understand. The following notations presented in the order in which they occur in the memoir, are taken from Wikipedia and the Minnesota Historical Society websites and include explanations of names, places, slang, and other miscellaneous items:

Chapter Two

1. **Fort Snelling, Minnesota:** is a former military fortification located at the confluence of the Minnesota and Mississippi Rivers in Hennepin County, Minnesota, United States. According to the Minnesota Historical Society, "During WWII the most common experience at Fort Snelling was that of the 'casual'—the recruit, the draftee or the returning veteran who was processed through Reception Station or Separation Point. For a new recruit, military service began with a physical examination, often indifferently done by a local doctor working under contract. After a couple of weeks to get his civilian affairs in order, the recruit would be on his way by bus or train to Fort Snelling. Arriving at the fort, recruits were marched to barracks and put to work with mop and broom. The over two hundred recruit hutments were Spartan quarters made more unpleasant by impersonal noncommissioned officers who sometimes showed outright contempt for the new soldiers. A thorough army physical followed the next day, as did the

all-important Army General Qualification Test. Scores on this test and results of the personal classification interview would determine the eager recruit's future. Recruits, however, gave little effort to the test, often delivered before breakfast. Fort Snelling recruits still scored well above the army average. This meant that a large number of recruits—37% in 1943—were assigned to the Air Corps. The practice of skimming the most intelligent recruits for air service was later criticized as it resulted in less intelligent and effective infantrymen. Following testing, recruits visited one of the clothing warehouses on post for as complete an issue of personal clothing and bedding as was on hand. In 1941 this sometimes meant left over WWI uniforms—supply became more regular shortly thereafter. The excitement of an army uniform faded in the next line as recruits were given their tetanus, smallpox and typhoid injections! After a personal interview with an army classification officer—questions on education, prior civilian jobs, hobbies and skills—the new recruit was formally classified. Until this decision was made, he perhaps was drilled, certainly pulled KP and latrine orderly duty, and he endured the required chaplain's lecture and orientation films.

When test scores and interview results had been compiled, the recruit's fate was sealed. He might be sent to an individual unit if his skills warranted. Those with high test scores likely were assigned to the Air Corps. The majority was designated for replacement training centers and eventual incorporation into existing units as replacements for casualties. Assigned to one of the ad hoc shipping companies at Fort Snelling, the fully processed recruit awaited his transportation orders. The whole process could take from three days to as long as two weeks. Over 300,000 young men were inducted here into military service during the war years. The Fort Snelling Reception Station grew to a peak in 1942 when its staff of over one thousand soldiers and civilians could fully process as many as eight hundred recruits each day. Later it would test officer candidates and send combat veterans home on furlough. One of the biggest problems at the fort was simply feeding and housing so many men. Fort Snelling was proud of serving meals to thirty-two hundred soldiers in seventy-five minutes and of turning the post field house into an eight hundred and fifty-bed dormitory on short notice. And in 1945 and 1946 the fort's efficiently operating Separation Point was the last taste of Army life for tens of thousands of the men who helped win World War II."

2. **Camp Wolters, Texas:** was a United States military installation four miles northeast of Mineral Wells, Texas. Originally named Camp Wolters, it was an Army camp from 1925 to 1946. During World War II, it was for a time the largest infantry replacement training center in the United States. After the war, the camp was deactivated for several years. (Wikipedia)

3. **Fort Bragg, North Carolina:** is a major United States Army installation, in Cumberland, and Hoke Counties, North Carolina, U.S., near Fayetteville. By 1940, the population of Fort Bragg had reached 5,400; However, in the following year, that number ballooned to 67,000. Various units trained at Fort Bragg during World War II, including the 9th Infantry Division, 2nd Armored Division, 82nd Airborne Division, 100th Infantry Division, and various field artillery groups. The population reached a peak of 159,000 during the war years. (Wikipedia)

4. **Higgins Boats** were a barge-like boat which could ferry a platoon-sized complement of thirty-six men to shore at nine knots where men generally entered the boat by climbing down a cargo net hung from the side of their troop transport and exited by charging down the boat's bow ramp.

5. **Landing Craft Infantry** were boats and seagoing vessels used to convey a landing force (infantry and vehicles) from the sea to the shore during an amphibious assault on enemy territory.
6. **G.I.:** is a term describing members of the U.S. armed forces or items of their equipment. It may be used as an adjective or as a noun. The term is now used as an initialism of "Government Issue" (or sometimes incorrectly as "General Infantry"), but originally referred to *galvanized iron*. The letters "G.I." were used to denote equipment made from galvanized iron, such as metal trash cans, in U.S. Army inventories and supply records. During World War I, U.S. soldiers sardonically referred to incoming German artillery shells as "GI cans." In that same war, "G.I." started being interpreted as "Government Issue" and said as an adjective of anything having to do with the Army. (Wikipedia)
7. **Bivouac:** is a temporary encampment with no or little lodging or shelter.
8. **Glory Boys:** a nickname used by those who regard the exploits of others with contempt.

Chapter Three

1. **Mortars:** A mortar is an indirect fire weapon that fires explosive projectiles known as (mortar) bombs at low velocities, short ranges, and high-arcing ballistic trajectories. (Wikipedia)

Chapter Four

1. **AT Grenades:** Anti-Tank rifle grenades capable of penetrating two inches of armor.

2. **Martha Raye (1916-1994):** was an American comic actress and standards singer who performed in movies, and later on television. In the early 1930s, Raye was a band vocalist with the Paul Ash and Boris Morros orchestras. She made her first film appearance in 1934 in a band short titled *A Nite in the Nite Club*. In 1936, she was signed for comic roles by Paramount Pictures, and made her first picture for Paramount. Her first feature film was *Rhythm on the Range* with crooner Bing Crosby. Over the next twenty-six years, she appeared with many of the leading comics of her day, including Joe E. Brown, Bob Hope, W.C. Fields, Abbott and Costello, Charlie Chaplin, and Jimmy Durante. She joined the USO soon after the US entered World War II. During World War II, the Korean War, and the Vietnam War, she travelled extensively to entertain the American troops, even though she had a lifelong fear of flying. (Wikipedia)

3. **United Service Organization (USO):** originated just before WWII and is a private, non-profit organization whose mission is to support the troops by providing morale, welfare, and recreation-type services (a touch-of-home) to the military.

4. **Messerschmitt Bf 109:** was a German World War II fighter aircraft designed by Willy Messerschmitt and Robert Lusser during the early to mid 1930s. It was one of the first true modern fighters of the era, including such features as all-metal construction, a closed canopy, a retractable landing gear, and was powered by a liquid-cooled, inverted-V12 aero engine. The Bf 109 first saw operational service during the Spanish Civil War and was still in service at the dawn of the jet age at the end of World War II, during which time it was the backbone of the *Luftwaffe's* fighter force. (Wikipedia)

Chapter Five

1. **Goums:** The Moroccan Goums, were the knife-wielding irregular troops who distinguished themselves fighting under French command in Tunisia, Italy, France, and Germany during World War II. Recruited from the hill tribes of Morocco's Atlas Mountains, the Goums were garbed throughout the war in the traditional djellaba of their homeland and were armed with long sharp knives, in addition to rifles, machine-guns and mortars. They terrified the enemy not only by their ferocity, but by their odd appearance. Their particular skill in mountain warfare prompted General Patton to request their participation in his Sicilian campaign, and they fought brilliantly in this and many other key campaigns. (referenced from Edward L. Bimberg's book *The Moroccan Goums.*)

2. **Boston Liberators, (B-24):** The most important and versatile military bomber aircraft in WWII built in a factory near Detroit Michigan. When the factory was in full production it produced a B-24 liberator every fifty-six minutes. The WWII Consolidated B-24 Liberator first saw combat in June of 1942. Nearly 18,500 Liberators were built during the war years, making it by far the most-produced American combat aircraft. It served in many roles beyond heavy bomber, transport, and anti-submarine patrol, and flew in Africa, Europe, India, the Atlantic, India and the Pacific Theatre. (Wikipedia)

3. **Panzer Division:** (German: *Panzerdivision*) was an armored (tank) division in the army and air force branches of the Wehrmacht and the Waffen-SS of Nazi Germany during World War II. The panzer divisions were the key element of German success in the Blitzkrieg operations of the early years of the war. A panzer division

was a combined arms formation, having both tanks (German *Panzerkampfwagen*, "armored fighting vehicle", usually shortened to "Panzer") and infantry as organic components, along with the usual assets of artillery, anti-aircraft, signals, etc. (Wikipedia)

4. **Stuka:** from *Sturzkampfflugzeug*, "dive bomber" was a two-seat (pilot and rear gunner) German ground-attack aircraft of World War II.

5. **Staff Sergeant** is just above Sergeant and is a non-commissioned officer. Staff Sergeants are generally placed in charge of squads, and ordinarily hold headquarters positions. Staff Sergeants are typically assigned as a squad leader or Company Operations Noncommissioned Officer in Charge at the company level, but may also hold other positions depending on the type of unit.

6. **Wadi:** (*wādī*; also: **Vadi**) is the Arabic term traditionally referring to a valley; in some cases it may refer to a dry riverbed that contains water only during times of heavy rain or simply an intermittent stream. (Wikipedia)

7. **Bayonet:** A blade adapted to fit the muzzle end of a rifle and used as a weapon in close combat.

8. **Dog Tag:** is the informal name for the identification tags worn by military personnel, named such as it bears resemblance to actual dog tags. The tag is primarily used for the identification of dead and wounded and essential basic medical information for the treatment of the latter, such as blood type and history of inoculations, along with providing religious preference. (Wikipedia)

9. **Sergeant Major** refers to both a military rank and to a specific administrative position. The rank refers to the highest enlisted rank in the U.S. Army. The holder of this rank is the senior enlisted member of the Army, and is appointed to serve as a spokesman to address the issues of enlisted soldiers to the Army's highest

positions. As such, they are the senior enlisted advisor to the Chief of Staff of the US Army. The exact duties vary, depending on the Chief of Staff.

Chapter Six

1. **C Rations:** The C ration, with a caloric value of 3700, was intended for operational needs of three to twenty-one days. This ration resulted from pre-World War II attempts to produce a stable, palatable, nutritionally balanced combat ration which would provide the individual soldier with three full meals per day. They primarily consisted of meat and beans, meat and vegetable hash, and meat and vegetable stew. The C ration was used for tactical situations in which the field kitchen could not be used. (Wikipedia)

According to U.S. Army Models (www.usarmymodels.com), the first version of the C rations offered a simple menu consisting of:

Package of Biscuits
Package of Graham Crackers
Package of Sugar Tablets
Meat Can of Ham (Breakfast), Chicken (Dinner), Turkey (Supper)
Fruit Bar (Breakfast), Caramels (Dinner), Chocolate Bar (Supper)
Powdered Coffee (Breakfast), Bouillon (Dinner), Lemon (Supper)
Piece Chewing Gum
4-Pack Cigarettes
Package of Toilet Tissue
Wooden Spoon
Matches

In early 1944 specifications for the C rations increased variety by alternating combinations of the "B," or bread, units, and the "M," or meat, units. An accessory pack included nine "good commercial-quality" cigarettes, water-purification tablets, matches, toilet paper, chewing gum, and an opener for the meat cans. A soldier's daily ration was three cans of B units, three cans of M units, and one accessory pack.

M unit varieties	B unit components
Meat and beans	Biscuits
Meat and vegetable	stew Compressed and premixed cereal
Meat and spaghetti	Candy-coated peanuts or raisins
Ham, egg, and potato	Powdered coffee
Meat and noodles	Sugar
Pork and rice	Powdered lemon or orange juice
Franks and beans	Cocoa powder
Pork and beans	Hard candies
Ham and lima beans	Jam
Chicken and vegetables	Caramels

Chapter Eight

1. **D Day:** The **Normandy Landings** were the landing operations of the Allied invasion of Normandy, also known as **Operation Neptune** and Operation Overlord, during World War II. The landings commenced on Tuesday, 6 June 1944 (**D-Day**), beginning at 6:30 British Double Summer Time. In planning, *D-Day* was the term used for the day of actual landing, which was dependent on final approval. The assault was conducted in two phases: an air assault landing of American, British, Canadian and Free French

airborne troops shortly after midnight, and an amphibious landing of Allied infantry and armored divisions on the coast of France commencing at 6:30. There were also subsidiary 'attacks' mounted under the codenames Operation Glimmer and Operation Taxable to distract the German forces from the real landing areas. The operation was the largest amphibious invasion of all time, with 175,000 troops landing on June 6, 1944. 195,700 Allied naval and merchant navy personnel in over 5,000 ships were involved. The invasion required the transport of soldiers and materiel from the United Kingdom by troop-laden aircraft and ships, the assault landings, air support, naval interdiction of the English Channel and naval fire-support. The landings took place along a fifty mile stretch of the Normandy coast divided into five sectors or beaches: Utah, Omaha, Gold, Juno and Sword. (Wikipedia)

2. **Croix de Guerre:** (English translation: *Cross of War*) is a military decoration of both France and Belgium, where it is also known as the ***Oorlogskruis*** (Dutch). It was first created in 1915 in both countries and consists of a square-cross medal on two crossed swords, hanging from a ribbon with various degree pins. The decoration was awarded during World War I, again in World War II, and in other conflicts. The croix de guerre was also commonly bestowed to foreign military forces allied to France and Belgium. The croix de guerre may either be bestowed as a unit award or to individuals who distinguish themselves by acts of heroism involving combat with enemy forces. The medal is also awarded to those who have been "mentioned in dispatches", meaning a heroic deed was performed meriting a citation from an individual's headquarters unit. The unit award of the croix de guerre was issued to military commands who performed heroic deeds in combat and were subsequently recognized by headquarters. (Wikipedia)

3. **Hedgerows:** A hedgerow is a fence of living trees, shrubs or other plants and may consist of a simple row or a pyramid of plant heights. Once off the beaches in France, the men hit the hedgerow country. These were not like the hedges back home, but a thicket of rock, dirt, and all manner of vegetation which formed walls in this part of France. Miles of this country had to be taken, and it was some of the most dangerous fighting in the war. (Wikipedia)

4. **Foxhole:** After the Battle of Kasserine Pass, U.S. troops increasingly adopted the modern *foxhole*, a vertical, bottle-shaped hole that allowed a soldier to stand and fight with head and shoulders exposed. The foxhole widened near the bottom to allow a soldier to crouch down while under intense artillery fire or tank attack. Foxholes could be enlarged to two-man fighting positions, as well as excavated with firing steps for crew-served weapons or sumps for water drainage or grenade disposal. (Wikipedia)

5. **K Rations:** The **K-ration** was an individual daily combat food ration which was introduced by the United States Army during World War II. It was originally intended as an individually packaged daily ration for issue to airborne troops, tank corps, motorcycle couriers, and other mobile forces for short durations. The K ration provided three courses: breakfast, lunch and supper. As it was based on an emergency ration, the K ration provided roughly 800-1,200 calories fewer than required by highly active men, especially those working in extreme heat or bitter cold, and malnutrition became evident.

- **Breakfast Unit**: canned entree (chopped ham and eggs, veal loaf), biscuits, a dried fruit bar or cereal bar, Halazone water purification tablets, a 4-pack of cigarettes, chewing gum, instant coffee, and sugar (granulated, cubed, or compressed).

- **Dinner Unit**: canned entree (processed cheese, ham, or ham & cheese), biscuits, 15 malted milk tablets (early) or 5 caramels (late), sugar (granulated, cubed, or compressed), salt packet, a 4-pack of cigarettes and a book of matches, chewing gum, and a powdered beverage packet (lemon (c.1940), orange (c.1943), or grape (c.1945) flavor).
- **Supper Unit**: canned meat, consisting of either chicken paté, pork luncheon meat with carrot & apple (1st issue), beef & pork loaf (2nd issue), or sausages; biscuits; a 2-ounce D ration emergency chocolate bar, Tropical bar, or (in temperate climates) commercial sweet chocolate bar; a packet of toilet paper tissues; a 4-pack of cigarettes; chewing gum, and a bouillon soup cube or powder packet.

In total, the three meals provided between 2,830 and 3,000 calories, depending upon components. As it was originally intended as an "assault" ration to be issued for short durations, the K ration was designed to be used for a maximum of 15 meals. The K-ration was produced by the Cracker Jack company with a waxed paper ration box, about the same size as the company's famous Cracker Jack box. (Wikipedia)

6. **Cobra: Operation Cobra** was the codename for the World War II operation planned by United States Army General Omar Bradley to break out from the Normandy area after the previous month's D-Day landings. Cobra was a great success that transformed the high-intensity infantry combat of Normandy into the highly mobile race across France. It led directly to the creation of the Falaise pocket and the loss of the German position in northwestern France. (Wikipedia)

7. **Flying Fortresses, (B-17):** The **Boeing B-17 Flying Fortress** is a four-engine heavy bomber aircraft developed for the United States Army Air Corps (USAAC), introduced in the 1930s. The B-17 was primarily employed by the United States Army Air Forces (USAAF) in the daylight precision strategic bombing campaign of World War II against German industrial, civilian, and military targets. The United States Eighth Air Force based in England and the Fifteenth Air Force based in Italy complemented the RAF Bomber Command's nighttime area bombing in Operation Pointblank, to help secure air superiority over the cities, factories and battlefields of Western Europe in preparation for Operation Overlord. The B-17 also participated, to a lesser extent, in the War in the Pacific, where it conducted raids against Japanese shipping and airfields. From its pre-war inception, the USAAC (later USAAF) touted the aircraft as a strategic weapon; it was a potent, high-flying, long-ranging bomber capable of unleashing great destruction, able to defend itself, and having the ability to return home despite extensive battle damage. With a service ceiling greater than any of its Allied contemporaries, the B-17 established itself as a superb weapons system, dropping more bombs than any other U.S. aircraft in World War II. Of the 1.5 million tons of bombs dropped on Germany by U.S. aircraft, 640,000 were dropped from B-17s. (Wikipedia)

Chapter Nine

1. **Bazooka:** is the common name for a man-portable recoilless rocket antitank weapon, widely fielded by the U.S. Army. Also referred to as the "Stovepipe", the innovative bazooka was amongst the first-generation of rocket propelled anti-tank weapons used in

infantry combat. Featuring a solid rocket motor for propulsion, it allowed for high-explosive anti-tank (HEAT) warheads to be delivered against armored vehicles, machine gun nests, and fortified bunkers at ranges beyond that of a standard thrown grenade or mine. (Wikipedia)

2. The **Battle of Hürtgen Forest** (German: *Schlacht im Hürtgenwald*) is the name given to the series of fierce battles fought between U.S. and German forces during World War II in the Hürtgen Forest, which became the longest battle on German ground during World War II, and the longest single battle the U.S. Army has ever fought in its history. The battles took place between September 19, 1944, and February 10, 1945, over barely fifty square miles, east of the Belgian-German border. The Hürtgen Forest cost the U.S. First Army at least 33,000 killed and incapacitated, including both combat and noncombat losses; German casualties were between 12,000 and 16,000. Aachen eventually fell on 22 October, again at high cost to the U.S. Ninth Army. The Ninth Army's push to the Roer River fared no better, and did not manage to cross the river or wrest control of its dams from the Germans. Hürtgen was so costly that it has been called an Allied "defeat of the first magnitude". The Germans fiercely defended the area for two reasons: it served as a staging area for the Ardennes Offensive (what became the Battle of the Bulge) that was already in preparation, and the mountains commanded access to the Schwammenauel Dam at the head of the Rur Lake (Rurstausee) which, if opened, would flood low-lying areas downstream and deny any crossing of the river. The Allies only recognized this after several heavy setbacks, and the Germans were able to hold the region until they launched their final major, last-ditch offensive on the Western Front, into the Ardennes. (Wikipedia)

3. **Battle of the Bulge or the Ardennes Offensive** (16 December 1944 - 25 January 1945) was a major German offensive launched towards the end of World War II through the forested Ardennes Mountains region of Belgium, and more specifically, of Wallonia. Germany's planned goal for these operations was to split the British and American Allied line in half, capturing Antwerp, Belgium, and then proceeding to encircle and destroy four Allied armies, forcing the Western Allies to negotiate a peace treaty in the Axis Powers' favor. The objectives for the offensive were not realized. In the wake of the defeat, many experienced German units were left severely depleted of men and equipment, as survivors retreated to the defenses of the Siegfried Line. With over 800,000 men committed and over 19,000 killed, the Battle of the Bulge became the single biggest and bloodiest battle that American forces experienced in World War II. (Wikipedia)

4. The **Waffen-SS:** was a multi-ethnic and multi-national military force of the Third Reich. It constituted the armed wing of the Nazi Party's *Schutzstaffel* ("Protective Squadron"). The Waffen-SS grew from three regiments to over thirty-eight divisions during World War II, and served alongside the *Heer* (regular army) but was never formally part of it. Adolf Hitler resisted integrating the Waffen-SS into the army, as it was to remain the armed wing of the Party and to become an elite police force once the war was won. At the post-war Nuremberg Trials the Waffen-SS was condemned as a criminal organization due to its essential connection to the Nazi Party and involvement in war crimes. (Wikipedia)

5. **Nordhausen Concentration Camp:** What GIs called Nordhausen was Mittelbau Dora—which was a sub-camp of Buchenwald. The Nordhausen-Dora complex of labor camps had been built in 1943 to supply labor for building V-2 factories in man-made caves dug

out of the Harz Mountains. Nazis locked those too sick to work in Boelcke Barracks, in the town of Nordhausen.

(Levinson, Leila. *Gated Grief: The Daughter of a GI Concentration Camp Liberator Discovers a Legacy of Trauma,* Cable Publishing, Brule, WI, 2011. P. 22

The extermination methods used by the SS were not the same as the ones used in the great extermination camps: there was no gas chamber but, in Nordhausen, the prisoners died by starvation and total lack of medical care. The camp of Nordhausen was a huge complex of installations and hangers made of concrete. There were absolutely no sanitary installations and the inmates had to stay in the hangars nights and days, without any food until they died. Even for a man in healthy condition, this could lead very fast to extreme weakness. For prisoners who were already exhausted and ill, these cruel conditions of life meant quick although miserable death. On April 3th, 1945, Nordhausen was bombed by the US Air Force. Since the camp was installed in concrete buildings and hangars, the US Air Force thought that it was a munitions depot of the German Army. This effective bombing killed a great many of helpless inmates because the SS forced them to stay in the hangars which were set ablaze by the bombs. Nordhausen was liberated by the 104th US Infantry Division on April 12th, 1945. When the first American GI's arrived in the camp, they discovered a gruesome scene. More than three thousand corpses were scattered, helter-skelter on the grounds. In several hangars there were no survivors and in others they found only two or three living inmates lying amongst dozens of corpses. The situation was so calamitous that the medic unit of the 104th Infantry Division had to request urgent medical reinforcements and supplies. More than four hundred German civilians living in the direct vicinity of the camp were forced by the GI's to evacuate the corpses. The medic units of the 104th Division did the best they could to save as many prisoners as possible, but even with the excellent care they received, numerous inmates died in the hours and days following the liberation of the camps. (www.jewishgen.org)

BIBLIOGRAPHY

Brennan, Barbara Ann. *Light Emerging: The Journey of Personal Healing.* New York: Bantam Books, 1993.

Cameron, Julia. *The Artist's Way: A Spiritual Path to Higher Creativity.* New York: Jeremy P. Tarcher/Putnam, a member of Penguin Putnam Inc., 1992.

Cortright, Susie Michelle. *"Journaling—A Tool For Your Spirit."* http://www.amberskyline.com/treasuremaps/journaling.html

Course in Miracles Published by the Foundation for Inner Peace in Tiburon, CA, 1975.

Dyer, Wayne W. PhD. *The Power of Intention.* Hay House, Inc., 2004

Louise Hay and Friends, *Gratitude: A Way of Life,* Hay House, Inc., 1996.

Ferrini, Paul. *Love Without Conditions.* Heartway Press, 1994.

Gabriel, Richard. *Military Psychiatry: A Comparative Perspective.* New York: Greenport Press, 1986.

Grossman, Dave, Lt. Col. *On Killing: The Psychological Cost of Learning to Kill in War and Society.* Back Bay Books / Little, Brown and Company, 1995.

Ingerman, Sandra. *Soul Retrieval: Mending the Fragmented Self.* San Francisco: Harper, A Division of HarperCollins Publishers, 1991.

Jampolsky, Gerald G., MD. *Love is Letting Go of Fear.* Bantam Books, 1970.

Jampolsky, Gerald G., MD. *Forgiveness.* Atria Books/Beyond Words Publishing Inc., 1999.

Kurtz, Ron. *Body Centered Psychotherapy: the Hakomi Method.* Mendocino, CA: LifeRhythm, 1990.

Levine, Peter A. and Frederick, Ann. *Waking the Tiger: Healing Trauma.* Berkeley, CA: North Atlantic Books, 1997.

Levinson, Leila. *Gated Grief: The Daughter of a GI Concentration Camp Liberator Discovers a Legacy of Trauma.* Brule, WI: Cable Publishing, 2011.

Lipton, Bruce, PhD. *The Biology of Belief.* Santa Rosa, CA: Mountain of Love/Elite Books, 2005.

Myss, Carolyn. *Defy Gravity: Healing Beyond the Bounds of Reason.* Hay House, Inc. 2009.

Rosenberg, Marshall B., PhD. *Nonviolent Communication: A Language of Love.* Encinitas, CA: PuddleDancer Press, 2003.

Ruiz, Don Miguel. *Love Without Conditions: Reflections of the Christ Mind.* Paul Ferrini, 1994.

Ruiz, Don Miguel. *The Four Agreements: A Practical Guide to Personal Freedom (A Toltec Wisdom Book.)* San Rafael, CA: 1 Amber-Allen Publishing, Inc., 1997.

Shay, Jonathan, MD, PhD. *Achilles in Vietnam: Combat Trauma and the Undoing of Character.* New York: Scribner, 2003.

Sheehy, Gail. *Passages.* New York: Ballantine Books, 1974.

Siegel, Bernie S., MD, *Love, Medicine, and Miracles: Lessons Learned About Self-Healing from a Surgeon's Experience with Exceptional Patients,* Harper and Row, Publishers, New York, 1986.

Stellman, J.M., and S. Stellman. 1988. "Post traumatic stress disorders among American Legionaires in relation to combat experience: associated and contributing factors." *Environmental Research* 47 (2), 175-210. Quote found in Grossmans ON Killing p 43.

Swank, R. L., and W. E. Marchland. 1946. "Combat neuroses: development of combat exhaustion." *Archives of Neurology and Psychology* 55, 236-47.

Tick, Edward, PhD. *War and the Soul.* Quest Books / The Theosophical Publishing House, 2005.

Vento, Carol Schultz. *The Hidden Legacy of WWII: A Daughter's Journey of Discovery.* Camp Hill, PA: Sunbury Press, 2011.